little war'' provide certain parallels with the United States' intervention in Vietnam which are duly noted, Welch is primarily concerned with their evaluation within the context of their own time and in terms of the diplomatic ambitions and social values of the United States at the turn of the century. This work successfully bridges diplomatic and social history to demonstrate that the reactions of these varied groups, with all of their confusion and ambiguity, served to mirror the aspirations and the prejudices of American society at the advent of the Progressive Era.

Richard E. Welch, professor of history at Lafayette College in Easton, Pennsylvania, is author of *Theodore Sedgwick: Federalist, George Frisbie Hoar and the Half-Breed Republicans,* and *Imperialists vs. Anti-Imperialists.*

Response to Imperialism

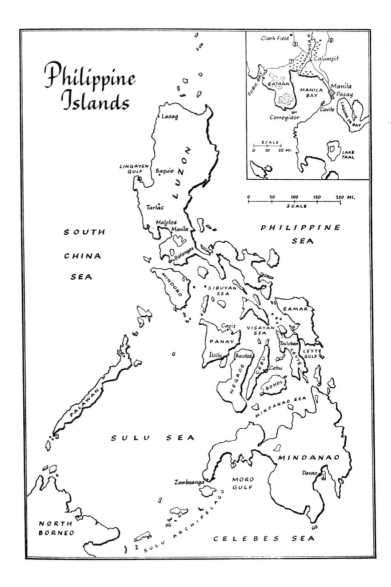

Philippine Islands

Laoag

LUZON

LINGAYEN GULF

Baguio

Tarlac

Malolos
Manila

Batangas

SOUTH

CHINA

SEA

MINDORO

SIBUYAN SEA

Capiz

PANAY

Iloilo

Bacolod

VISAYAN SEA

CEBU

Cebu

NEGROS

BOHOL

PHILIPPINE
SEA

SAMAR

Tacloban

LEYTE
GULF

LEYTE

MINDANAO SEA

PALAWAN

SULU   SEA

MINDANAO

Zamboanga

MORO
GULF

Davao

NORTH
BORNEO

SULU ARCHIPELAGO

CELEBES SEA

0   50   100   150   200 MI.
SCALE

Inset map

Clark Field

Calumpit

SUBIC BAY

BATAAN

MANILA
BAY

Corregidor

Manila
Pasay

Cavite

LAGUNA DE BAY

SCALE
0   10   20 MI.

LAKE
TAAL

Response to Imperialism

The United States and the Philippine-American War, 1899–1902

by Richard E. Welch, Jr.

The University of North Carolina Press   Chapel Hill

Frontispiece from Theodore Friend, *Between Two Empires*
(New Haven: Yale University Press, 1965), printed by permission
of Yale University Press.

© *1979 The University of North Carolina Press*
All rights reserved
Manufactured in the United States of America
ISBN 0-8078-1348-6
Library of Congress Catalog Card Number 78-11403

Library of Congress Cataloging in Publication Data

Welch, Richard E.
   Response to imperialism.

   Bibliography: p.
   Includes index.
   1. United States—History—War of 1898. 2. Philippine Islands—
History—Insurrection, 1899–1901.
I. Title.
E721.W4   959.9'031   78-11403
ISBN 0-8078-1348-6

To my children

C. W. S.
R. E. W. III
C. W. M.
E. M. W.
M. C. W.   *with love and admiration*

Contents

Illustrations

Acknowledgments

I am indebted to all of the libraries and institutions cited in the bibliography and most particularly to the staffs of the Library of Congress (Manuscript Division), the National Archives (Diplomatic Division), the Massachusetts Historical Society, the University of Michigan Library (Michigan Historical Collections), the University of North Carolina Library (Southern Historical Collection), the Duke University Libraries, the Harvard University Libraries and Archives, the New York Public Library, the Boston Public Library, the Columbia University Libraries, the U.S. Army Military History Institute (Carlisle Barracks, Pa.), the Boston Athenaeum, the David Bishop Skillman Library of Lafayette College, and the Newburyport Public Library (Newburyport, Mass.).

I would also express my appreciation to the President and Board of Trustees of Lafayette College and to its Committee on Advanced Study and Research for grants of time and money. I am equally indebted to the secretary of the Lafayette History Department. Mrs. Carl L. Cooper has typed many drafts with constant good humor and an eagle eye for inconsistencies of citation, spelling, and capitalization.

My greatest obligation, of course, is to Christina.

Richard E. Welch Jr.
Lafayette College

Introduction

The Philippine-American War was a colonial war, fought for the purpose of retaining a Pacific archipelago ceded to the United States by Spain in December 1898. The war began on Saturday evening, 4 February 1899, when shots were exchanged between American and Filipino patrols on the outskirts of Manila. Over the next forty-one months 126,500 Americans saw service in the Philippines, 4,200 were killed, and 2,800 wounded.

Once labeled "the Filipino Insurrection" and treated as an anticlimactic footnote to the Spanish-American War, it has more recently been analyzed by historians determined to trace the roots of American economic imperialism and find analogies to the Vietnam War. The Philippine-American War has obvious chronological relationship to the war with Spain, and the bitter struggle of the American army with the guerrilla forces of Emilio Aguinaldo offers certain parallels with American involvement in Vietnam. America's first war in Asia should not be dismissed, however, as a minor episode in the diplomatic history of the McKinley administration, nor should it be viewed as a prophetic foretelling of American diplomatic history in the presidential years of Lyndon B. Johnson. The war and its impact on American society can be understood only when assessed within the context of its own times and with a conviction of its value as a mirror for the social beliefs and political divisions of turn-of-the-century America. A major element of its historical significance is to be found in the evolving response of various groups of Americans to the origins and conduct of the war and its official justification.

The renewed interest in the Philippine-American War that was exhibited by several scholars in the Vietnam decade, 1965–75, was predictable. Historians by training look for parallels and demonstrations of continuity in history. Some historians, however, have not been content to search for parallels between the Philippine-American War and American intervention in Vietnam but have insisted that the conquest of the Philippines furnished a model for subsequent intervention by the United States in the Pacific and Far East. If it is a mistake to exaggerate analogies between two wars separated by a half-century and more of complex international developments, it is a far more serious error to exaggerate the legacy of the Philippine-American War in an effort to discover moralistic lessons in a past reshaped to assure its relevance to the presumed needs of the present.

There are, as noted, certain obvious similarities between the Philippine and Vietnam Wars. In both instances American troops were fighting men of different color in an Asian guerrilla war. In Vietnam as in the Philippines, American soldiers expressed a racist scorn for "gook" and "gugu"; in Vietnam as in the Philippines there were acts of torture and charges of military atrocities. The Philippine and Vietnam Wars were wars of counterinsurgency, at least in part, with American soldiers seeking to isolate the guerrilla forces from the civilian population by a policy of protection and reprisal. The garrison policy of General Arthur MacArthur was similar in intent to the "hamlet protection policy" of General William Westmoreland, and the geographic and climatic obstacles met by the American soldier in Vietnam were not unlike those experienced by the American army in Luzon and Samar. There is, indeed, a pattern of sorts to the military conduct of all American wars against underdeveloped peoples—whether they be Indians, Filipinos, Nicaraguans, or Vietnamese. But the student who would explain our ill-fated involvement in Indochina by means of the precedents of the Philippine-American War is in danger of escalating historical parallelism into historical fiction.[1]

Where parallels break down and dissimilarities are most pronounced is in the contrasting international context of the two wars and the nature of the protest movement they inspired. The Philippine War was fought at a time when America was only beginning to assert its diplomatic claim as a world power. The Vietnam War was fought in an era characterized by American globalism and a nuclear balance of terror. The Philippine-American War followed a short and popular military victory over Spain; the Vietnam War followed the "loss" of China, stalemate in Korea, and French surrender at Dienbienphu. The Filipino republic and Aguinaldo's insurgent army received no assistance from any foreign country; in the Vietnam War the North Vietnamese received arms and equipment from the Soviet Union and China. The Philippine War was essentially the product of a policy of insular imperialism; the Vietnam War, the product of a global crusade against communist expansion.

Although both wars generated dissent and division within the Ameri-

1. An example of such escalation is provided by Professor Howard Zinn in his "Preface" to Daniel B. Schirmer's relentlessly present-minded account, *Republic or Empire*. See also Luzviminda Francisco, "The First Vietnam."

can public, there were marked differences in the nature, breadth, and tactics of the two protest movements. Any student of the anti-imperialists of 1900 must initially be impressed by the similarity of various of their arguments and concerns with those of the "doves" of the 1960s. In both instances there was antipathy to "the arrogance of power" and the growth of militarism, fear of the political and constitutional consequences of reckless foreign adventures, and warnings against the overextension of American resources. But in contrast to the anti-imperialist movement of the Philippine-American War, the protest against American involvement in Vietnam steadily grew in size and violence. Its tactics of public demonstrations and vigils, sit-ins and mass marches, obstructionism and verbal abuse stand in sharp contrast to the self-imposed restraint of Erving Winslow and other officers of the Anti-Imperialist League. If a majority of the academic and literary communities in both periods denied the war's necessity and justice, professors and writers exhibited more public anger in the latter years of the Vietnam War than was ever demonstrated by their predecessors. It is difficult to compare Charles Eliot Norton and Noam Chomsky and impossible to equate the protest of William Dean Howells with that of Norman Mailer. The campus strikes and trashings of the late 1960s would have been unthinkable on the campuses of Harvard, Chicago, and Stanford during the Philippine-American War.

There is, moreover, an important difference in the depth of dissent in the two periods. The opponents of the Philippine-American War saw the subjugation of the Philippines as a departure from the path of rectitude; many of the dissenters of the 1960s saw American aerial bombardment of North Vietnam as the logical expression of a corrupt and repressive society. The Anti-Imperialist League did not view the Philippine-American War as a reflection of the evils of "the system"; for some of the more determined dissenters of the 1960s, the Vietnam War was the culmination of a long-term policy of counterrevolutionary design. In 1900 a patriotic faith in the essential benevolence and superiority of the American republic forbade violence and muffled dissent. A strong note of moral concern and moral righteousness links the two protest movements, but they differed widely in temper and tactics.[2]

The significance of the Philippine-American War for American history is not to be found in strained analogies with the Vietnam War nor in exaggerated efforts to see that war as a model for American economic

2. This point is made with persuasive detail by Robert L. Beisner in his essay, "1898 and 1968: The Anti-Imperialists and the Doves."

diplomacy and military actions in the Pacific and the Far East over the past two generations. Recent American history has demonstrated clearly enough the danger of determining diplomatic policy by means of misapplied historical "lessons." The historian of the Philippine-American War should resist the temptation to exaggerate its "lessons" or its legacy. The product of a particular juxtaposition of events at the end of the 1890s, the Philippine-American War finds its major significance not in strained analogies to future diplomatic crises but in its contemporary impact.

This study will analyze the response of various groups and components of American society to overseas imperialism and the Philippine-American War in an effort to determine the contemporary effects of that war. Its goal is to relate a dramatic episode in the nation's military and diplomatic past to the characteristics and needs of American society of the time. The Philippine-American War was a source of division but for a majority of Americans not a source of shame, and the response it inspired sheds light on the strength of such social forces as racial prejudice and patriotic pride and the values and beliefs of the American people at the end of the nineteenth century.

American soldiers did not wage war in the Philippines in order to provide precedents for American policy makers or parallels for American historians. But the fact that they did wage war for some forty-one months with majority support from an American public, troubled, divided, but—on balance—determinedly optimistic, is important to an understanding of American society as well as American diplomacy at the beginning of the Progressive Era.

Response to Imperialism

CHAPTER I

The Decision to Take the Philippines

The U.S. Congress on 19 April 1898 authorized President William McKinley to use the army and navy of the United States to force Spain to renounce its sovereignty over the island of Cuba. Some twelve days later and some 9,000 miles away, Commodore George Dewey opened fire on the Spanish squadron in Manila Bay.

The juxtaposition of these events has inspired understandable suspicion. Why did the first battle in a war fought to free Cuba take place in the Western Pacific? If the decision for war was inspired by popular indignation over Spanish barbarities against the Cuban insurgents and by a sense of humanitarian obligation to stop the bloody struggle on that Caribbean island, why were we blowing up Spanish ships in Manila harbor? When Dewey instructed the *Olympia*'s captain, "You may fire when ready, Gridley," was he not also instructing the historical profession to look to the Pacific if it would understand the decision to go to war against Spain in the spring of 1898?[1]

Several historians have heard the command. They insist that the more fundamental causes of the Spanish-American War are to be found in American ambition and self-interest in Asia; some indeed believe that the McKinley administration had already determined to secure the Philippines when war began. They offer different judgments, however, about the nature of the self-interest that explains the war's origins. Some believe U.S. policy was directed to the acquisition of Pacific bases for the sake of the navy and long-term strategic needs, and emphasize the part of Theodore Roosevelt, Assistant Secretary of the Navy, and his friends Senator Henry Cabot Lodge and Captain Alfred T. Mahan.[2] Other historians look to McKinley's many friends and advisers who were businessmen and suggest that America's economic needs and ambitions best explain the Spanish-American War and the presence of an American squadron at Manila. Business leaders, convinced that the home market was inadequate to the needs of expanding industrial production, persuaded the administration that an island empire would increase exports and foreign commerce and provide protection and stimulus for the China trade.[3]

[3]

Such interpretations possess understandable appeal. It is natural to be suspicious of happenstance and alert to the possibility of self-interest if not conspiracy. It is equally natural for the historian to look for consistency and consequently to argue that the justifications later urged by the administration in behalf of acquisition of the Philippines, during the debate over the Treaty of Paris, must define the motives that brought Dewey to Manila Bay. The disconcerting probability is that they do not. Dewey was at Manila Bay because the Navy Department had in the period June 1896–June 1897 fashioned various contingency plans for a possible war against Spain, and in each plan an attack on Manila had been projected.

The earliest of these plans carried the signature of an obscure naval lieutenant, William Wirt Kimball. According to this plan, were the United States to find itself at war with Spain, any American squadron in the Pacific should try to capture Manila. The declared motive was to attack Spain wherever she was vulnerable and, incidentally, deprive the Spanish of Manila as a naval base and presumed source of revenue. If Manila were occupied it could serve as a hostage and offer assurance that a monetary ''war indemnity'' could be satisfactorily arranged at the war's end.[4]

Now it was certainly within McKinley's authority as chief executive to have cancelled these contingency plans or have refused to give assent on 24 April 1898 to the telegram ordering Dewey to proceed to Manila and ''commence operations againt the Spanish squadron.''[5] The fact that he did not shows that McKinley was well aware of the location of the Philippine Islands, but it does not oblige one to believe that McKinley asked for war with Spain because he wished to acquire islands in the Pacific. Once war came, he was not long in deciding that he wished to have the chance to acquire some part of the Philippine archipelago, but Dewey's presence in Manila Bay on 1 May 1898 was not part of any grand scheme to promote the economic or strategic interests of America in the Far East. It was primarily the result of a war plan that was itself based on the far-from-novel theory that in war you try to hurt the enemy wherever he is vulnerable.

If McKinley's responsibility for Dewey's naval victory was modest, the same cannot be said for the executive order of 4 May that ordered 5,000 troops to San Francisco and then to the Philippines to occupy Manila.[6] Subsequently, in a letter to his Secretary of War, McKinley sought to define the purpose of this expeditionary force:

> The destruction of the Spanish Fleet at Manila, followed by the taking of the naval base at Cavite . . . and the acquisition of the control of the bay, have rendered it necessary, in the further prosecution of the measures adopted by this Government for the

purpose of bringing about an honorable and durable peace with Spain, to send an army of occupation to the Philippines for the two-fold purpose of completing the reduction of the Spanish power in that quarter and of giving order and security to the islands *while in the possession of the United States*.[7]

McKinley's words can, of course, be read as no more than a long-winded justification for seizing the opportunity provided by Dewey's victory. They may also be read as the words of a man wishing to widen his future choices. The latter reading would appear the more accurate. McKinley had not determined by mid-May 1898 that he wished the United States to acquire any part of the Philippines. He had already decided that it would be safest for the United States to be in control of Manila, so that when a decision was made concerning the disposition of the islands, the United States would be in a position to dictate matters according to its own view of what was right. In the interim the United States must assume responsibility for assuring good order; the Spaniards, paralyzed by Dewey's victory and the renewed insurgency of the Filipino natives, could not be trusted. And so the decision was made—not without calculation but without sufficient thought—to send an occupying force to the Philippines.

A corollary of McKinley's decision was his instruction that these troops should exclude the Filipino insurgents from any share in the capture and occupation of Manila.[8] Although this order has furnished ammunition for those who believe that the administration intended from the beginning to acquire the Philippine archipelago, it is more likely that McKinley again sought only to preserve his choices. There can be no doubt that McKinley had little understanding of the insurgents and their ambitions. Dewey had been remiss in forwarding information respecting their strength and intentions. Though aware that the Filipinos had won several skirmishes with the Spanish and were constructing trenches about Manila, McKinley found it difficult to conceive that these little brown men could object to the authority and good intentions of their American friends. They must not be troublesome as the United States assumed responsibility in the Philippines. Decisions as to the extent and duration of that responsibility could await an assessment of national duty and political advantage after information about the islands had been obtained and American public opinion evaluated.[9] In the interim the U.S. army could operate more efficiently if it were not forced to share its authority with the ragtail soldiers of Emilio Aguinaldo.

A point of particular bitterness for Aguinaldo and his followers lay in the fact that the surrender of Manila to the American forces on 13 August was prearranged with the Spanish. Dewey and Major General Wesley Merritt were indeed guilty of collaboration with the enemy. Operating from an understandable wish to avoid bloodshed, Dewey had engaged in indirect negotiations with the Spanish commandant. After a token resistance, sufficient to meet the demands of Spanish honor, the white flag would be raised and the Americans, unaccompanied by their Filipino allies, would march into the city. Hearing rumor of this arrangement, the Filipinos tried to prevent their scheduled exclusion. The presence of certain Filipino troops on the flank of the American "attack" generated some gunfire and gave unexpected credence to the Battle of Manila.[10]

Throughout the summer and autumn of 1898, America's Philippine policy was the preserve of William McKinley and the executive branch of the government. Congress did nothing before the debate over the Treaty of Paris, and although Lodge and other expansionist-minded senators volunteered advice, there is little evidence that they influenced the decision to take the Philippine Islands. The United States acquired the Philippines by the act and decision of McKinley, and if that decision was reached only gradually it was the result of a careful assessment of personal, political, and national advantages. There was no grand design, but there was calculation.[11] In the weeks between mid-June and early October, McKinley decided that America should acquire a commercial entrepot and naval base at Manila; should acquire the island of Luzon; should acquire the entire Philippine archipelago.

On 16 September McKinley instructed his commissioners, now leaving for the peace conference in Paris, to secure Luzon. Three weeks before he began his swing through the Midwest and Plains states, he had rejected such policy options as military withdrawal, a temporary protectorate, or a naval base and enclave at Manila.[12] The only decision that remained was whether or not to demand the other islands of the archipelago. The response of the cheering crowds in Ohio, Illinois, and Nebraska did not require such a demand, but popular applause and military advice confirmed his belief that herein lay the course of maximum political advantage. On 28 October McKinley cabled his peace commissioners in Paris to secure U.S. annexation of the Philippine Islands.

McKinley claimed that there was no honorable alternative to annexation, and many historians have concurred.[13] But did he correctly interpret his alternatives, and did not the United States have more options than McKinley allowed?

The first alternative, as McKinley later phrased it, was "to give them back to Spain." That phraseology—which has been adopted by most students of American Philippine policy—embodies the undeclared assumption that a victorious American army of liberation was in possession of the islands and that any return to status quo ante bellum would represent a gift from America. The assumption is false. Even if one ignores the circumstance that American troops received the surrender of Manila only after the armistice was signed in Washington, the fact remains that on 28 October— and for a considerable time thereafter—U.S. physical possession of the Philippines was confined to the bay and city of Manila. The rest of Luzon and most of the other islands in the archipelago were under the moderately effective control of Aguinaldo's insurgents and their sympathizers. Had McKinley decided ''to give them back to Spain,'' it would have meant hauling down the American flag, but so restricted was the American presence that few flags would have been lowered.

It is uncertain that McKinley was accurate in his assertion that such a course would have outraged the moral sensibilities of the American people. After a time—and after administration spokesmen and editors had repeatedly declared that the people would not tolerate such a dishonorable course—it is probably true that public opinion made this alternative impossible. But in the summer of 1898 citizens of the United States, most of whom had only the vaguest knowledge of the Philippines before Dewey's victory, were not demanding with united voice that despicable Spanish dons never again set foot on Filipino soil. Had Dewey sailed into Cadiz there would have been cheers for the raising of the American flag but no demand for the permanent expulsion of the Spaniards, and for some Americans in the summer of 1898 Manila was quite as unknown and unsought as Cadiz. Had McKinley wanted, and had he decided to do so early enough, he could have convinced the American public that the United States had only taken Manila as a hostage and it was now proper to return the Philippines to a repentant Spain.

It is interesting to speculate upon the probable consequence of such a course. The Filipino insurgents would have continued their resistance; the Spanish would probably have sent over to the Philippines the tattered remnants of their defeated Cuban army; there would have been more bloodshed and a probable military deadlock and home-rule status for the Filipinos. One need not consider such a hypothetical conclusion dishonorable for the United States or disadvantageous for the Filipinos.

There was a second alternative. We could avoid the obligations of colonial rule by selling or otherwise alienating the islands to some other power. McKinley's argument here seems persuasive. Such a sale would not only deny ourselves commercial advantage but would stir up a hornets' nest of international animosities and quarrels.

A third alternative, leaving the Philippines to the Filipinos, was dismissed with equal dispatch. In McKinley's judgment the Filipinos were incapable of governing themselves. Perhaps he wished to think poorly of the Filipinos; certainly he was too quickly convinced of their political incapacity and too ready to dismiss the reality and aims of the Philippine revolution. He was encouraged in measure by the fact that available information about the Filipino people was strongly biased. It is known that McKinley read John Foreman's article in the July 1898 issue of *Contemporary Review*, and Foreman, allegedly the Englishman most knowledgeable about the Philippines, saw the Filipinos as political infants and believed that American withdrawal would lead to civil war and anarchy in the islands.[14]

If withdrawal was considered and rejected, the alternative of an American protectorate was never seriously considered. Most historians have taken McKinley's lead and either overlooked this alternative or dismissed it as an impractical and clumsy variety of colonial rule.[15] Several have suggested that the experience of the United States with the tripartite protectorate arranged for the Samoan Islands in 1889 probably influenced McKinley to ignore this option.[16] This is conceivable, although the parallel is weak. Surely the populace of Tutuila had not claimed a right of self-determination or issued a proclamation of independence. In any case, one can argue that the alternative of a limited and temporary protectorate was available. The Filipino leaders would suggest this alternative in negotiation with the American military shortly before the outbreak of the Philippine-American War. The United States could have proclaimed its willingness to recognize the independence of the islands, provide naval protection for a specified time, and assist the Filipinos in the establishment of their government during a transitional period terminable at the decision of the Filipinos. Such a limited protectorate would not have furnished a guarantee against future American embarrassment as the result of Filipino inexperience or foreign intrigue. It was worthy of more study, however, than it received.[17]

McKinley never made mention at any time of a fifth alternative: neutralization of an independent Philippines by either a unilateral American guarantee or international agreement. There were precedents in the European conventions guaranteeing the neutrality of Belgium and Switzerland, but McKinley was not alone in disregarding them. It was not until the summer of 1899 that this "solution" would be championed by his anti-imperialist opponents, and by that date McKinley's decision had become national policy.

McKinley's decision to annex the Philippines was not alone the result of a process of elimination. Two considerations that received little attention in his public pronouncements are crucial to an understanding of that decision. They are his suspicion that other nations might seek territory in the Philippines if we did not acquire all of the islands, and his growing conviction that annexation of the Philippines could provide economic advantage for America and political advantage for his administration.

Both Britain and Germany had some measure of influence in determining McKinley's policy. The British advised that the United States should keep the Philippines or sell them to Britain. McKinley was not an Anglophile, and it is doubtful that British desires alone would have weighed heavily. Though anxious for the national honor, McKinley did not associate national disgrace with an inability to follow the British colonial example. The British helped convince McKinley, however, that the Philippines could serve as ''a golden apple of discord.'' Were America not to annex the Philippines, Britain would contest their annexation by any other nation, and particularly Germany.[18] McKinley was never as persuaded of German ambition as was Theodore Roosevelt, but he believed that the mutual suspicions of Britain and Germany made advisable the removal of temptation.[19] Germany was more of a warning than a threat; it symbolized the possibility of international conflict in the Western Pacific were we to withdraw from the Philippines. McKinley seems to have entertained no fear of a direct contest between America and Germany. Nor did he fear a confrontation with the Japanese. The Japanese declared their satisfaction with the prospect of American rule in the Philippines, and McKinley gave no credence to reports from Manila that Japanese army officers were serving with the Filipino insurgents.[20]

McKinley was not a geopolitician nor a disciple of Mahan, and international rivalries did not determine his decision to acquire territory in the Western Pacific. They were, however, significant in determining the amount of territory he would demand. One of the reasons McKinley decided to acquire the entire archipelago was fear that if America took only Luzon, the other islands might become a source of temptation for England, Germany, and Japan, and this would make our possession of Luzon troublesome and costly. The suspected ambition of other nations did not figure importantly in the key decision to acquire Luzon. National economic advantage probably did; the political advantage of his party and administration certainly did.

McKinley was aware by the summer of 1898 that many trade journals were offering optimistic forecasts of the value of the Philippines as a source of customers and raw materials. McKinley's correspondence for 1898 does not offer much evidence that he shared this optimism—indeed, it would not be until the autumn of 1899 that he would emphasize the economic value of the Philippines—but from the beginning he realized that to deny American capital the prospect of colonial profits would be unwise. He was aware that self-appointed spokesmen for the business community were forecasting that Manila would serve as the vestibule for an expanded American trade with China and insisting that such an accommodation was necessary because the European powers had begun to carve eastern China into spheres of influence. McKinley's nights were not disturbed by visions of "the fabled China market," but he hoped that the Philippines would prove to be a source of economic advantage.

Many groups influenced McKinley's decision to annex the Philippine Islands—naval officers concerned for American strength in the Pacific, church groups determined to expand their missionary enterprises and carry the True Gospel to the Filipinos, business correspondents who saw economic advantage for themselves and the nation in the acquisition of the islands—but McKinley was a politician, and the most important influence was his calculation that annexation promised the greatest political gain and offered the fewest political dangers. Once he had made this assessment, he sought to foster public acceptance for colonial expansion. McKinley was neither an indecisive man nor a far-sighted man; he worked within the framework of the immediate future. Acquisition of the Philippines appeared likely to bring economic profit for the country and political profit for party and administration. McKinley had in effect made his decision by the end of September 1898. He would have reversed that decision only if public opinion had proven strongly antagonistic. Leaving himself an escape hatch by assuming a posture of indecision, he waited for annexationist sentiment to gain increasing support, and he did not wait in vain.[21]

McKinley knew his countrymen and accurately predicted their response. He knew the Filipinos not at all and would misjudge their response with tragic persistence. When on 28 October he sent his revised instructions to the American peace commissioners in Paris, armed Filipinos were patrolling fourteen miles of trenches surrounding the city of Manila. The Filipino insurgents had constructed those trenches when the Spanish flag flew over the Macalañan Palace; they continued to occupy them after the American flag was raised on 13 August. They exhibited a continuing determination to remain until the red, blue, and white flag of Filipino independence replaced the Stars and Stripes and the Philippine revolution —now three years old—was acknowledged victorious.

Although the origins of the Philippine revolution may be traced back to sporadic revolts against Spanish rule in the seventeenth century, its official date of origin is August 1896. The first modern colonial revolution in Asia, its inspirations were the now familiar trinity of economic change, rising expectations, and a growing sense of national identity. There was in addition the issue of the Catholic friars and their association with the corruption and restrictions of Spanish domination.

The Spanish friars became a source of resentment as a result of their political control of the barrios and monopolization of large areas of arable land. In the eyes of a slowly expanding Filipino professional class, the Spanish religious orders were seen as a hindrance to commercial growth and political participation. The nineteenth century had seen an increase in Philippine trade and an accompanying Western orientation on the part of a small group of educated, middle-class Filipinos, the "illustrados." Influenced by European doctrines of nationalism and liberalism, these men began to seek more autonomy, and they saw the feudal estates and political authority of the Spanish friars as both threat and symbol. The execution of the anticlerical reformer, Dr. José Rizal, had the usual backlash effect of stiffening opposition. The Philippine revolution now had its martyr, and petitions were succeeded by insurrection.

In recent years there has been an effort by several Filipino scholars to describe the revolution that began in 1896 as a class revolution directed by the masses. This effort would appear misdirected. The goals of the revolution were provided by the illustrado class, and though Andres Bonifacio, leader of the Katipunan, probably saw himself as a spokesman for the peasant masses, the chief element of social revolution was a call for the forced sale of the friars' estates. The Katipunan was a secret society representing an uneasy mixture of Free Masonry, nationalism, and anticlericalism. It provided the core of the guerrilla army that waged war against Spanish garrisons on Luzon in 1896–97. But leadership of the revolution was drawn from the illustrados, particularly after a convention at Tejeros in March 1897 replaced Bonifacio as head of the revolutionary army with a more successful military figure, Emilio Aguinaldo y Famy.

The son of a middle-class family in economic decline, Aguinaldo was born in the province of Cavite in 1869. When the Philippine revolution broke out he was an ill-educated, highly intelligent young man of 27. He had served as mayor of his barrio of Cavite Vienjo and had joined the Katipunan shortly after the execution of his early hero, Rizal. When at the start of the revolt he took command of a small group of insurgents from his home province, Aguinaldo was, in common with his fellow revolutionaries, a Filipino nationalist but not a separatist. He wished the tribes of the islands to think of themselves as a single people, but he did not call for an independent Philippine republic. In its first phase the Philippine revolution represented a call for restriction on the power of the friars, land reform, and greater participation by the Filipinos in the government of the islands.

The insurgent bands had limited military success in 1896, but by the summer of 1897 Aguinaldo saw his poorly equipped forces being pushed back by Spanish troops into the mountains of Bulacan province. Faced with a shortage of arms and the prospect of Spanish reinforcements, he prepared to make a stand in a mountain stronghold known as Biak-Na-Bato. The Spanish governor general, embarrassed by the cost of the insurrection and convinced that the natural defenses of Aguinaldo's stronghold would require an unacceptable loss of Spanish troops, now decided to negotiate with the despised insurgents, using as go-between an ambitious Manila lawyer, Pedro A. Paterno.

The Pact of Biak-Na-Bato, which ended the first phase of the Philippine revolution, was never given formal, written expression, and its terms would later be the source of much controversy. According to the Spanish version, Aguinaldo and other leaders were bought off, promising in return for a bribe to leave the islands permanently. In the Filipino version the Pact embodied a series of Spanish promises as well as an "indemnity." The Spanish promised to expel the religious orders, give the Filipinos representation in the Cortes in Madrid, grant freedom of press and association, and assure equal treatment to Filipinos in political appointments and administration of justice. It was only after receiving these promises—the Filipino version continues—that Aguinaldo agreed that the insurgents would surrender their arms and the insurgent leaders go into exile at Hong Kong. The arrangement whereby these leaders would receive 800,000 pesos was not a bribe but an indemnity, to reimburse those who had lost property during the rebellion and serve as a reserve for financing its renewal should the Spanish not carry out the specified reforms.

In December 1897, Aguinaldo and some forty companions embarked for Hong Kong, taking with them a Spanish draft for 400,000 pesos. This sum he deposited in a Hong Kong bank, ignoring all suggestions by such of his followers as Isabelo Artacho that it be divided and distributed. The second payment of 400,000 pesos was never made; nor did the Spanish enact any political or religious reform. Guerrilla warfare again erupted in central Luzon in February 1898. Full-scale resumption of the insurrection would await the return of Aguinaldo under protection of the U.S. Navy.

At approximately the same time that the U.S. Congress was instructing McKinley to wage war on Spain and liberate Cuba, Aguinaldo decided to avoid a possible court suit by Artacho by temporarily taking up residence at Singapore. His arrival was a source of excitement for E. Spencer Pratt, the U.S. consul at Singapore. Pratt decided that he would exhibit initiative and gain promotion by persuading Aguinaldo to join hands with the United States and extinguish Spanish authority in the Philippines. In secret meeting, arranged with the help of a British businessman named Howard Bray, Pratt urged Aguinaldo to meet Commodore George Dewey and come to an understanding with the commander of the Asiatic squadron of the U.S. Navy.

Many controversies center about the figure of Aguinaldo, and foremost among them are those relating to promises that Aguinaldo did or did not receive from Pratt and Dewey. In all probability Pratt did promise Aguinaldo that if he went to the Philippines and cooperated with Dewey he could be assured that the United States would look with favor on his plan to establish an independent Philippine republic.[22] Pratt had little concern for Philippine political independence, but he saw Aguinaldo as a provocateur who could assist the American military. Aguinaldo had no interest in the task unless it furthered the Philippine revolution. The goal of revolution he now defined as national independence.

When Pratt had his first talk with Aguinaldo, Dewey was at Hong Kong making final preparation for his attack on the Spanish fleet in Manila Bay. Receiving Pratt's wire indicating Aguinaldo's willingness to cooperate, Dewey replied that Aguinaldo should come to Hong Kong as soon as possible.[23] Arriving at Hong Kong, Aguinaldo was informed that Dewey had already departed and that arrangements would soon be made for his transportation to Manila. Aguinaldo took advantage of the delay to purchase arms with funds from the insurgents' account at the Royal British Bank and prepare a proclamation urging the Filipinos to rise against their oppressors and cooperate with their new friends.

By 14 May the U.S. revenue cutter *Hugh McCulloch* had returned to Hong Kong to bring news of Dewey's victory at Manila Bay and furnish passage for Aguinaldo. Five days later he was at Cavite, and the following day was piped aboard the U.S.S. *Olympia*.

No student of the Philippine-American War can afford the posture of certainty when evaluating the hour-long conference of Dewey and Aguinaldo in the wardroom of the *Olympia* on 20 May. The later versions of the two participants bear no resemblance. Aguinaldo insisted that Dewey had begged his cooperation and sought a military alliance with the Filipino insurgents. Dewey suggested that he had never viewed Aguinaldo as other than a self-serving little beggar who might be of limited use in keeping the Spanish land forces occupied until the arrival of an American occupation force, and declared on oath that he had never proposed an alliance or given Aguinaldo any promise that America would recognize his claims as ruler of an independent Philippine republic.

George Dewey was not a liar. He was an ambitious and intellectually limited naval officer, who was neither certain about his country's policy in the Philippines nor seemingly very interested in it. Although he initially thought that the United States would wish no more than a coaling station at Cavite, he was probably too cautious to make any alliance with Aguinaldo and too aware of the complexities of military-civilian relationships to accede to Aguinaldo's demands for assurances respecting U.S. policy. Dewey's remark to a Senate committee, some four years later, that he was unaware of the political goals of Aguinaldo was inaccurate at best.[24] He did know of Aguinaldo's aspirations for Philippine independence, but his relations with the Filipino chieftain were characterized more by uncertainty than calculated deception. He was not kept informed with respect to the evolution of administration policy and, while under instruction to make no commitment to the insurgents, was aware that the initial success of American troops would largely depend on the cooperation of the Filipinos. Dewey decided to obtain a maximum of Filipino military assistance while making a minimum official commitment to Filipino nationalism. The month of June 1898 saw the American admiral ignoring an invitation to attend a ceremony at Cavite where Aguinaldo proclaimed Philippine independence. At the same time he issued instructions that Spanish arms captured at Subig Bay be turned over to Aguinaldo and American small craft be placed at the disposal of the insurgents.[25]

Aguinaldo took notice of the absence of any American representative at the ceremonies on 12 June marking the declaration of Philippine independence. One sees in the next six months a note of increasing urgency in the efforts of Aguinaldo and his chief adviser, the crippled but fiery Apolinario Mabini, to construct a government and ward off the fear as well as the fact of American colonial ambition. An initial ''military dictatorship'' was superseded by a Philippine Revolutionary Government established by proclamation on 23 June.[26] This government made provision for a presidential executive, a unicameral legislative body, and a semiautonomous committee of the legislature to serve as a supreme court. The town of Malolos, some forty-five kilometers northwest of Manila, was chosen as the seat of the new government, and elections were ordered for ''the first revolutionary congress.''[27]

By mid-January 1899 a constitution had been drafted and approved by an elected constituent assembly. It was promulgated on 21 January, and two days later the Republic of the Philippines was formally inaugurated. A blend of British and American practice, the constitution embodied the four ideals of the Philippine revolution: national emancipation, representative government, individual liberties, and separation of church and state. Its promulgation represented both a culmination and an act of defiance. A month earlier—by an executive letter of instruction of 21 December—

Inauguration of the Philippine Republic at Malolos, 23 January 1899 (from Teodoro M. Kalaw, The Philippine Revolution, *reprinted by permission of the Philippines Press)*

McKinley had proclaimed American sovereignty throughout the Philippine archipelago.

When he issued this order McKinley was well aware of Aguinaldo's insurgents and their claims. It is probable that he still underestimated the extent of territorial control exercised by Aguinaldo's forces, but in McKinley's opinion it was unimportant how much territory the insurgent government claimed. The issue was whether there existed a government. Was it not the fanciful scheme of a single faction of the Tagalog tribe, a faction determined to impose itself on a disorganized and helpless people? The limited information available appeared to support such a judgment, and racial stereotypes heightened the temptation to emphasize the incapacity of the Filipinos.[28] McKinley entertained no sense of guilt in brushing aside the claims of Aguinaldo's "republic." Once it had been determined what was the safest policy politically, the most intelligent policy economically, and the wisest policy strategically *for America*, then the "little brown men" must necessarily accept its implementation. They could be assured that McKinley would pursue a colonial policy characterized by a Christian concern for their material welfare.

Convinced of the necessity and intelligence of his decision to acquire the Philippines, McKinley could not believe that Aguinaldo's insurgents would be so stupid as to resist the power and benevolence of the United

President William McKinley, author of the Executive Order of 21 December 1898 (courtesy of the Library of Congress)

States. McKinley appears to have entertained the self-contradictory notions that Aguinaldo was an evil, self-seeking bandit chieftain and that he could be as easily managed as an office-seeker in Canton, Ohio. McKinley's understanding could not exceed his experience. He was incapable of imagining the suspicion and determination of the Filipino insurgents occupying the fourteen miles of trenches that surrounded the American-occupied city of Manila.

General Emilio Aguinaldo, president of the Republic of the Philippines, 1899–1901, (U.S. Signal Corps Photo. No. 111-SC-98358, courtesy of the National Archives)

By the precedents of international law, McKinley's order of 21 December extending American military rule throughout the Philippine archipelago was illegal. Granting that no foreign nation had recognized Aguinaldo's republic, the fact remains that sovereignty remained with Spain until ratification of the Treaty of Paris. On 21 December the Senate had only just begun to debate the Treaty of Paris, and as of that date the armistice of 12 August 1898 was still in force and the United States was sovereign nowhere in the archipelago outside "the harbor, city, and bay of Manila."[29] McKinley never indicated an awareness of the illegality of his act. He would probably have insisted that he was operating under the wartime powers of the chief executive, and reminded his critics that his proclamation referred all questions concerning the permanent government of the islands to Congress.

McKinley's instructions of 21 December offered no prophecies respecting the political future of the Philippines, nor did it offer the promise of self-government. American military government would be extended throughout the islands, and its agents were ordered to protect the natives "in their personal and religious rights." The purpose of the United States was "the benevolent assimilation" of the Filipino people, substituting for arbitrary rule "the mild sway of justice and right."[30]

The significance of McKinley's executive order can hardly be overestimated in an analysis of the origins of the Philippine-American War. It represented the culmination of his evolving decision between the months of May and October to secure in the Western Pacific a colony as well as a naval base. It represented McKinley's rejection of the political claims of the insurgents. McKinley wished annexation and unrestricted sovereignty, and he was prepared to present the Senate with a fait accompli. If the Senate were now to refuse to confirm the Treaty of Paris, it would be repudiating the declaration of the nation's commander-in-chief as well as the achievement of his peace commissioners.[31]

Following one of the longest and most intelligent debates in its history, the Senate approved the Treaty of Paris on 6 February 1899 by vote of 57 to 27. Many factors enabled McKinley to obtain the necessary two-thirds majority, but perhaps foremost was his ability to persuade Republican senators of the rightfulness of the administration argument. That argument was similar to the reasons that had inspired McKinley's decision to demand the cession of the Philippine archipelago, but there were omissions and differences of emphasis. The factors of political safety and partisan advantage were not articulated in the Senate debate, nor was the administration's concern for German ambition and international rivalry given more than passing notice.

Administration spokesmen in the Senate unfailingly emphasized the incapacity of the Filipinos and denied that there was either a Filipino government or a Filipino nation. This assertion was basic to half of their argument, that respecting American duty in the Philippines and the lack of a satisfactory alternative for meeting that obligation except by annexation and control. Providence had decreed that we must fulfill our responsibility to civilization by uplifting those heathen, backward people. The other half of their argument stressed the value of the Philippines to the economy, defense, and diplomatic authority of the United States. Ownership of the Philippines would bring great commercial advantage and provide the equivalent of a leasehold on the continent of Asia. The islands would furnish a coaling station and naval base and by enhancing American military strength would assure the respect of other powers. Duty and advantage were the contrasting if complementary themes of the administration argument in the debate over the Treaty of Paris. To this argument were added three corollaries, patriotic, racist, and prophetic in nature.

Were the treaty to be rejected, the president and the country would be discredited in the eyes of the world. Patriotism demanded that the labors of our soldiers and diplomats receive senatorial endorsement. Confirmation of the treaty would not burden America with another race problem, for annexation would not mean amalgamation. The Filipinos would receive the benefit of American institutions but need never share direction of those institutions. We must, finally, look beyond the needs of the present to the requirements of America in a new century. Overseas expansion would demonstrate adaptation to the laws of social progress, and would have a broadening and uplifting effect on the American spirit. As our horizons broadened, the opportunities for service of our young people would grow, domestic problems be alleviated, and our sense of national purpose be strengthened.

The different themes of the administration position were not particularly harmonious, but they were sufficiently persuasive. Perhaps a few votes were bought with patronage; possibly William Jennings Bryan's muddled advocacy of treaty confirmation influenced two Western senators, but the two most influential factors in determining the vote in the Senate were the arguments furnished the Republican majority by William McKinley and the executive order of the previous December. In the name of the Republic, McKinley had laid claim to the Philippines. The Senate was faced not with a decision to acquire the islands but with a decision of whether or not to repeal their annexation. To reject the treaty would be an act not of abstention but of renunciation; to confirm was but to accept the status quo. McKinley had so arranged matters that psychological inertia as well as the calls of duty, profit, and strategic advantage favored ratification.

Had he gone further? Had he arranged the additional security of a Filipino attack on the American flag and soldier? When the Senate voted on the afternoon of 6 February, it was aware that some forty hours earlier the Filipino insurgents had "attacked" the American line at Manila. Although it cannot be proved that this news changed a single vote, it is a matter of record that several senators who cast affirmative votes declared that they did so in support of the brave American soldier as well as his commander-in-chief, and McKinley offered the opinion that the outbreak of hostilities made additionally certain the confirmation of the treaty.

The New York *World* in its lead editorial of 6 February suggested that it was "an amazing coincidence" that the shooting occurred "just at the exact moment when the first news of it would still be fresh in the minds of the Senators as they cast their votes,'' and its suspicions have been frequently echoed. Several Filipino historians have quoted with approval the judgment of Apolinario Mabini, in his memoir of the Philippine revolution, that McKinley, frustrated by the Democratic minority in the Senate, ''decided to stage what is called a coup d'etat.''[32] Similar judgments have recently been offered by such critics of American colonialism as William J. Pomeroy and Daniel B. Schirmer. Schirmer offers the most extended charge of American responsibility. In his view President McKinley, General Elwell S. Otis, and American corporate capitalism conspired separately and in unison to provoke hostilities with Aguinaldo's troops.[33]

There was within a period of forty hours ''an amazing coincidence'' of events in Manila and Washington. The historian, wary of coincidence, is inclined to suspect a causal relationship. No single communication from Washington to Manila exists to substantiate such a relationship. So confused were the lines of communication between McKinley and Otis that it appears highly unlikely that McKinley could have arranged a provocation had he wished it. The charge that McKinley instigated a clash between Philippine and American pickets in an effort to secure passage of the treaty fails for lack of evidence.

McKinley did not conspire to initiate the Philippine-American War, but he must bear primary responsibility for its initiation. He did not anticipate the outbreak of hostilities, but his refusal to offer the Filipinos the promise of future self-government made war inevitable. Support for that judgment is found in the story of the deteriorating relations of Aguinaldo and the American military in the period between McKinley's executive order of 21 December 1898 and the night patrol of Private Willie Grayson on 4 February 1899.

When General Otis received McKinley's executive order, he realized that its assertion of American sovereignty would anger the insurgents and inspire support for the revolutionary government at Malolos. He unwisely decided to edit McKinley's message before ordering its distribution, and then saw his deception revealed when the original document was published by an unwitting subordinate. This episode confirmed the suspicion of Aguinaldo respecting American intentions, and it was now that Aguinaldo gave approval to Mabini's campaign seeking to associate the American occupation forces and the hated friars. General Otis and his soldiers, though Protestant heretics, would restore the friars to their authority and power as a means of suppressing the Filipino people.

General Otis, successor to Merritt as commander of the American forces in Manila, had become by December 1898 the symbol of American duplicity and intransigence in the eyes of Aguinaldo. Having little conception of the American constitutional practice of civil control, Aguinaldo always credited American commanders with an independence of authority they did not possess. Although his initial confidence in Dewey had long since eroded, he retained a grudging admiration for the hero of Manila Bay; in the beagle countenance and martinet posture of Otis he saw only an enemy. The distinction Aguinaldo made between Dewey and Otis was natural but exaggerated. Any difference was the result of comparative military position and responsibility. Neither man began to fathom the determination of the insurgent leaders to secure Philippine independence, and Dewey was prepared to work with Otis as the latter laid plans for the chastisement of the insurgents should they decide to resist American sovereignty by force of arms.

Otis, commanding officer of a force ringed by insurgent trenches, developed an increasing antipathy toward the Filipino insurgents. He became convinced that only military defeat would subdue their arrogance and pretension, and not unnaturally desired control over the timing of military action. But Otis, like Dewey, was not a free agent; he labored under the orders of Washington to avoid provocation of the insurgents while according them neither concessions nor recognition. A less prejudiced and more able man might have found the task impossible.

It was with reluctance that Otis received in the early days of January a delegation of "prominent Filipinos" and their request that he appoint three officers "to meet a committee appointed by General Aguinaldo to confer with regard to the situation of affairs and to arrive at a mutual understanding of the intent, purposes, aim and desires of the Philippine people and the people of the United States."[34] Otis viewed the negotiation that followed as little more than a delaying action, made necessary by conflicting instructions from the War Department, but on 9 January he appointed Brigadier General R. P. Hughes to serve as chairman of a committee of three officers to hold discussions with a committee of like size headed by Florentino Torres.[35] Four separate meetings were held, and each followed an identical pattern. The Americans demanded that the Filipinos submit a detailed exposition of their political aims. The Filipino commissioners replied that General Aguinaldo could accept nothing less than independence, but the Americans could be assured that he would be prepared to make concessions in behalf of economic friendship and the needs of the American navy.[36] When the Americans demanded more precision, the Filipinos countered by requesting a statement of American intentions, and were told by General Hughes that he was authorized only "to ascertain the desire of the Philippinos'' and had no authority to make pledges in behalf of the president of the United States.

Aguinaldo was apparently prepared in mid-January 1899 to accept an arrangement whereby Philippine independence would be qualified by restrictions not dissimilar to those later imposed on Cuban sovereignty by the Platt Amendment. The previous month had seen the secession of the more conservative elements from the revolutionary government at Malolos, and their defection had seemingly shaken his confidence. Despite the urgings of Mabini, Aguinaldo was prepared to accept a limited American protectorate. The temptation is consequently great to bewail the intransigence of the American military commissioners, and their failure to seize the propitious moment. Must they not bear responsibility for the long and grisly Philippine-American War?

The negotiation between the committees of General Hughes and Florentino Torres probably never held any possibility but failure. The American military officers had neither diplomatic authority nor the power to grant concessions. If Otis saw the negotiation as a delaying action and Aguinaldo hoped that it might offer a reprieve from the alternative of war or surrender, the beliefs of neither Otis nor Aguinaldo were of primary importance. William McKinley ignored those meetings—never authorizing a reply to the two cables sent by Otis describing their initiation and progress—and without the interest and authorization of McKinley the negotiation could be no more than a charade.

McKinley alone could make sufficient concessions to Filipino nationalism to arrest the likelihood of armed struggle, and McKinley was determined to place no restriction on the rights of American sovereignty. The motives that had determined him to seek annexation of the islands now persuaded him against the ''weakness'' of restricting America's future freedom of action in the islands. He was prepared to grant the Filipinos individual liberties but not national freedom. His irreconcilable difference with the Phillipine Revolutionary Government revolved about this distinction. McKinley would insist throughout that freedom did not mean national freedom. A just-minded president was prepared to protect the rights of individual Filipinos, but there was no Filipino nation, and so there could be no acknowledgment of Philippine sovereignty. McKinley's decision in January 1899 to send an investigating commission to the Philippines did not indicate that he was prepared to negotiate with Aguinaldo. The Schurman Commission was not to make concessions to the insurgents; it was authorized to recommend ways to conciliate the Filipinos, undermine support of the Tagalog chieftain, and enable the United States to proceed with its projects of benevolent indoctrination.

There was, in short, no basis for compromise between the McKinley administration and the Filipino insurgents in the month of January 1899. This fact was underlined by the reception granted the memorial of Felipe Agoncillo.

Following fruitless labors at the peace conference in Paris, Agoncillo had been ordered to Washington and instructed to work for defeat of the treaty while making a final effort to gain concessions from McKinley. When the President refused to receive him, Agoncillo prepared a long memorial in which he described the course of the Philippine revolution, the history of Philippine-American relations, and the grounds on which Aguinaldo's government based its claim to recognition. It remains today the most cogent expression of the rights of the Philippine republic.[37] Agoncillo was allowed to deliver his memorial to the office of the Secretary of State and then curtly dismissed. The memorial was never answered—at least not by Secretary John Hay or President McKinley. Its answer came from the rifle of Private Grayson shortly after ten o'clock on the night of Saturday, 4 February 1899. By that time the opposing ambitions of the Philippine revolution and the McKinley administration could find resolution only in battle.

CHAPTER II

War

The outbreak of hostilities between Filipino and American troops at Santa Mesa on the evening of 4 February was ordered by neither McKinley nor Aguinaldo.[1] McKinley's initial reaction was one of surprise and Aguinaldo's one of irritation and dismay. But for their soldiers war was a source of relief. A series of disputes and war scares had strained the nerves and patience of officers and men on both sides. For the American soldier, the Filipino insurgent with his blue cotton tunic, white trousers, and bare feet was a bumptious "nigger" playing soldier. Unrequited insults must be revenged and their authors whipped. A soldier correspondent subsequently remembered that "upon the part of the rank and file of Americans," there had developed a "feeling of intense personal hatred of their tormentors and an earnest desire to be turned loose upon them and kill them."[2] Similar feelings were entertained by Aguinaldo's soldiers. Conscious of the scorn with which they were regarded by the American soldiers—and increasingly aware of the derogatory connotation of the epithet, "nigger"—they found diminishing satisfaction in the exchange of insults. The greedy Americans who had come to the islands in the false guise of liberators were braggarts and must be thrashed.[3] Although Aguinaldo on the afternoon of 5 February sent emissaries to General Otis to suggest a cease fire, his soldiers as well as their enemies wanted war. General Otis declared the war must go on to its natural conclusion: the defeat and unconditional surrender of the insurgents. Rebuffed, Aguinaldo now publicly scorned the idea of an armistice. The requirements of military morale dictated a proclamation pledging battle until the Philippine Republic was acknowledged and victorious.

The Filipinos had no hope of military victory in the Philippine-American War, but the success of the American army was by no means certain. Aguinaldo's troops did not have the experience or equipment to drive the American army from the islands. Their only hope lay in the possibility that the United States might decide that subjugation was so costly in lives and money that it would give up and withdraw. The American army, for its part, faced a difficult and in some ways unprecedented task. Never before had Americans fought outside North America; in the Philippines they would fight in jungle terrain 7,000 miles from home. Excepting perhaps the wars against the Indians, the U.S. army had never sought to subjugate a people who laid claim to national independence. Now it would be required not only to subjugate but to pacify the Filipinos; not only to defeat them in battle but to make them accept American rule. The wonder is not that the war lasted for forty-one months but that it did not last longer.

The years of the Philippine-American War find their dividing line with the month of November 1899. At that point Aguinaldo ordered the insurgent army to dissolve into guerrilla bands and sought to gain independence by the erosion of America's will rather than defeat of its army. The period from February to November 1899 may itself be divided into three phases. Between the initial battle of 4–5 February and the end of April, there was an erratic series of American military successes that enabled General Otis to extend the area of American control some thirty miles north and east of Manila. The months of May–September saw the rainy season, limited activity, and a sharp decline in American military morale. The fall of 1899 saw the American army mount a three-pronged drive into the central plain of Luzon which secured over a hundred miles of territory but failed in its central mission of capturing Aguinaldo and the core of his army. The most interesting of these three phases was perhaps the first. The first three months of the war revealed both the superiority and the limitations of the American army in the Philippines.

Forty-eight hours after Private Grayson had "shot my first nigger," the divisions of General Arthur MacArthur and General Thomas Anderson had charged the trenches of the Filipino troops encircling Manila, captured the water works, burned a dozen barrios, and gained control of an arc of territory forming the natural topographical defense line for the capital city.[4] General Otis now ordered a halt and the consolidation of the new American line, but one week later, responding to the urging of MacArthur, he allowed the Second Division to capture the rail center of Caloocan, seven miles to the north. Aguinaldo's chief general, Antonio Luna, ordered the Filipino troops at Caloocan to resist to the last man, and when the trenches there were overrun, dead Filipinos were found stacked like cordwood. In the first two weeks of the war the Filipinos, fighting with bewildered bravery, suffered over 3,000 casualties.

The American advance was shortly distracted by the abortive uprising of the Sandatahan, an underground Filipino militia in Manila. The attack fell victim to ill-timing and poor coordination. When 500 insurgents under Major Francisco Roman slipped around the left of one of MacArthur's brigades and began to infiltrate the city, the Sandatahan failed to receive notice and were not in position. Fires designed to distract the Provost Guard were confined to the Tondo district by the newly organized fire-fighting service, and two dozen Filipino sharpshooters appointed to gun down the fire fighters were quickly captured. By the evening of 23 February, the last of the fires had been extinguished, communication destroyed between the Sandatahan agents in Manila and the insurgent troops, and portions of the latter routed in two short engagements at the Chinese cemetery and San Pedro Makati. Aguinaldo had belatedly ordered other troops to attack MacArthur's front, but American artillery and ten-inch shells from the *Monadnock* made short work of their efforts. By mid-afternoon the insurgents had withdrawn, having made their first and final effort to wrest Manila from American control.[5]

Another lull in military activity now followed, as Aguinaldo sought to strengthen the defenses of his capital at Malolos and Otis awaited rein-forcements from the United States. General Lloyd Wheaton engaged in a brief punitive expedition, burning a few barrios and garrisoning Pasig and Pateros, but it was only with the last days of March and the arrival of fresh troops that Otis authorized an assault on Malolos.[6] In a pitched battle the American forces overran the earthworks before Malolos on 30 March, and the next day they occupied the city. They found a ghost town. Aguinaldo and his government had decamped under cover of darkness, making tracks for San Isidro. Otis had believed that with the capture of the enemy capital and the scattering of its political functionaries, Aguinaldo would see the hopelessness of opposition and the rebellion would be over. He failed to order the immediate pursuit of the insurgent army, and when emissaries did not arrive proffering Aguinaldo's unconditional surrender, Otis felt cheated.

General MacArthur's division would remain at Malolos for several weeks, and Antonio Luna was given the opportunity to collect his scattered forces and to call upon municipal presidents to raise new recruits "for the salvation of our outraged country." A decree of the Malolos government had made all Filipino citizens between the ages of 18 and 35 subject to conscription, and small bands of peasant sons were soon wending their way toward Calumpit, where Luna planned to mass his troops in anticipa-tion of the next American offensive. The Filipino recruits had little training in marksmanship—they saw the back sights of the Mauser rifles as need-less obstructions and threw them away—and were difficult to discipline. Their loyalties were largely local, and Luna often found it impossible to persuade them to take orders from any but their provincial officers. His

greatest difficulty, however, was ammunition supply. Aguinaldo had established two small arsenals where empty cartridge cases saved from combat
were brought to be refilled, but the bullets produced were often defective.
In the early months of the war it was bullets rather than rifles that were in
desperately short supply in the insurgent ranks.

Otis never lacked supplies, but in the eyes of some junior officers he
lacked courage. He was viewed by his more impatient subordinates as
"Grandma Otis" and judged a "nervous Nelly." Otis did display an
excessive concern for the safety of his lines of communication, but in light
of the difficult terrain of central Luzon and the initial size of the American
army, his apprehensions were understandable. An unimaginative fussbud-
get, Otis was neither a fool nor a coward.

Few commanders in American military history have possessed such
unrestricted political-military authority over so large a region as did Elwell
S. Otis, "Commander Eighth Corps Area, Pacific, and the Philippines."
Otis was both oppressed by his responsibility and determined not to share
it. A student of law as well as military science, he saw unnecessary risk as
faintly illegal. His reports to Washington were filled with prophecies respecting the imminent collapse of the rebellion, but he worried continu-
ously that the insurgents would cut his supply lines or encircle an advance
detachment. In appearance Otis looked like a great beagle dog grown fat.
He had the temperament of a bureaucrat and enjoyed paper work. Every
evening after dinner he would return to his office on the first floor of the
Malacañan and read through the hundreds of reports that he demanded
daily of his subordinates. He worked endless hours, took advice poorly,
and lacked the ability to delegate authority. Perhaps his overriding fault
was his determination to control the tactical maneuvers as well as the
strategy of battle, while never moving outside the walls of Manila.

In April 1899 Otis decided to concentrate his combat power by mas-
sing the bulk of his forces north of Malolos and then advance on Calumpit.
The American troops were to execute a double flank movement and trap
General Luna's army. Calumpit was captured, but thanks in part to Otis's
interference with the orders of his junior officers, the main insurgent force
escaped. The capture of Calumpit provided another example of the success
and frustration that characterized the American military effort in the winter-
spring of 1899. In a typical exercise of rationalization, Otis would later
inform Washington that he was pleased that the insurgent army had not
been crushed too quickly or completely. Had it been eliminated immediately
the Filipinos would not have had the opportunity to experience its tyran-
nical ways and so become disenchanted with "Tagalo rule."[7]

Otis also offered this opinion to the Schurman Commission, which

General Elwell S. Otis, "Nervous Nelly" (U.S. Signal Corps Photo No. 111-SC-90854, courtesy of the National Archives)

had finally arrived at Manila on 31 March 1899. Otis and Admiral Dewey had been appointed members of this commission, to serve with Jacob Gould Schurman, its chairman, Charles Denby, and Dean C. Worcester, but neither the general nor the admiral had much use for it. Dewey seldom attended its sessions, and Otis tried his best to ignore its existence, seeing it as a threat to his undivided political and military authority.

Having been appointed before the outbreak of hostilities and possessing only investigative authority, the role of the Schurman Commission was at best anomalous. Two of its civilian members, Denby and Worcester, were quite prepared to accept the view that American-Philippine relations were now exclusively a military problem, but Schurman, president of Cornell University, had ambitions of playing the peace maker. After distri-

A Filipino trench after the battle of Calumpit, April 1899 (U.S. Signal Corps Photo no. 111-RB-1288, courtesy of the National Archives)

buting a proclamation stressing America's benevolent intentions in the Philippines, Schurman sought interviews with Filipino residents in Manila in an effort to discover a basis for a peace settlement. Discounting Mabini's counterproclamation of 15 April, warning the Filipinos against cooperation with a nation "who hate mortally the colored race," Schurman became convinced that there was a growing counterrevolutionary movement among the insurgents. The fall of the Mabini cabinet appeared to give substance to his hope.[8]

Discouraged by the loss of the small insurgent treasury at Malolos and the subsequent defeat at Calumpit, members of Aguinaldo's government had sought a scapegoat and turned against the uncompromising Mabini.

Aguinaldo was persuaded to accept Mabini's resignation as premier, and Pedro A. Paterno and Felipe Buencamino formed a cabinet pledged to explore the possibility of a negotiated peace. On 10 May 1899 the Paterno cabinet sent out feelers to Otis and the Schurman Commission. The intransigence of military leaders on both sides cut short the hopes of Paterno and Schurman. General Luna threatened to arrest any Filipino officials collaborating with the enemy, and General Otis refused to see Paterno's emissaries and vetoed all talk of an armistice. A majority of the Schurman Commission accepted his advice and recommended to Washington that the war be prosecuted until the insurgents surrendered and acknowledged American sovereignty. By the end of May, the Paterno ministry had reversed course, and on 2 June it issued a manifesto promising the continuation of the war until independence was acknowledged.[9] By that date both sides had re-pledged their allegiance to a military solution and the political role of the Schurman Commission became increasingly meaningless.

The month of May had seen not only the abortive negotiations of the Paterno ministry but an effort by the American army to extend its lines south of Manila. Otis gave General Henry Lawton authority to try to expand American military power in the area of Cavite. After a series of skirmishes with the elusive enemy, Lawton asked for permission to send troops into Batangas province. The rainy season had begun, and Otis denied his request. Having scorned any solution other than that of military victory, Otis now appeared to doubt that he had troop strength sufficient to risk military defeat. Lawton returned to Pasay in an angry mood. His sense of frustration became increasingly typical of the American army over the next four months.

The months of June through September saw little military action by the American forces in Luzon, and this ineffective in result. Towns were captured only to be abandoned, for Otis was reluctant to detach units for garrison duty. The onset of the monsoon season accentuated problems of disease as well as transportation, and American military morale reached perhaps its lowest point in the war.[10] The sick rate for some units was as high as 40 percent. By the end of September, the American army had been fighting for eight months and had secured only 120 square miles of Luzon's total area of 42,000 square miles. Letters of American troopers reflected a mounting impatience. They were tired of the dampness and the rain. From June to October no less than 70 inches fell; rice paddies became lakes, and ground not under water was a thick black paste of mud. Dry beds were a luxury; dry shoes a dream. They wanted victory or they wanted home.

With October, a new phase of the war began that appeared to promise both. Rumors circulated that a great drive would soon be underway that would succeed in capturing Aguinaldo and his miserable army. At last Grandma Otis was going to turn them loose.

Otis was justifiably proud of his strategic plan. It was sufficiently complex so that it might serve some day as a sandtable exercise in a West Point classroom. The American force would be divided into three main units under Generals MacArthur, Lawton, and Wheaton. The force under General MacArthur would serve as a battering ram to drive the insurgents up the central plain of Luzon, while the regiments under Lawton and Wheaton, operating in a great pincer movement, would shut off any retreat for Aguinaldo into the Benguet mountains of northern Luzon. MacArthur's force was to move along the railroad on the western flank of the plain, capture the new insurgent capital of Tarlac, and chase the main body of insurgents toward the Lingayan Gulf. Concurrently, Lawton was to make a wide sweep to the east, sealing off the mountain passes bordering the eastern edge of the plain. Near Dagupan on the shore of Lingayan Gulf his advance units were to make contact with the troops of General Lloyd Wheaton, which would have been ferried to Lingayan by sea. That meeting would seal the trap, and Aguinaldo and his force would have the choice of surrender or annihilation.

Early November saw the plan in operation, and almost to the end it operated like clockwork. MacArthur's troops pushed steadily forward from San Fernando and Angeles toward Tarlac. They were forced to abandon use of the railroad after Angeles, but on 12 November Tarlac was captured and a week or so later the town of Bayonbong, the last whilom capital of the Philippine Congress. Meanwhile Lawton, appreciating the need for speed and finding it difficult to navigate his great wagon trains and artillery through a terrain of hills and ravines, had detached flying columns of cavalry under General S. B. Young. Young's cavalry packed two weeks' rations in their saddle bags and set forth to close the mountain passes of the Caraballo and Sierra Madre mountains.

Aguinaldo, after a series of delaying actions, fell back toward Dagupan, hoping to reach the village of Pozorrubio before its occupation by the Americans.[11] Pozorrubio was the key to the northernmost pass leading to the Benguet mountains and asylum.

General Wheaton had an excellent chance to capture Aguinaldo and failed. This usually bold officer was unaccountably slothful in performing his role in the November campaign. He disembarked with his brigade at San Fabian on 7 November, but instead of hacking his way directly to Dagupan, sent a reconnaissance force to Rosario. This company reported back that there was no sign of the insurgents, although had they occupied the town rather than reconnoitered its outskirts they would have found

Aguinaldo hidden in the house of the police chief. By the time Wheaton thought to establish barricades on the road north to Dagupan, Aguinaldo had reached Pozorrubio and begun to head toward the Tila Pass. General Young's cavalry arrived at Rosario sixty hours after Aguinaldo's departure; a day later he met a patrol company from Wheaton's brigade. The cordon had been established, but too late to cut off Aguinaldo's retreat.

General Wheaton contented himself with a letter to Otis recommending that all insurgents henceforth be treated as outlaws, but General Young made one final effort to capture Aguinaldo by ordering a battalion under Major Peyton C. March to continue the pursuit. This final effort provided the occasion for the sacrificial stand of General Gregorio del Pilar at Tila Pass on 2 December 1899. Hearing of the annihilation of del Pilar's band, Aguinaldo ordered a forced march from Cervantes through Kayan to Bontoc. By the end of December he was established in new and secret headquarters at Palinan in the heart of the mountain jungle of Isabella province.[12]

Otis reported to Washington that the November campaign had achieved its goals and the rebellion had been broken. The insurgent army had been scattered; its commander was but a bandit in hiding.[13] The insurgent army had been scattered, but peace was not at hand. What Otis judged to be the end of the rebellion was only the transformation of the Philippine-American War into its longer and more difficult guerrilla phase. After a council of war at Bayambang on 13 November 1899, Aguinaldo ordered the insurgents to dissolve as a formal army. The Filipino soldiers were to return to their home provinces and pursue the war as organized bands of guerrilla warriors.

The guerrilla phase of the war would last from December 1899 to July 1902, and for the first eleven months of that period Aguinaldo often held the initiative. Using a rotating company of couriers and an elaborate underground network, Aguinaldo would exercise a surprising measure of control over operations in the northern half of the Philippine archipelago. The islands were divided into provincial districts, zones, and subzones and guerrilla commanders appointed for each. Command structure would remain centralized, but battle tactics were to be determined locally. Guerrilla units were ordered to maintain themselves by soliciting the support of the native civilian population, and they were instructed to try to establish parallel governments in cities and pueblos under nominal American control. Often, indeed, the same Filipino officials appointed by the Americans would serve as tax collectors, supply agents, and recruiters for the guerrillas.[14]

The guerrilla strategy was to protract the war, undermine the will and morale of the American army, and make the war so costly for the United States that its citizens would demand an end to American occupation. To promote that strategy, the guerrillas were to avoid open combat unless they clearly outnumbered the American detachment and pursue tactics that would assure support from their countrymen while subjecting the Americans to continual harrassment:

> [Our purpose] will be to worry the Yankee in the Pueblos occupied by them, to cut off their convoys, to cause all possible harm to their patrols, their spies and their scouts, to surprise their detachments, to crush their columns if they should pass favorable places and to exterminate all traitors. . . . The guerrillas shall make up for their small number by their ceaseless activity and their daring.[15]

Aguinaldo encouraged the revival and expansion of the old Katipunan society, and ordered its village committees to serve as supply and propaganda agencies and as informers against collaborators.[16] Collaborators were initially turned over to the local guerrilla commander for summary court martial, but soon the Katipunan, and its offshoot the Magdudukuts ("The Secret Avengers"), were allowed to forego this formality. American soldiers who surrendered were promised good treatment and eight silver dollars for each rifle they brought with them.

Few American soldiers deserted to the ranks of the enemy. When they found that the war was not over but only transformed, their reaction was one of anger rather than discouragement. Many had been scornful of policies of "benevolent pacification," and had cooperated only half-heartedly in education and reconstruction projects.[17] Now they saw the covert aid given the guerrillas by the natives as proof that the uncivilized and ungrateful Filipinos understood only brute force.[18] Otis himself lost faith in the pacifying effect of public works and proclamations. After assuring Washington that the insurgents were only bandits-in-hiding, he requested 10,000 more troops.

The year 1900 saw the American army in the Philippines steadily augmented until it reached a total of 70,000 officers and men. That year also saw the Americans seek to counter the new insurgent strategy by shifting from a divisional tactical system of organization to a territorial occupational pattern. Otis finally accepted the fact that to capture a town was purposeless unless it was garrisoned. The American army would have to do garrison duty at the same time it sought to extend its search-and-destroy operations over the entire archipelago. By the spring of 1900 the archipelago had been divided into four military districts: the Department of Northern Luzon under General Wheaton, the Department of Southern Luzon under General John Bates, the Department of the Visayas under General Robert Hughes, and the Department of Mindanao and Jolo under General William A. Kobbé. (A separate command was created for the city of Manila under General J. Franklin Bell.) Although the establishment of these districts demonstrated that American troops were now in control of all of the major towns of the Philippines, the countryside often remained under the effective authority of the insurgents. Only occasionally, as at Santa Cruz, Laguna, did the insurgents accept invitation to open battle, but American casualties continued to increase and so did the temptation of junior officers to authorize the "water cure" in an effort to gain information about the enemy and discourage his supporters. By the summer of 1900 the practices of counterterror were increasingly common.

Counterterror never received official sanction by military headquarters in Manila, and acceptance of the "water cure" as a proper military weapon varied widely between regions and officers, but the diaries and contemporary letters of American soldiers reflect a growing conviction that all Filipinos were their enemies, deserving of any form of punishment that would assure surrender. If racial prejudice had initially inspired dislike for the gu-gus, the guerrilla tactics of the insurgents inspired angry contempt. The patriotic exploits of Sumpter and Marion in the American Revolution were forgotten. Guerrilla warfare was now defined as alien, cowardly, and treacherous. General William Shafter might rationalize his anger by informing his correspondents that it was necessary to slaughter the guerrillas in order that "the remaining half of the population could be advanced to a higher plane of life," but Private William Eggenberger was content to damn the enemy for his inability to "fight like an American." Corporal Frederick Presher spoke for many of his comrades when he justified reprisals on the ground that "the looks of the gu-gus" were sufficient "to convict them of almost any crime under the sun." The water cure would bring the war to a quicker end and return the American soldier to "God's country." Corporal Presher had no use for squeamish civilians and anti-imperialist critics. They gave comfort to the guerrillas and were partially responsible for their continued resistance.[19]

Secretary of War Elihu Root and William Howard Taft were too intelligent to attribute the difficulties of the Philippine campaign to anti-imperialist pamphlets. On occasion they spoke harshly of home-front obstructionists, but they believed the key to suppressing the "insurrection" lay in a policy of attraction. American rule must seem conducive to the interests of propertied and respectable Filipinos. These men would then turn against Aguinaldo and furnish the American occupation with expanding support from the native population. When Taft was appointed to head the second Philippine Commission in April 1900, Root was still under the impression that the war was drawing to a close and that Otis's optimistic portrait of affairs could be trusted. His instructions to Taft picked up the theme of benevolent assimilation; the Filipinos should receive personal liberties and political tutelage. The commission was not to interfere with military operations, but Otis would now bear the title of Military Governor and the commission would gradually assume responsibility for the political and economic reconstruction of the islands.

Root had predicated his instructions on the harmonious cooperation of the Taft Commission and the American military. He must have known, however, that Otis would take umbrage at any diminution of his authority, and there was more alacrity than regret in the War Department's acceptance of Otis's request that he be recalled from the Philippines. The succession in May 1900 of Arthur MacArthur as military governor was only a limited gain for harmony. MacArthur was a far abler officer than Otis, but he shared with his predecessor an ill-concealed scorn for the interfering civilian. Relations between MacArthur and Taft were always stiff and frequently testy. The fault lay not alone with MacArthur, nor was the contest one between the hard-nosed militarist and the humane civilian. Taft was more anxious to assert American civilian authority in the Philippines than to display clemency toward the Filipinos, and MacArthur was intelligent as well as pompous.

MacArthur almost alone among the ranking American officials in Manila realized the extent of Aguinaldo's hold on the Filipino population. He did not take refuge in the delusion that Aguinaldo was but a tribal chieftain whose authority was the product of terror alone. The inability of the Americans to find a single native willing to serve as an informer and disclose Aguinaldo's whereabouts demonstrated that his authority found its chief source in ethnic loyalty. But MacArthur was also convinced that many insurgents, despite their personal allegiance to Aguinaldo, were weary of the war. On 21 June he issued an amnesty decree. For a ninety-day period any guerrilla who surrendered his weapons and acknowledged the sovereignty of the United States would be granted amnesty and free transportation to his home province. The only exception was for those "who have violated the laws of civilized warfare." The vagueness of this reservation was perhaps one reason why the number of those taking advantage of the amnesty proposal was so small. Not only did relatively few surrender their arms and pledge allegiance to the United States, but these very months of June–August saw a new wave of raids and ambushes by guerrilla forces and an expansion of guerrilla activity to the southern islands.

Subject to increasing pressure from Washington to end the war and aware that the same Washington authorities wished no news of military severities to disturb public opinion at home, MacArthur was in an unenviable position. He decided that a new pacification policy was in order. Army garrisons would be dispersed over the islands with the mission of coercing those who aided the guerrillas and protecting those who collaborated with the Americans. Intelligence operations would be expanded, surveillance improved, and insurgent agents executed. The goal of the new policy would be to isolate the guerrillas from their base of supply in the villages and end the alliance of the barrio and the guerrilla camp. Mac-Arthur delayed the formal announcement of the new policy until the complication of the American presidential election had passed, but he had determined its necessity by October 1900.

It would be a mistake to see this new policy as an example of military sabotage directed against the wishes and wisdom of the Taft Commission. Taft was prepared at this point to call for military severity against the insurgents, even while he criticized the army for not cooperating sufficiently with the administration's policy of attraction. Taft's humanitarian precepts often succumbed to the heat of Manila, and occasionally he sounded like General Lloyd Wheaton as he talked of the "useful effect" of a few hangings.[20] If MacArthur's new policy was purposefully severe, it was representative of a mood of frustration that embraced civilian commissioners as well as army generals.

McKinley's victory in the election of 1900 served to discourage Aguinaldo and to free MacArthur. On 20 December 1900, MacArthur issued new instructions whereby guerrillas who assumed civilian disguise would be treated as "war rebels" who had divested themselves of the character of soldiers. Neutrality was no longer an option available to Filipino men of property. Henceforth all Filipinos who failed to offer active assistance to the American army would be considered suspect, and fear of insurgent reprisal would provide no excuse for anyone furnishing sustenance to the guerrillas. Army garrison units would occupy all towns known to have given aid to the insurgents and would be accorded powers of summary punishment over Filipino officials who violated their oath of allegiance. There would be no indiscriminate terror, but the power granted an occupying army by General Order No. 100 would be exercised to the full.[21]

The next phase of the Philippine-American War, December 1900–
April 1901, would see the new policy executed vigorously and would
reach its climax with the capture of Aguinaldo. That capture would not end
the war, but by the spring of 1901 there was no longer any doubt of the
war's outcome.

The first effect of the new and harsher tactics of the American army
toward Filipino civilians suspected of double-dealing was to strengthen the
resolution of the insurgent leaders. Aguinaldo proclaimed that military
brutality was now official American policy, and he issued an order on 17
January 1901 enumerating American atrocities and calling "in self-
defense" for a policy of retaliation. Judged by their long-term goal, however, the new American tactics were successful.

Part of their success was the result of timing. They came at a point
when the American army was at its peak strength and so able to occupy and
garrison an increasing area; when propertied Filipino conservatives were
becoming convinced that they had more to lose from American anger than
guerrilla retribution; and when the insurgent guerrillas were short of supplies and increasingly discouraged. Having fought for nearly two years,
many were weary of war and increasingly doubtful that the Americans
would withdraw. Regionalism and class interest had gradually eroded the
strength of Philippine nationalism, and the military power of the United
States was accompanied by the declining authority of Aguinaldo.[22]

January 1901 saw the deportation to Guam of Mabini and thirty-eight
other revolutionaries, and the adoption by the American army of new rules
whereby the property of guerrilla sympathizers was subject to confiscation
and American troops were given authority to fire all barrios that persisted
in offering asylum to the insurgents. The next month saw the newly formed
party of the Americanistas, the Federal Party, gain converts among the
harassed Filipino middle class, and on 14 March American control in
central Luzon was signalized by the surrender of General Trias. Trias had
been one of the boldest and most effective of the insurgent generals, and
his capture was seen as a sign of the effectiveness of the new pacification
policies. The surrender of Trias was quickly overshadowed, however, by
news of General Frederick Funston's capture of Aguinaldo.

For over a year the Americans had sought by every means possible to
discover the hiding place of Aguinaldo in the mountain fastnesses of north-
eastern Luzon. The capture of one of Aguinaldo's couriers, Cedilio Segismundo, offered the wanted opportunity. Finding ways to make him speak,
his American interrogators discovered that Aguinaldo was at Palinan in
Isabella province and had instructed Segismundo to dispatch a company of
loyal insurgent soldiers to reinforce his personal guard. Funston, a short,

wiry, red-headed officer from Kansas with a carefully cultivated reputation for derring-do, persuaded MacArthur to allow him to lead a detachment of eighty-one Macabebe Scouts, disguised as Tagalog insurgents, to Aguinaldo's headquarters. Funston and four other American officers would pretend to be prisoner-captives of the "insurgents," who would be under the apparent leadership of Segismundo, a Filipino mercenary by the name of Hilario Tal Placido, and Lazaro Segovia, a former Spanish secret service officer who would masquerade as a guerrilla captain. The Macabebe soldiers with their officers and "prisoners" would be shipped to Casiguran Bay and once ashore attempt to make their own way along 50 miles of jungle trail to Palinan.

Combining duplicity with courage, Funston's mixed band made a forced march through difficult terrain and by 22 March were only 6 miles from Palinan. There they learned that Aguinaldo, fearful of letting American prisoners enter the insurgent headquarters, had dispatched a patrol of soldiers to take charge of the prisoners. The Macabebes hid Funston and the other American officers in the bush and informed the loyalist soldiers that the captive Americans were back in Casiguran.

The loyalists pressed on to Casiguran, and the next afternoon Tal Placido marched the new recruits into Palinan. Aguinaldo's guard lined up to offer a military salute of welcome, and the Macabebes carefully maneuvered into position around them. At Segovia's signal the Macabebes opened fire, and within minutes Aguinaldo was thrown to the floor of his bedroom and informed that he was a prisoner of the American army.[23] Funston led his small force and their prisoner back to Casiguran Bay where they met the U.S.S. *Vicksburg* steaming into the harbor exactly on schedule. On the morning of 28 March an astonished General MacArthur was informed that Emilio Aguinaldo was now under guard in a room of the Malacañan.[24]

On 1 April, Aguinaldo took the oath of allegiance, and on 19 April he agreed to sign a manifesto calling upon his countrymen to forego further resistance and accept the fact of American rule. Aguinaldo's manifesto and capture received wide publicity, and Funston was the hero of the hour.[25]

Although some historians have sought to diminish the importance of Aguinaldo's surrender,[26] the capture of the symbol as well as the leader of the Philippine struggle for independence marks the beginning of the last chapter of the Philippine-American War. Guerrilla war by its very nature is never over while there are men in the field capable of inciting renewed hope and effort, and there were in April 1901 guerrilla forces operating in Samar and in the Batangas and Laguna provinces of Luzon, but Aguinaldo's manifesto had the effect of removing the mark of treason from the act of surrender. In short order, General Tinio surrendered in northern

Emilio Aguinaldo boards the U.S.S. Vicksburg *after his capture, 26 March 1901 (U.S. Signal Corps Photo No. 111-SC-85795, courtesy of the National Archives)*

Luzon, Generals Mascardo, Alejandrino, and Lucon in central Luzon, and General Cailles in Laguna. By the summer of 1901 the only two organized and sizable guerrilla units still in the field were those of General Malvar in Batangas and General Lukban in Samar.[27] Both would figure largely in the anticlimactic and bloody final period of the Philippine-American War, a period that would witness the perversion as well as the victory of the American army's pacification policy.

The last year of the Philippine-American War began on a note of pacific optimism as William Howard Taft was inaugurated civil governor of the Philippines on 4 July 1901. Concurrently, General Adna R. Chaffee succeeded MacArthur as commanding general. Chaffee, scorning Malvar's

Frederick Funston takes his ease on the U.S.S. Vicksburg, *having success-fully completed his mission (U.S. Signal Corps Photo No. 111-SC-83545, courtesy of the National Archives)*

claim as the new leader of the Philippine revolution, predicted that a slight tightening of the screws would soon bring the last of the insurgents to heel. Less than three months later there occurred the Massacre of Balangiga, followed in turn by the campaign of General Jacob H. Smith to make Samar "a howling wilderness."

On the morning of 28 September 1901, the seventy-four men of Company C, 9th Regiment, U.S. Infantry, were surprised at breakfast by a band of insurrectos, many of whom had earlier infiltrated the town of Balangiga on Samar Island in the guise of a detail of laborers. At a signal arranged by the police chief of the town and the local priest, these workers turned on the unarmed soldiers standing in mess line and proceeded to kill thirty-eight and wound eleven, mutilating many of their victims with a ferocity unusual even for guerrilla warfare.

The Balangiga Massacre revived the hopes of the remaining bands of Filipino guerrillas in Samar and Leyte, and the American army, jolted from its conviction that the war was virtually over, felt a natural sense of rage.[28] "Hell Roaring" Jake Smith was given command of the army and marine units assigned to revenge Balangiga, and he openly proclaimed his determination to pursue a policy of destruction and terror. One can assume that Smith wished the submission of the native population and not their torture, but the orders he gave brought in their wake atrocities as well as pacification. The most famous of these atrocities centered about the conduct of a marine major, Littleton W. T. Waller. Major Waller would be charged with ordering the death of eleven native guides under the provocation that during a long march through central Samar they had found some edible roots and had kept this knowledge from the famished American troops who had accompanied them. Later, during a lengthy court-martial in Manila, Waller would claim that in ordering the assassination of the eleven Filipino guides he was only acting in the spirit of instructions given him by General Smith: "Kill and burn and the more you kill and burn, the better you will please me."[29]

While American forces in Samar were creating a new wilderness, Taft in Manila gave his approval to a sedition law (4 November 1901) that made it illegal to advocate Philippine independence and General Chaffee ordered General J. Franklin Bell to mount a campaign to crush General Malvar's guerrilla forces in Batangas, a province that had been a center of insurgent activity since the war's beginning.

Bell's campaign in Batangas would become a textbook example of effective military pacification. By a series of thirty telegraphic orders of 8 December–23 January, he instructed his junior officers to herd the civilian population into concentration centers, to burn all crops and slaughter all cattle that might furnish sustenance to the guerrilla force under Malvar, and then to undertake an unrelenting chase of the guerrillas through the Batangas highlands. Any able-bodied male who left his garrisoned compound after sundown without permission would be shot; prisoners of war would be executed in retaliation for any acts of murder and assassination—on a one-to-one basis; and each officer was encouraged to make existence so "insupportable" for the disloyal population of Batangas that no rational man would wish the war's continuance.[30] By the middle of April, hundreds of Filipinos had died in the camps of Batangas, propertied civilians had been subjected to levies and confiscations, and the guerrillas had been starved into submission. The surrender of Malvar on 16 April marked the end of organized opposition to American rule in the Philippines.

A few guerrillas still conducted small-scale raids, and before long the Moros in the southern islands would take up arms in defense of religious rights and customs, but the dream of a Philippine republic had been effectively crushed. In recognition of that fact, Congress passed on 1 July 1902 the Philippine Government Act, and Theodore Roosevelt on 4 July declared the "insurrection" ended and proclaimed executive clemency for the Filipinos.

Aguinaldo in his captive's quarters in Manila sought to take comfort from the fact that over the past four years his countrymen had demonstrated the existence of a Filipino nation and this fact was not to be obliterated by defeat. Taft expressed his conviction that with victory the benefits of American rule would be fully revealed and the Filipinos find contentment in material progress. Neither Aguinaldo nor Taft lingered on the costs of the war, for they were tragically high for both peoples.

Casualty figures are at best only estimates. But the author of the most detailed American history of the war has concluded that 126,500 Americans saw service in the "Philippine Insurrection," the peak strength of the American army at any single time was 70,000, and this army suffered battle losses of over 4,200 men killed and over 2,800 wounded.[31] This represented a casualty rate of 5.5 percent, one of the highest of any war in American history. The financial cost of the war was over $400 million, a figure twenty times the purchase price paid Spain. The insurgents suffered battle losses of 16,000–20,000 killed. In addition, perhaps 200,000 Filipinos died of famine, disease, and other war-related calamities.[32]

The American public was not aware of the extent of losses on either side. Opponents of the war in the United States who sought to describe its human and financial costs were called pessimists or liars. Confused in tactics and insufficient in numbers, these opponents failed to change the nation's diplomatic and military policy, but their labors helped make certain that the Philippine-American War was a source of division and dispute for the American people.

CHAPTER III

The Anti-Imperialist League and the Charge of Treason

The opinions and labors of the Anti-Imperialist League provide an important but easily exaggerated element in American response to the Philippine-American War. America's response would exhibit more support than dissent, and the Anti-Imperialist League did not speak for all dissenters.

The League was founded with the object of preventing the Spanish-American War "from being perverted into a war for colonial spoils," and throughout its history the League was essentially a protest movement against overseas imperialism, not against the military subjugation of the Filipino people. The two became connected in the years 1899–1902, but the League continued to be more concerned with ridding America of the Philippines than denouncing the Philippine-American War. Many members of the League were prepared to attack the war and the conduct of the American army, but as an organization the League was essentially a product of the fight over the Treaty of Paris, and its overriding purpose was to repeal the Philippine cession. The League, in brief, was more typical of opposition to the Treaty of Paris in the winter of 1898–99 than of opposition to the Philippine-American War of 1899–1902, and the opponents of the Treaty of Paris were not identical in inspiration or numbers with the opponents of the Philippine-American War. American dissent to the Philippine-American War was more uncertain and sporadic, more complex and diverse, than the publications of the League would suggest.

The League furnished, nonetheless, not only the loudest expression of organized protest but the chief target of attack for the administration, the military establishment, and the more fervid supporters of the war. Consequently, it forms a natural starting point for any analysis of dissent in the Philippine-American War and the animus it aroused.

The Anti-Imperialist League had its origins in Boston and retained a strong New England flavor throughout its existence. Its initial founders were all members of the Massachusetts Reform Club, its constitution was fashioned in the office of the Boston mugwump, Edward Atkinson, and among its charter members were such descendants of the antislavery crusade as Erving Winslow, Moorfield Storey, Gamaliel Bradford, Winslow Warren, David Greene Haskins, and William Lloyd Garrison, Jr. Declaredly nonpartisan, its constitution welcomed to membership all who would join the battle against imperialism and the extension of American sovereignty over noncontiguous territory.[1] During its losing battle in the winter of 1898–99 to secure the defeat of the Treaty of Paris in the Senate, the League officers had encouraged the establishment of branches in a dozen other cities in the East and Middle West and had sought to assume a more national character. That effort was climaxed in October 1899 with the decision to shift the headquarters of the League from Boston to Chicago and to rechristen the organization, the American Anti-Imperialist League. By that date the League claimed a membership of over 30,000.[2] Its membership was concentrated in the Northeast, however, and its most active division was the charter organization in Boston, now titled the New England Anti-Imperialist League. Winslow was the secretary and guiding spirit of the Boston organization. The League was too heterogeneous in membership ever to speak with a single voice, but its most persistent spokesman was Erving Winslow.[3] A solemn, bespectacled, and well organized individual with a great capacity for work and worry, Winslow saw the anti-imperialist crusade as the natural culmination of all of the reform movements of the Gilded Age. To the neglect of his business as an importer and commission merchant, the sixty-year-old Winslow decided to devote the rest of his life to the battle against overseas imperialism. In personal correspondence with hundreds of members of the League and as editor of a majority of its pamphlet publications, Winslow sought to shape the League's response to the Philippine-American War.

In Winslow's view, the object of the Anti-Imperialist League was to make clear to the country that the war was unnecessary as well as unrighteous. The League should force the administration and Congress to suspend hostilities,[4] arrange a conference with the Filipino leaders, and formally promise the Filipinos the right of self-determination. The United States should completely withdraw, after aiding the Philippine republic to reestablish effective governmental authority. The prime goal of the League was to free America from the Philippines and from the self-destructive policy of imperialism, but an auxiliary goal was to assist the Filipinos and to make redress for the wrongs that had been done them. The Filipinos were not enemies of the American people, and sympathy for their cause was an act of patriotism as well as conscience. The army that had fought for humanity in Cuba must not be an instrument of aggression in the Pacific, and it was the task of the Anti-Imperialist League to defeat those who would use the flag to conceal avarice and folly.

Winslow's recitation of the dangers of imperialism was unchanging throughout the Philippine-American War, but there was less certainty in his analysis of the motives of his enemies and an occasional note of caution in his expressions of support for the Filipinos. At times Winslow would suggest that colonialism was the work of "the wealthy corporations and promoters, who alone would profit by it," but he never offered a detailed analysis of the economic causation of colonial expansion and frequently implied that colonialism was the product of political ambition and the decline of public morality. The Filipinos were fighting for liberty "with a courage and persistence which makes them worthy of it, if any people ever were," but there was no reason for the League to give ammunition to its enemies by praising the guerrilla tactics of Aguinaldo. The League did not wish the military victory of the insurgents, only the political freedom of the Filipinos. The restraints of official position and family background made Winslow loath to associate the crusade of anti-imperialism with pacifism or radicalism. He wished to see the membership of the League embrace all sections of society, and he was fearful lest social and political radicals blacken its name or confuse its purpose. The League must smite the imperial monster with all boldness, but there was no reason to offend the sensibilities of the refined by publishing "A Psalm of Empire," for it mocked the style of the Songs of David and smacked of agnosticism.[5]

The Puritan heritage of Winslow was not shared by all members of the Anti-Imperialist League, but he fairly represented the League in his attitudes respecting racism, economic expansion, and diplomatic isolation. While offended by racial slurs against the political competence of "the little brown men," Winslow reflected a note of *noblesse oblige* in his expressions of sympathy for the followers of Aguinaldo. They were chiefly praised for their desire to imitate the ideals of Thomas Jefferson and the political wisdom of the Founding Fathers of the American Republic. By the definitions of his day, however, Winslow was not a racist, and neither, by the same criteria, was he an economic imperialist. He was a free trader who opposed the use of military force or economic coercion in behalf of the expanding commercial interests of the United States. Those interests would be best served by lowering tariff rates and avoiding military adventure. A peaceful foreign policy implied, however, neither parochialism nor isolation. By abstaining from colonial adventures the United States would increase its authority in the councils of the world. Winslow insisted that not only did the League not wish America to retreat from the world, it had no wish to see America ignore its obligations to the Filipinos. We should arrange for the international neutralization of the Philippine Islands. Having disrupted the natural evolution of Filipino nationalism, we were now obliged to protect Filipino independence as well as acknowledge it.

Winslow and the other officials of the League were educators at heart. As educators they had a great faith in meetings, committees, and the printed word.[6] With their pamphlets and broadsides they sustained the hope of the faithful; they were much less successful in expanding their ranks. Winslow made efforts in Massachusetts to attract black and Irish-American organizations, as well as members of various "Young Men's Democratic Clubs," but though these organizations often passed resolutions in behalf of liberty and justice, few of their members formally joined the League. The Brahmin stooped to conquer, but with little success.

With the summer of 1900, there came signs of increased urgency in the labors of Erving Winslow and of worrisome division among the officials of the Anti-Imperialist League. The prospective presidential election provided the sense of urgency and source of division. A call was made for a new Liberty Congress to be held in Indianapolis in early August, and Winslow laid plans for the Congress to endorse the candidacy of the Democratic nominee, William Jennings Bryan.[7] Although a majority of the League officials agreed with him, Carl Schurz, Oswald Garrison Villard, and Moorfield Storey seriously considered the idea of a third-party ticket, and Jay Chapman publicly refused to accept the decision of the Liberty Congress to endorse Bryan. Winslow as much as any man was responsible for that endorsement, and the subsequent defeat of Bryan reduced the influence of Winslow and the membership of the Anti-Imperialist League.[8]

If Winslow more than any other man typifies the organizational labors of the Anti-Imperialist League, there were two of his allies who might have claimed equal importance: George S. Boutwell and Edwin Burritt Smith.

Boutwell was president of the League from its origin until his death in 1904, being reelected to the office after the League shifted its national headquarters to Chicago and again upon its return to Boston. Boutwell was nearly eighty when first elected, and it is customary to dismiss him as little more than a figurehead. It is true that his past history as a charter Republican lent a desired dignity to an association begun by mugwump reformers, and it is equally true that he left to Winslow and Smith the day-to-day operations and correspondence of the League, but Boutwell was not a doddering incompetent. Indeed his labors for the League had a rejuvenescent effect. He was a far more active figure in 1900 than he had been twenty years earlier, and more reform-minded than he had been since the days of the Free Soilers. In addresses and magazine articles he castigated "syndicated wealth" as the parent alike of imperialism and the trusts and denounced the Philippine-American War as a "brutal war of subjugation." Boutwell's age lent a certain immunity, and he was prepared to risk the charge of disloyalty. McKinley was his chief target, for from the beginning he saw McKinley as author and director of "the work of transforming this republic into an empire." As between Aguinaldo and McKinley, "Aguinaldo is in the right and the President is in the wrong." The Filipinos were not rioting against recognized authority;[9] rather they were engaged in a popular rebellion like that of our forefathers of 1776. Their cause was just, and it was the history of popular rebellions that they should succeed. On America's part the war was being prosecuted "for the conquest and the enslavement of eight million people," and was without moral justification of any kind. The honor of the war would rest not with our own soldiers "who have died bravely in this war of Criminal Aggression," but with those "whom our soldiers have slain."[10]

It is more difficult to determine the opinions and arguments of Edwin Burritt Smith of Chicago, secretary of the executive committee of the American Anti-Imperialist League. Smith's role was that of the coordinator and bureaucrat. His correspondence was second only to Winslow's,[11] but his publications and public addresses were relatively few. Smith's major contribution, apart from his labors as a fund raiser and program chairman for numerous conferences, was as editor of a series of pamphlets published by the Chicago Liberty League and sponsor of its major publishing effort, *The Truth About the Philippines from Official Records and Official Sources*. The latter was written by Henry Hooker Van Meter and was a strange blend of tome and tirade. Though badly organized, it offered source material for League publicists, and Smith saw that it was widely distributed throughout the country. Smith was concerned not only with the harmful effects of the war on the republican institutions of the United States but also with its impact on the American soldier in Luzon. Appended to Van Meter's thick volume was a chart indicating the location of "1,109 licensed liquor saloons" in Manila. Regret was expressed that it was impossible to show on the same map the "200 houses of ill fame or the 600 opium dens."[12]

An additional dimension to the response of the Anti-Imperialist League to the war may be gained from an analysis of the roles and opinions of three other figures: Carl Schurz, Moorfield Storey, and Edward Atkinson. None of these men was a spokesman of the League organization, and each supplemented his labors for the League with independent efforts of his own making, but in the eyes of the public they were more conspicuous than Winslow, Boutwell, or Smith. Because they were honorary vice presidents of the League, their independent actions would be identified with the League and its response to the Philippine-American War.

By 1899 Carl Schurz had been engaged in political protest and controversy for over forty years. One of the most prominent of the anti-imperialists, he was also one of the most bitter and consistent. It was primarily on political and constitutional grounds that Schurz denounced the administration and its war. The President had never asked nor received the consent of Congress, and the Constitution reserved to Congress the power to declare war. The McKinley administration was conducting a war of "bare-faced, cynical conquest," and its conduct was illegal and unconstitutional. In his draft resolutions for a protest meeting at Cooper Union on 24 May 1900, Schurz proclaimed that it was "the plain duty of the American people to stop the bloody war against the inhabitants of the Philippines, to recognize their right and title to freedom and independence . . . and to withdraw our armed forces from those islands as soon as they may no longer be needed to . . . protect the people thereof in setting up and maintaining an independent government." To continue our present course was to risk the destruction of the American Republic.[13] Schurz saved his most savage scorn for those who, though unhappy about the war, believed that there was now no option but to see it through. We had no right to begin the war, and so surely no right to continue it. The notion that a nation must proceed in a career of crime in obedience to the force of inertia was the epitome of stupidity.

Moorfield Storey would match Schurz's scorn for those who rationalized their greed by the rhetoric of duty and pragmatic necessity. "Every day of continued warfare in Luzon [was] . . . a fresh national sin." Unlike Schurz, however, Storey was suspicious of proposals for a temporary American protectorate in the Philippines. The only way we could help the Filipinos was to leave them alone; they did not need our assistance in establishing order and an effective government. "There was no reported disorder in the Philippine Islands . . . when the Philippine Government was in control, and there is none now save such as is caused by our armies."[14] More than most of his anti-imperialist allies, Storey was prepared to believe evil of the conduct of the American soldier in the Philippines and was accordingly convinced that the more swift and complete the American withdrawal, the better for the Filipinos. Storey first gained national attention for his investigation of American military atrocities, and that investigation did much to confirm his belief that the role of the American army was essentially one of coercion and brutality; it could never serve as an instrument for the political or economic progress of the Filipino.

If Storey was more bold than most anti-imperialists in his readiness to accuse the American soldier of torture and brutality, he was atypical of his countrymen in his immunity to racism. A friend of the black man in America, Storey had only scorn for those who called the Filipinos ''niggers'' and treated them as such. All races were equal in the eyes of God and all peoples possessed the right of national self-determination. Prideful of his descent from New England abolitionists, Storey saw a parallel between the slave holders of antebellum days and the contemporary imperialists. He saved for his scrapbooks an editorial in the Baltimore *Sun* that compared McKinley to a slave catcher: ''In what respect does Mr. McKinley differ from Simon Legree, unless, indeed, that which would be a crime in an individual, visited upon the person of a single offending slave, becomes excusable in the ruler of millions when visited upon a few thousand of brown men in a distant land?''[15]

Storey was too racially egalitarian and too uncompromising an anti-militarist to be representative of the Anti-Imperialist League. Such officials as Erving Winslow respected his talents and feared his candor. For Edward Atkinson, they showed less respect and greater apprehension.

Atkinson's role in the Anti-Imperialist League is often exaggerated. His temperament as well as his particular brand of anti-imperialism made it necessary for him to play a lone hand. Though a laissez-faire liberal like so many of the League officials, Atkinson was more ambitious for the nation's expanding economic power than most and one of his chief arguments against colonialism was its dangers for the growth of the American economy. Money spent on armies and navies and the physical protection of colonies meant heavy taxation, and heavy taxation discouraged investment at home and abroad. The natural ambitions of the American investor and entrepreneur and the operations of the law of comparative advantage should be left free to assure America's economic power and prosperity. An economic expansionist, Atkinson was also an exponent of moral certitudes. McKinley was not only wrong but the incarnation of evil. Every life destroyed in the Philippine Islands by order of ''that pious fraud [was] an act of murder; every dwelling or village destroyed an act of arson; every piece of property taken an act of robbery.'' Congress should not only oppose McKinley's war, it should refuse to appropriate money for the army and so coerce the presidential tyrant to withdraw all American troops from the Philippines.[16]

The individuality of Atkinson's views and the intemperateness of his prose made Erving Winslow and the League reluctant to serve as the distributing agency for Atkinson's writings. Winslow found offensive Atkinson's explicit depictions of the venereal diseases of Asia to which American soldiers would fall victim and was reluctant to give League endorsement to Atkinson's efforts to dissuade young Americans from enlisting in the army. Atkinson was soon organizing his own mailing list and distributing his pamphlets independently of the League. Discovering that a serial publication could be sent as second-class mail with a large saving in postage, he distributed these pamphlets as successive issues of *The Anti-Imperialist*. Each issue of the latter would contain three of his longer and more inflammatory tracts plus revisions, statistical appendixes, and other new material sufficient to justify its classification as a serial. By means of an ingeniously compiled mailing list of some 23,000 names, Atkinson was soon able to give his pamphlets a broader geographic distribution than any single production of the Anti-Imperialist League. Rather like a magazine publisher of today, Atkinson sought to reach "the influential men," and his list contained not only the addresses of 4,000 public libraries in the United States but clergymen, congressmen, labor leaders, college presidents, and more than 200 newspaper editors.[17] Andrew Carnegie and others occasionally helped defray the expenses of distribution,[18] and noninstitutional subscribers were asked to pay five and then seven cents a copy, but the modest fortune Atkinson had secured as a textile manufacturer, cotton broker, and inventor of the Aladin cooking oven furnished his chief resource. As a pamphleteer, Atkinson gained prominence but not profit.

That prominence was initially the result of Atkinson's decision in April 1899 to test the suspected censorship policies of the McKinley administration by mailing copies of his articles, "The Hell of War," "Criminal Aggression," and "The Cost of a National Crime" to seven officials in the Philippines: George Dewey, Jacob Gould Schurman, Dean Worcester, General Harrison Gray Otis,[19] General Henry W. Lawton, General Marcus P. Miller, and the correspondent for *Harper's Weekly*, John S. Bass. The manner in which the administration overreacted confirmed his darkest suspicions. On 2 May Postmaster-General Charles Emory Smith ordered the San Francisco postmaster to remove Atkinson's "seditious pamphlets" from the Manila mail. Atkinson proclaimed the McKinley administration guilty of a "rape of the mails" and was most gratified. He informed Senator George F. Hoar that he had forced the government to show its mailed fist and its determination to crush opposition and deprive dissenters of their constitutional rights.[20]

Atkinson's long-winded pamphlets were not treasonous by the definition of the Constitution, but their declared aim was to show the injustice of the army's assignment and its certain failure. The climate and diseases of the tropics could only bring misery to the American soldier; many would be driven insane by the brutalities of the campaign; those who survived would return home crippled and contaminated. Atkinson did not advocate desertion by the uniformed soldier, but he was determined to discourage enlistments and restrict the army's ability to serve as an instrument of colonial subjugation. He wrote Hoar that his goal was "to prevent any but dead-beats and degenerates [from] enlisting in this 'accursed war.' "[21] There was reason why the McKinley administration should see Atkinson as its enemy, but it was stupid to make him a martyr. The receipt of three pamphlets by seven men in Manila—six of whom were on the federal payroll—was not going to incite a mutiny. The government should have ignored Atkinson's grandstand play. Instead it extended military censorship from Manila to San Francisco, and by elevating Atkinson's pamphlets to the status of "forbidden fruit" increased their circulation tenfold.

Several expansionist papers predicted this development and criticized the government's action; others believed that loyalty to the Philippine policy of the administration required the defamation of Atkinson and his depiction as the new Aaron Burr. For the Chicago *Times-Herald*, Atkinson was the worst of the "Boston school of slanderers." His action in mailing his vile pamphlets was clearly treasonable; for "men who lend aid and comfort to the enemies of their country. . . are guilty of treason." The Worcester *Spy* agreed, arguing that as "no agitator would be allowed to go from camp to camp, haranguing the soldiers and inciting them to mutiny," Atkinson could not be allowed "to attempt the same purpose by means of printed addresses and pamphlets."[22] Reactions of this sort were partly responsible for Erving Winslow's decision to issue a public letter disclaiming on behalf of the League any responsibility for Atkinson's action.

Atkinson never forgave or forgot Winslow's letter. Their dispute reflected not only temperamental antagonism but their differing answers to a central and difficult question: At what point does dissent in wartime risk identification with treason and thereby lessen its chance of success? The failure of the members of the Anti-Imperialist League to reach common agreement is not surprising. It is a question that has beset every antiwar movement in American history, and perhaps it is a question that can never be answered in advance.

Some members of the League were prepared to declare publicly their support for Aguinaldo and their wish that he might be victorious. McKinley's ambitions were dangerous and should meet defeat. "My country right or wrong" was the cant of jingoists; the true patriot was the man who obeyed his conscience.

Supporters of the war found such statements false and disloyal. There was no difference, they declared, between advocacy of Aguinaldo's cause and enmity toward the American army, and enemies of the army were enemies of the nation. For Theodore Roosevelt such anti-imperialists were "simply unhung traitors," and the Grand Army of the Republic passed resolutions at its encampment in the summer of 1899 proclaiming members of the Anti-Imperialist League to be "unworthy of the name of American citizens." They were half-men—"Aunties"—and true descendents of the hated Copperheads of Civil War days.[23] *The New York Times* sneered that the Anti-Imperialist League should "send rifles, Maxim guns, and stores of ammunition to the Filipinos," for it would then "be more openly and frankly treasonable"; and during the presidential campaign of 1900 the New York *Tribune* insisted that the death of "every American soldier that is killed during these months" could be laid to the door of the anti-imperialists.[24]

More hurtful to the cause of the anti-imperialists than denunciations in the cribbed editorial columns of the *Times* and *Tribune* were the full-color cartoons displayed on the covers of such journals as *Puck* and *Judge*. Joseph Keppler, Jr., the cartoonist for *Puck*, was a fervant expansionist and one of the few men since Thomas Nast able to extract humor from bile. He sought to portray anti-imperialism as a cross between treason and transvestitism. The "Aunties" were dressed in skirts and poke bonnets and made to curtsy before arrogant Filipino clowns or attempt ineffectually to block the path of the valorous American soldier.[25] The most famous and libelous cartoon appeared in the Republican magazine, *Judge*. It showed an evil, grinning Aguinaldo, standing with his foot on the back of a dead soldier. The caption read, "What is behind Aguinaldo, that fiend who has slain many American Soldiers?" By raising the flap, the reader could discover behind the face of Aguinaldo the smiling countenance of William Jennings Bryan.[26]

John Barrett, former minister to Siam, and Congressman Lemuel Quigg competed with one another in slandering the Anti-Imperialist League and charging its membership with collective treason, but the most sweeping indictment was that penned by a little-known Vermont lawyer, Fred C. Chamberlin. The title of his essay made clear its theme: *The Blow from Behind, or Some Features of the Anti-Imperialistic Movement*.[27] The Fili-

Spoil-Sports of the Anti-Imperialist League, as seen by a Republican loyalist (from Judge, *24 February 1900)*

pino insurrection, wrote Chamberlin, would have been crushed in short order had not Aguinaldo been falsely encouraged by disloyal citizens in America. The words and acts of the anti-imperialists had cost the lives of hundreds of American soldiers—"stabbed in the back as they stood out there on the firing line." Aguinaldo had been incited and misled by the "copperhead sentiments" of his American allies and their collusion with members of the Filipino junta. He was able to continue his bloody banditry only because of the aid and support he received from the members of the Anti-Imperialist League. One did not see the name of any soldier or veteran on the lists of the League; for all anti-imperialists were cowards, "the first in peace and the last in war."[28]

When the patriots directed their fire against particular dissenters, they usually aimed at men only tangentially related to the Anti-Imperialist League. They attributed all opposition to the League, however, and erroneously believed that it gave sanction and inspiration to every dissenter. Gamaliel Bradford, in a speech before a small Connecticut "peace conference" in August 1899, called for a "moral alliance with the Filipinos" by all American citizens who opposed the war. His critics not only ignored the qualifying adjective but insisted that he had exposed the true sentiments of the Anti-Imperialist League.[29] Congressman John J. Lentz, at a meeting of "Peace Democrats" at Cooper Union in New York, proclaimed Aguinaldo one of the world's heroes and a spiritual brother to Patrick Henry. The Philadelphia *Press* demanded that the Anti-Imperialist League deny its latest spokesman.[30] The most extreme example of associative guilt, however, centered about the quixotic figure of Morrison I. Swift.

Swift was a highly individualistic socialist, and the only time he ever marched in line was in 1893 when he briefly joined the army of General Jacob Coxey. He scorned the Anti-Imperialist League and damned it for its bourgeois timidity.[31] He saw the Philippine War as the natural offspring of the plutocracy, the trusts, and the avarice of international bankers. McKinley's object was to get more territory for the millionaires to exploit. Whoever yielded to the dictation of the tyrant McKinley made himself an "accomplice of villains," and it was "the duty of every true citizen" to disobey the commands of the administration and see that "the arch-Ripper" was impeached and imprisoned.[32]

With a few like-minded souls, Swift formed in Los Angeles "The Filipino Liberation Society." Initially unknown and ignored, it gained a brief period of notoriety thanks to the excitability of Brigadier General Joe Wheeler. Emulating the efforts of Edward Atkinson, Swift had sent a few copies of an antiwar petition to the Philippines, and one of these fell into the hands of the feisty ex-Confederate. The petition asked for the signature of all who would denounce this foul and unjust war and pledge their energies to expunge "the greatest crime in our history." Wheeler sent his copy to General Otis, and Otis forwarded it to Washington by cable. Swift was assured of a place in the expanding "Roll of Dishonor," and Erving Winslow on behalf of the Anti-Imperialist League was soon disavowing any connection with Morrison I. Swift.[33]

There can be little doubt that accusations of treason worried the officials of the League. It is probably also true that these accusations discouraged some Americans from formally joining the organization. The editors of two German-American papers sought to make clear that their opposition to the war implied no wish for the military defeat of "their bride America." Yet the denunciations of its enemies afforded the League publicity and a satisfying sense of martyrdom. Certainly there were more important causes for the failure of the Anti-Imperialist League than the obloquy of its opponents and the charge of treason.

The charge of treason was the product of anger and intolerance, but was it without validity? The more undeviating supporters of the war insisted that the League was guilty of inspiring the Filipinos to continue their insurrection and guilty of seeking to undermine the morale and discipline of the American army. The first part of the indictment may be disproved rather easily; the second part is more open to debate.

The leaders of the Philippine "insurrection" were inspired by a determination to serve as rulers of an independent Philippine republic. Their goal and determination would have been the same had the Anti-Imperialist League never been formed or its members never uttered a word of protest against the war. Aguinaldo undoubtedly hoped that anti-imperialist protests would influence public opinion in America, and during the spring and summer of 1900 he issued several manifestos predicting the victory of "the anti-imperial party" in the American presidential election. At no time, however, did Aguinaldo suggest that the duration of the Filipino struggle depended on the success of the anti-imperialists in America.[34] It was on the guerrilla tactics of his soldiers, not the pamphlets of Erving Winslow, that Aguinaldo placed his hope of eroding the will of the American government.

Did the anti-imperialists undermine the morale and discipline of the American army in the Philippines and so afford its enemies indirect aid and comfort?[35] A few members and sympathizers of the League did openly seek to discourage army enlistments; others encouraged state legislatures to demand the return of volunteer units when their tour of duty was finished; and still others predicted the moral deterioration of the army and its surrender to tropical vices.[36] Such activities probably depressed a few enlisted men while infuriating more, but there is little evidence of a direct connection between antiwar sentiment in America and military morale in Luzon. Soldier morale was more influenced by rain, jungle rot, and the elusiveness of the guerrillas than by a few "treasonable telegrams" and admonitory pamphlets.[37] The soldier is usually quick to disdain civilian opinions on military matters, and there is no reason to believe that the handful of soldiers who heard of Moorfield Storey's anti-atrocity tract were thereby inspired to disobey the orders of their superior officers.

One must conclude that although a few members of the Anti-Imperialist League were prepared to undermine the morale of the army, the better to end "a war of criminal aggression," they had in fact little influence on the military effectiveness of the American army. On both counts, the charge of treason fails from lack of evidence.

If the League did not influence the course of events in Manila, neither did it alter administration policy in Washington. Its labors, however, were not without significance. Not only did the League serve as the publishing medium for some of the most eloquent expressions of protest against the Philippine-American War, but it provided as well the organizational structure for a large part of that protest.

The major weakness of the League was its lack of political power. The eloquence of its pamphleteers could force the administration to revise its defense, but the League did not enlist the political authority that could coerce the administration to alter its policy. The League suffered too from the heterogeneity of its membership. Civil service reformers and retired politicians, free traders and prohibitionists, municipal reformers and pacifists, labor leaders and academics could cooperate with one another on occasion, but the organizational effectiveness of the Anti-Imperialist League was hurt by this diversity and the divisions it encouraged.

A strong idealism characterized many members of the League, but a number joined from motives of fear. These tended to fall away when certain of the more selfish of those fears were assuaged by acts and promises of the McKinley and Roosevelt administrations. Those who joined because of racist fears respecting the admission of the Filipinos to the rights of American citizenship or economic fears respecting a possible influx of cheap Filipino labor and sweatshop Filipino goods tended to fall away when the Republican majority in Congress made clear its determination to sustain immigration and tariff barriers and restrict the Filipino to civil liberties exercisable in the Philippines.

Even the more dedicated members of the League divided over questions of emphasis and tactics. Some were full-fledged pacifists, others wanted only to stress the evils of this particular war. Some wished to associate the war with the monopolistic ambitions of the trusts, others were stockholders in those same trusts. There were disputes over the propriety of associating anti-imperialism with partisan politics, and there was confusion concerning the emphasis to be given to the needs and welfare of the Filipino people.

Acknowledgment of the fears and divisions of the League need not inspire contempt for its goals and tactics. Some of its leaders were naive, but more were courageous. Theirs was not a failure of will but of political strength. Like other protest groups in American history, they lacked a recognized role in the political system. The Anti-Imperialist League had friends in Congress who would present its memorials and petitions and occasionally address its meetings, but no active politician ever served any branch of the League in other than an honorary capacity. The League asked fundamental and necessary questions about the principles and future of American political society, but whatever their skill as propagandists, its members were poor politicians operating without a secure political base. They were unable to defeat the inertia of congressional politics or inspire among the urban middle class apprehensions sufficient to overcome sentiments of national pride and optimism.

CHAPTER IV

War and Politics

At no time did the Philippine-American War become the dominant issue between the two major parties, but the Republicans were inescapably associated with the administration's goals of military victory and benevolent indoctrination, and Democratic politicians were frequently critical of the duration of the war and its conduct. Only briefly during the presidential campaign of 1900 did the Democratic party give criticism official expression, but a distinction may be drawn between the majority position of the Republican and Democratic parties. The response of professional politicians to the Philippine-American War had a partisan flavor.

Taking their lead from the national administration, most Republican politicians insisted that the war was the product of the duplicity of a small minority of Filipinos led by a would-be tyrant. Aguinaldo had attacked the American army without provocation and there was no honorable course but to chastise this Tagalog bandit and suppress his insurrection. America had legally acquired sovereignty over the Philippines from Spain, and that sovereignty must be acknowledged. We had never stooped to negotiate with those in armed rebellion, begging their good conduct with promises; nor should we now. Once American authority was acknowledged throughout the archipelago, we would train the Filipinos and endow them with such rights and liberties as they were capable of exercising, but our benevolence must await their submission.[1]

Republican spokesmen usually denied that our expansion into the Western Pacific represented a new departure, and few were prepared to adopt the imperial vision and oratory of Senator Albert J. Beveridge. For the most part they justified the annexation of the islands and the military chastisement of the Filipinos on the grounds of necessity. There was no alternative in either instance. Annexation was the only honorable course after Dewey's defeat of the Spanish fleet in Manila Bay; suppression of the Tagalog rebellion was required by the needs of the untutored Filipinos as well as the demands of American honor.

[58]

Honor, duty, and necessity were the ingredients of an argument of wider political appeal than Beveridge's talk of raw materials and Pacific supremacy, and they furnished the most constant theme of Republican oratory. It was a theme reiterated time and again by William McKinley in his speaking tour through the Middle West and Plains West in the fall of 1899. "Our sons" were in the Philippines "because in the providence of God, who moves mysteriously, that great archipelago has been placed in the hands of the American people." Hostilities would cease "when those who commenced them will stop," but they would not cease until our flag "shall float triumphantly in every island of the archipelago under the undisputed and acknowledged sovereignty of the republic of the United States." We had never in our proud history given "a bribe for peace," nor would we now. Rather we would put sufficient men behind the flag in Luzon to maintain our authority and fulfill our responsibilities.[2]

The administration's defense of its Philippine policy became more strident in response to anti-imperialist attack, and not only did McKinley take to the stump but various of his cabinet officers as well. The most effective of these was Elihu Root. In a series of set speeches over the next year, Root described the beneficial intent of American colonial policy and elaborated the administration argument respecting the incapacity of the Filipinos. There was "no Philippine people." The islands were inhabited by more than eighty different tribes, speaking more than sixty different languages. The alleged government of Aguinaldo at Malolos was never acknowledged by a majority of the Filipinos, and the period of attempted Tagalog domination in Luzon, between June 1898 and February 1899, "was marked by the worst evils of semi-civilized misgovernment." We would do the cause of liberty an ill service were we to deliver "the patient and unconsenting millions of all other tribes" into the hands of "the assassin Aguinaldo . . . and the authors of the [Manila] massacre order."[3]

In Congress the most eloquent Republican supporter of the war was Henry Cabot Lodge. Lodge assumed personal responsibility for defending the goals and conduct of the American army, and in his speech of 7 March 1900 presented the most detailed defense of American Philippine policy ever offered the U.S. Congress.[4] It was a speech that blended the initial arguments of the imperialists respecting American duty and responsibility with a heightened emphasis on the strategic and economic advantages of the Philippines. The unexpected protraction of the war made it necessary to remind the American people of expanding markets as well as the onward march of Anglo-Saxon civilization, and Lodge's sonorous prose gave obeisance to profit and to service.

The Republican party was not united in behalf of the administration's

Philippine policy or the war, but the dissenters were an ineffective minority. They were unable to determine the party's position in any of the forty-five states, and their efforts were increasingly muffled as the war continued. Their ineffectiveness was due as much to their lack of influence as their lack of numbers. They tended to be members of an older generation. George Boutwell, Benjamin Harrison, George Edmunds, John Sherman, George Hoar, Eugene Hale, and Thomas Reed were Republicans whose authority and power lay in the past; the "Young Men's Republican Clubs" had other party heros. Hoar and Hale alone were office holders in the year 1900, and each was already eclipsed by a younger senatorial colleague. Thomas B. Reed, once czar of the House, might have provided a source of power for Republican dissent, but he had retired from political life and was content to express his scorn for the war and its military goals in private letters to sympathetic correspondents.

Although there were a few Republicans in Congress who questioned the war, their protests were uncoordinated and their motives often confused. Senator Henry M. Teller, after a brief flirtation with imperialism, turned against the administration's Philippine policy, but he appeared to be concerned primarily with the beet sugar industry of Colorado and the need to restrict the importation of Filipino produce. Congressmen Samuel Mc-Call and Henry U. Johnson and Senator Walter Mason gave greater attention to questions of justice, but their protests were occasional and directed against the policy of imperialism rather than the Philippine-American War. They shied away from criticism of the army or the military conduct of the war.

Of the Republican anti-imperialists in Congress, George Frisbie Hoar was comparatively the boldest. A social conservative convinced of the God-given superiority of the Republican party, he was prepared to praise Aguinaldo, proclaim the political competence of the Filipinos, and accuse the army of misconduct. Aguinaldo was a brave and honest man, and his detractors should remember that Commodore Dewey had sought his aid. The Filipinos had taken up arms in defense of their republic, and there was no "greater and more pestilent delusion than the notion that a strong people may take away the liberty of a weak one, if . . . [it] happens to think the weak one not fit for liberty." Our attempt to despoil the Filipinos of their freedom and independence was a story of "shame and dishonor," and no part of that story was more shameful than the brutalization of our soldiers.[5]

Suggestions of misconduct by the American army brought a quick response from several of Hoar's Republican colleagues. He was charged with talking like a copperhead Democrat.

The response of the Democratic party to the Philippine-American War was significantly influenced by its apprehension of being labeled the copperhead party. The opposition of many Democratic politicians was restricted by their memories of the party's struggle during the Reconstruction decade to prove its patriotism. They did not now wish to give their political opponents the opportunity to wave another bloody shirt. Even those Democrats who believed the Philippine war to be unjust as well as unnecessary flinched when Republican papers printed Aguinaldo's commendation of "the great good Democratic party" and his prayers for its political success.[6] Fear of the copperhead label was part cause for the refusal of Senator Augustus Bacon and other Democratic leaders to accept the suggestion of Edward Atkinson that they vote against army supply bills and thereby force the administration to stop the war. Bacon and the Democratic minority in Congress continued to vote in favor of appropriation bills and measures authorizing increased enlistments in the army and navy. If they disliked American military objectives, they were not prepared to take responsibility for reducing the chance of American military success. Criticism was within the American tradition; obstruction in wartime was not.[7]

The national committee of the Democratic party carefully abstained from any alliance with the Anti-Imperialist League, and only in the election of 1900 was it prepared to make opposition to imperialism "the paramount issue." There were many Democrats who disliked the administration's Philippine policy, and there were some who were prepared to criticize the Philippine-American War, but the institutional response of the Democratic party to the war was neither emphatic nor consistent.[8] It was characterized by uncertainty, selective criticism, and sectional differences.

Democrats in the East tended to be more suspicious of the fruits of imperialism than those in the Far West. Democratic-Populists in the Plains West were more ready to see Bryan identify the party with anti-imperialism than were the Democrats of the Deep South. There were in all cases, however, intraregional differences. The Dixie Democrats best illustrate those differences, and Senators John T. Morgan of Alabama and Benjamin R. ("Pitchfork Ben") Tillman of South Carolina can serve as biographical examples.

Senator Morgan was an admitted expansionist. Morgan believed that the welfare of the South was linked to the industrial growth of the United States, and that it would be self-defeating for either the South or the Democratic party to resist the demands of American nationalism. Expansion was the cure for disunity and the best assurance of the prosperity of the South and the nation. Once they acknowledged American sovereignty, the Filipinos would enjoy American textiles as well as American justice.

No red-blooded American would wish to see the flag lowered where once it had been raised, and Southern Democrats should emulate "Fightin' Joe" Wheeler, who now served in Luzon as proudly as once he had at Shiloh.[9] Many Southern Democratic politicians agreed with Morgan, either from a conviction that the administration's Philippine policy was right or a belief that to oppose it would be politically unwise. Others, however, agreed with Senator Tillman that colonial expansion was dangerous, the war inglorious, and opposition to both the best course for the white southerner and Democrat.

Tillman publicly declared his conviction that the white man always had and always would "walk on the necks of every colored race he comes into contact with." Talk of "benevolent assimilation" was ridiculous. The only relation possible between American and Filipino was that of dominance and subjugation, and the United States did not need "another race problem." The southerner with his superior experience in this area should be the first to recognize this fact and protest "the subjugation of the Filipinos and the establishment of a military government over them by force." The South must oppose "incorporating any more colored men into the body politic," and remind northern imperialists and missionaries that our first duty was not to the Filipinos but to the safety of the American republic. To continue to send "thousands and tens of thousands of reenforcements" to the Philippines in an effort to expunge some dishonor supposedly done the American flag was to risk "familiarizing our people with despotic methods" and to imitate Mahomet who pursued converts with a scimitar.[10]

A similar mixture of racist fears and antimilitarist convictions can be found in the speeches of John Sharp Williams, a congressman from Mississippi, and Edward W. Carmack, junior senator from Tennessee.[11] Carmack went further than Tillman in his opposition to the conduct of the American army. Where Tillman projected the probable use of "despotic methods," Carmack proclaimed military atrocities a fact. His suspicions of the military were matched by suspicions of the trusts, and he never failed to make an appeal to partisan animosities as well as racial anxieties. But if his motives were mixed, Carmack stood witness that many Southern Democrats were opposed to the acquisition of the Philippines and a minority were prepared to oppose a war that had as its goal the retention of those islands.[12]

Certain of the Gold Democrats were also prepared to judge the war unwise, but they were probably outnumbered by others who supported the war. Whereas Abram S. Hewitt, Thomas Mott Osborne, Louis Ehrich, and John Carlisle were anti-imperialists, Richard Olney, John Palmer, Perry Belmont, and a majority of the Gold Democrat editors of the Northeast believed in the propriety of economic expansion and saw no alternative to the military chastisement of Aguinaldo. Belmont wished to see the Democrats in Congress assume a greater role in prescribing the terms of pacification and bringing "the armed rebellion" to a swift conclusion, but he believed the Constitution posed no impediment to our pursuit of "the vast mission for the advancement of mankind."[13]

The Populist-Democrats of the Plains West furnished the core of Bryan's strength in the Democratic party and the group most united in its suspicion of imperial adventures. If they were reluctant to associate anti-imperialism with antimilitarism, they showed from the beginning little enthusiasm for the Philippine-American War. For some Populist Democrats distaste turned to opposition as they increasingly identified the war with the political needs and ambitions of the Republican party. Governor William Poynter of Nebraska was ready in April 1899 to label it "a war of conquest" and to deny that it would bring "new glory to our flag," and fourteen months later this view gained tacit adoption in the platform of the Nebraska Demo-Pop convention.[14] The virtue and necessity of the war was increasingly questioned by certain German-American and Irish-American communities in the Plains states. They associated colonial wars and conquests with the example of the British Empire. America should never ally itself with England, "the hereditary and implacable enemy of . . . human liberty throughout the world"; nor allow deceitful John Bull to place the burdens of imperialism on the back of Uncle Sam.[15]

Other Bryan Democrats, who were neither "hyphenates" nor former Populists, agreed that colonial wars should remain the monopoly of the Old World. Congressmen Joe Bailey, Champ Clark, and William H. Fleming were supporters of William Jennings Bryan, and each in his varying way criticized the war.[16] None were members of the Anti-Imperialist League, but all subscribed to the view of Senator Bacon that the war could be ended immediately if the administration promised the Filipinos that we would recognize their status as an independent nation once we had helped them establish a stable government.

This judgment represented the majority opinion among Bryan Democrats, and it became official party policy in the Democratic Convention of 1900.

There was guerrilla action throughout the years of the Philippine-American War between the Democratic and Republican parties but only one formal battle. This was the campaign of 1900, and it was a confrontation without a climax. Anti-imperialism would be denied the popular referendum it had seemingly been promised.

In July 1900 the redemption of that promise appeared likely. At least a half-dozen magazine editors were planning symposia articles on "The Philippines and the Election" for their next issue. The Democrats had formally declared that imperialism and the administration's Philippine policy was "the paramount issue" facing the American electorate, and the Republican convention, though avoiding explicit advocacy of colonialism, had taken a position of whole-hearted support for the diplomatic and military policies of William McKinley. The Philippine planks of the two major parties were not "Tweedledum and Tweedledee," as some historians have mistakenly insisted,[17] but were significantly different.

The Republican platform declared that with the destruction of Spanish authority in the Philippines it became the duty of America "to provide for the maintenance of law and order, and for the establishment of good government and for the performance of international obligations. Our authority could not be less than our responsibility; and wherever sovereign rights were extended it became the high duty of the Government to maintain its authority, to put down armed insurrection, and to confer the blessings of liberty and civilization upon all the rescued peoples." The Democratic platform proclaimed imperialism "the paramount issue" of the campaign and declared: "We favor an immediate declaration of the nation's purpose to give to the Filipinos, first, a stable form of government; second, independence; and third, protection from outside interference such as has been given for nearly a century to the republics of Central and South America."[18] The Democratic plank was cautiously phrased, but it was neither a sell-out nor a rhetorical variation of the Republican position. It did not demand immediate independence for the Philippines and implied that recognition of Philippine sovereignty must await the establishment of "a stable form of government," but the essential theme of the Philippine plank of the Democratic party was a denunciation of imperial expansion. The essential theme of its Republican counterpart was a defense of a foreign policy of colonial expansion. Those historians who judge "the protectorate scheme" of the Democratic platform to be indistinguishable in effect from the "imperial benevolence" of the Republican platform ignore a crucial difference. The limited protectorate projected by the Democrats was presumably to be arranged with the voluntary consent of the Filipinos.

Certainly those delegates of the Democratic convention most opposed to McKinley's Philippine policy did not believe that they were supporting a plank that was simply imperialism in disguise.[19] They were men less well educated than their recent critics, but their understanding of their own motives and intentions was not necessarily inferior. When the platform was read, no plank received greater applause than that elaborating the party's intentions respecting the Philippines. According to the reporter for *The*

New York Times, "the crowd screamed" as a 75-foot flag was unfurled and the delegates saw "printed in huge letters" the words, "A Republic Can Have No Colonies."[20] These anti-imperialist delegates left the Democratic convention convinced that their platform excoriated the imperialism of the Republican party and offered a distinct and constructive alternative.[21]

In one sense, however, the Democratic platform was a compromise. If the Democrats were prepared to declare imperialism "the paramount issue," they were not prepared to insert a condemnation of the Philippine-American War. Some delegates believed the war disgraceful, more were convinced that it was unnecessary, but to condemn it was to divide the convention and give the Republican slanderers additional ammunition. It was safer to offer a way to end the war than to denounce it.

The failure of the Democratic party platform to criticize the Philippine-American War was the first of many developments that lessened the likelihood that the presidential election of 1900 would assume the character of a referendum, but the omission did little to lessen the Republican assault on the Democratic alternative.

That assault began with McKinley's letter of acceptance, in which he indicated his belief that the Democrats proposed not only a different policy but one of great vulnerability:

> The American people are asked by our opponents to yield the sovereignty of the United States in the Philippines to a small fraction of the population . . . a fraction which wantonly attacked the American troops in Manila. . . . We are asked to protect this minority in establishing a government. . . . We are required to set up a stable government in the interest of those who have assailed our sovereignty and fired upon our soldiers, and then maintain it at any cost or sacrifice against its enemies within and against those having ambitious designs from without.

The American people could be assured that the Republican party wished only to do for the Filipinos better than they could do for themselves, but American sovereignty must be acknowledged. The suggestion of the Democratic party that the United States try to bribe the insurgents with promises concerning future American policy was not only dishonorable but dangerous. It encouraged the insurgents to continue their guerrilla warfare. Most blameworthy were those opponents of the nation's Philippine policy who would charge our soldiers with brutality. Such men were the enemies not only of the army but of truth. "Every step of the progress of our troops has been marked by a humanity which has surprised even the misguided insurgents."[22]

McKinley had given the marching orders for his party's attack on the

"Take Your Choice" –the flag raiser or the man who would cut down "Old Glory" (from Judge, *12 May 1900)*

Democratic alternative. That alternative was to be ridiculed and associated with opposition to the war and encouragement of the insurgents. The Republicans were to deny that imperialism was a valid campaign issue while making an issue of the anti-imperialists and the presumed consequences of their dissent. This strategy had been foreshadowed earlier by the Wisconsin senator, John C. Spooner, when he had explained to the Senate that imperialism was "a forced and fictitious issue" that could not be considered a proper subject for political debate, and then called upon all loyal Republicans to denounce and defeat the anti-imperialist agitation that had "prolonged the insurrection . . . and cost many, many lives."[23] In his campaign tour in the fall of 1900, Theodore Roosevelt would deny that the United States was pursuing a policy of imperialism and would castigate the anti-imperialists for their lack of patriotism. Only fools would confuse the healthy and historic expansion of America with imperialism, and the anti-imperialists were worse than fools. They were champions of Filipino bandits and "miscreants" who urged cowardly surrender.[24]

Roosevelt reserved his harsher appellations for his private correspondence, but the second echelon of Republican orators were not always as circumspect. Some proclaimed Bryan to be the tool of Aguinaldo and the Filipino insurgents as well as the ally of Atkinson and the Boston anti-imperialists. Rumors were floated that the insurgents were negotiating a formal alliance with Bryan and the Filipino junta was raising a campaign fund in his behalf.[25]

The latter weeks of the campaign, however, found the Republicans tending to ignore the evil allies of Bryan and the iniquity of the Democratic alternative. It seemed less necessary to assault the latter, for the Democrats themselves gave it less emphasis.

For Bryan the subordination of the issue of imperialism in the last weeks of the campaign represented less a retreat than a return. Domestic issues were those that most readily inspired his moral certitudes. His denunciations of McKinley's Philippine policy were sincere, but his primary concern was always for the farmer subjugated by the money interests of the East rather than the Filipino subjugated by the American army of the Pacific. At the Kansas City convention he made clear his personal priorities when he had threatened to refuse the nomination if the Democratic platform did not explicitly reaffirm the party's advocacy of Free Silver.

In his letter of acceptance, Bryan had given much space to the issue of insular imperialism. He had attacked the economic arguments of the expansionists, and expounded at length on the safety and justice of a limited American protectorate. A pledge to protect the Filipino republic from outside aggression would be "neither difficult nor expensive"; for if the

Bryan's "Allies," from an Expansionist perspective (from Judge, *11 August 1900)*

Filipinos showed "as much determination in opposing the sovereignty of other nations as they have shown in opposing our sovereignty," they would require little assistance.[26] But even in his letter of acceptance, Bryan refrained from any direct attack on the war policy of the McKinley administration. As the campaign proceeded, references to the Filipino and to American injustice abroad diminished and increasing attention was given to the farmer and economic problems at home. Bryan might still believe that "no nation can endure half Republic and half Empire," but by October he seldom mentioned the Philippine archipelago or the Democratic alternative of a limited protectorate.

Bryan, the "Filipino Negro," and our "southern Negro" (from Judge, *3 November 1900)*

The campaign efforts of his supporters witnessed a similar evolution. There were exceptions. Bourke Cockran, in an address delivered in Boston only a few days before the election, gave forthright praise to the Filipinos' refusal to submit to American piracy, and declared that it should be a subject of rejoicing "that the people of the Philippines are resisting our efforts to subjugate them."[27] But most Democratic orators and editors followed Bryan's lead and played down the Philippine issue as the campaign moved toward its conclusion. When they saw that even the party faithful found it difficult to see McKinley as both a timid politico in the pocket of Mark Hanna and a military tyrant on horseback, they tended to discard the latter image and concentrate on the domestic sins of the Republican nominee. The editor of the *Atlanta Constitution*, who in September had thundered against McKinley for perverting "a war for the rights of the revolutionists in Cuba into a war for the suppression of the same class of revolutionists in the Philippines," was by the third week in October content to chide McKinley for his favoritism to the bankers of the Northeast.[28]

It was not, of course, Bryan's political priorities alone that prevented a partisan confrontation on the issues of imperialism and military pacification. The nature of the American political system and an understandable reluctance by Democratic politicians to court the charge of copperheadism played their part, and so, too, did the relationship of the Democratic party and the black American. The reliance of the party on the white majority of the South made it difficult for the Democrats to sustain a denunciation of Republican treatment of "tropical races." The Democratic party made little effort to appeal to the black voter on the score of racial justice for the Filipino, and the "domestic racism" of many Democratic politicians— Bryan among them—weakened their advocacy of self-determination for the Filipino people.

The attempt of Erving Winslow to forge an alliance between the Anti-Imperialist League and the Democratic party was doomed to failure.[29] The Democrats were fearful of too close an alignment with League members who had been charged with treasonous deeds, and many members of the League found increasing fault with Bryan as the campaign proceeded while others denied from the outset his right to serve as the champion of anti-imperialism.[30] Not only did economic conservatives find it difficult to support Bryan, but so, too, did some of the more single-minded members of the League. Edward Atkinson shed curses alike on Bryan and McKinley, and Carl Schurz, though prepared to vote for Bryan, judged the necessity a "real martyrdom." Schurz and others were particularly disappointed at Bryan's decision to emphasize silver rather than the Philippines in the last month of the campaign.[31] In defense of their reluctance to work in his behalf, some members of the Anti-Imperialist League persuaded themselves that Bryan's policy for the Philippines differed little from that of McKinley. If this belief was incorrect, it was probably shared by many voters in the election of 1900.

By the time the voters went to the polls on Tuesday, 6 November, neither major party wished to make American policy in the Philippines "the paramount issue." Historians have agreed with unaccustomed unanimity that it was not.[32] The implication that it was irrelevant to the results of the election is, however, misleading. One of several factors explaining McKinley's comparatively easy victory would be the success of the Republicans in defusing the issue of imperialism while identifying the administration with the U.S. Army in the Philippines. The Republicans successfully damned the Philippine plank of the Democratic platform and set against the picture of a vacillating Bryan that of a rocklike McKinley, unwavering in his respect for the American soldier. In one of his many retrospective analyses of the election results, Bryan suggested that his party's Philippine plank had cost him votes, and he was probably right.[33] The election was not a referendum on imperialism or the war, but McKinley's skillful attack on obstructionists and dissenters in the early weeks of September increased the majorities he received in November. McKinley wrapped himself in the flag and clasped hands with the boys in khaki. It was a politically advantageous posture, particularly among newly acquired party members in the Mississippi Valley and on the West Coast. Superior organization, prosperity, and fear of "Bryanism" assured success for the Republican ticket, but the diplomatic and military policies of McKinley enlarged the margin of victory.

Bryan's defeat in the presidential election of 1900 discouraged the national organization of the Democratic party from sustaining its identification with anti-imperialism, but in Congress the war and the administration's Philippine policy occasionally inspired partisan conflict over the next eighteen months. The ranks of the Democratic dissenters steadily thinned and Gorman and Bacon lost interest, but Tillman, Carmack, and a few others sought to associate the Democratic minority with anti-imperialism. The winter–spring of 1902 saw them seeking party votes in behalf of an investigation of military misconduct by the American army in the Philippines. The Senate Philippine Committee was authorized to hold hearings, and those hearings were characterized by continuous partisan bickering between the majority and minority members. Carmack and Chairman Lodge made no effort to conceal their mutual disdain and Senators Charles A. Culberson and Albert J. Beveridge baited each other with increasing animus. In the Senate as a whole, however, neither military atrocities nor their investigation became a clear-cut partisan issue.

The hearings of the Senate Philippine Committee came to an inconclusive end in June 1902, shortly before the Republican majority secured passage of the Philippine Government Act. The Senate Democrats selected this bill for a last-stand effort, realizing that once Congress approved a form of civil government for the territory of the Philippines, however restricted the rights of the island inhabitants, accusations of military tyranny would appear irrelevant if not anachronistic. The bill passed by an almost straight party vote, 42–29, with only a single Democrat voting for passage. For many of the Democratic leaders opposition was more symbolic than vigorous, but this could not be said of Senators Tillman and Rawlins. Tillman proclaimed his conviction that "the inordinate greed of . . . some men to get ungodly and indecent wealth [lies] . . . at the bottom of this bill," and Joseph Rawlins denounced the bill as a partisan trick hurtful to the interests of small businessmen, Democrats, and Filipinos, all of whom must bear the costs of corporate greed and carpetbagger-style territorial government.[34]

Its chief defender was Henry Cabot Lodge, who insisted that the measure gave the lie to those who had sought to associate Republican policy with a desire to tyrannize over our colonial wards.[35] His exposition of the bill's virtues convinced neither Thomas M. Patterson, the Democratic senator from Colorado, nor the editors of the New York *Evening Post*,[36] but some six months later the *Atlantic Monthly* printed an article by a young Princeton professor that appeared to endorse both the Philippine Government Act and the argument of Senator Lodge. Woodrow Wilson wished to see Americans govern their colonial wards in a democratic spirit, but the Filipinos for their part "must obey as those who are in tutelage." Liberty must be balanced by the needs of order, and Wilson feared that this cardinal principle had been forgotten by those who had cheered on "the Filipino rebels in their stubborn resistance to the very government they themselves live under and owe fealty to." The Filipinos could not expect to have liberty without first learning "the discipline of law." For the moment, they were as "children," and we were their tutors "in these deep matters of government and justice."[37]

In the year 1902 Wilson was not a spokesman for the Democratic party. It consequently exceeds poetic license to assert that his article demonstrates that after the passage of the Philippine Government Act, imperialism in the Philippines was no longer a subject of partisan division. There is nothing fanciful, however, in the observation that in the congressional elections of November 1902, no prominent Democrat raised the issue of the Philippines and its future. President Roosevelt had declared the Philippine-American War ended with his proclamation of 4 July, and the Democratic party was not prepared to sustain the debate over the necessity and justice of that war.

The historian who interprets the response of parties and politicians to a controversial issue exclusively in terms of the two major parties usually risks error in behalf of simplicity. Partisan response to the Philippine-American War may be analyzed, however, almost exclusively in terms of the major parties and their politicians, for none of the third parties took a distinctive position in support of or opposition to McKinley's Philippine policy and the war it inspired. The Prohibition party did not see fit to defend or attack the war, and when it mentioned the Philippines it was only to express its concern about the dispensing of beer in the army canteens and the expanding number of saloons in Manila. It was apparently more worried about the sobriety of the army than its mission.[38] The Socialist Labor party made no effort to denounce the war or offer praise for the struggle of the Filipino, preferring to concentrate on economic injustice and class warfare at home, and the small anti-Fusionist rump of the Populist party similarly ignored the Philippines and the "insurrection" of the Filipinos.[39]

An exception of sorts to the lack of interest shown by third parties was the Social Democratic party. This party offered no praise of Bryan or the alternative Philippine policy offered by the Democratic party, insisting that the major parties were equally capitalist and so, of necessity, equally imperialist. But some of its members did condemn the war. The editor of the *Haverhill* (Massachusetts) *Social Democrat* saw the Philippine-American War as one with the wars in China and South Africa. In all three cases the big capitalists had ordered out the military in an effort to gain new markets. But workers in the United States should concentrate on "the imperialism of the factory." Once that had been ended by the victory of socialism, foreign wars of exploitation would be a thing of the past.[40]

Recent efforts to portray the Socialists as the only true enemies of insular imperialism and the Filipinos' best friend are exercises in exaggeration.[41] A few socialists spoke out against the Philippine-American War, but most viewed the anti-imperialist crusade as merely a sideshow to the class struggle at home. Eugene Debs diluted Marxist doctrine with several parts of midwestern isolationism and virtually ignored the Philippines during the campaign of 1900.

It seems fair to conclude that the third parties refused to allow colonialism and the Philippine-American War to displace those issues about which they felt a particular proprietary claim. To the degree that McKinley's Philippine policy inspired partisan division, that division was confined almost exclusively to the Republican and Democratic parties.

The politicians of the Democratic party exhibited neither unity nor consistency, and few were bold enough to move beyond criticism of imperialism to denunciation of an imperialist war, but it was the Democratic party that provided the source of dissent in national politics. The anti-imperialist Republicans were too few and lacked party authority; the officials of the Anti-Imperialist League were educators with little political power. The only sizable body of anti-imperialist politicians were members of the Democratic party. Their labors, though sufficient to publicize the presumed errors of McKinley's policy, were insufficient to defeat or reverse it. Only for a brief period during the campaign of 1900 was the national organization of the Democratic party prepared to declare the relationship of the Philippines and the United States a "paramount issue." Bryan shied away from a direct confrontation, and his defeat made certain that the opposition of Democratic politicians in the last years of the war was sporadic, uncertain, and increasingly ineffective.

CHAPTER V

Business, Labor, and
the Influence of Economic Self-Interest

Several historians identified with that elastic classification known as the "New Left" have suggested that as American foreign policy has always reflected the goals of dominant economic groups, so McKinley's decision to annex the Philippines and subjugate the Filipinos is to be explained by the ambitions of American manufacturers and investors. They see the Philippines providing an example of the power of economic self-interest to determine foreign policy and the domestic response to diplomatic developments.

A crude paraphrase of their views might go in this fashion: The evolution of industrial capitalism in the United States saw the growth of trusts and brought increasing political power to the representatives of Big Business. The quest for aggrandizement that stimulated industrial combination at home inspired a policy of expansion abroad for by the 1890s the capitalist economy of the United States appeared threatened by its own productivity. Manufacturers sought new markets, as did American investors desirous of a higher rate of return, and the Philippine archipelago was judged a most valuable possession. Not only would the islands provide a new market for American goods and capital, but they would serve as an entrepôt for the still more important market of China. Business consequently favored a policy of territorial colonialism and demanded the annexation of the Philippines. As the needs of capital expansion had inspired McKinley's Philippine policy, Business praised that policy and supported the military effort to subjugate the Filipinos.

There are obvious variations among these historians and their arguments. If a reasonably accurate summary of the views of Daniel B. Schirmer, such a paraphrase offers an incomplete representation of the more sophisticated analysis of such authors as Thomas J. McCormick.[1] For all their differences, however, these historians emphasize the paramount importance of economic self-interest in their analyses of both the inspiration

[75]

of our Philippine policy and the response of Business to that policy. They
see Big Business as firm in its belief that the Philippines had to be retained
for the greater gain and safety of American capital. Conversely, some of
them imply that representatives of the laboring masses, aware of the essential connection between monopoly at home and militarism abroad, stood
opposed to the subjugation of the Philippines.[2]

It is a picture that offers a good deal of surface persuasiveness. It
would appear logical that Big Business would acclaim the Philippine policy
of William McKinley and that Labor might recognize a parallel between
tribulations of the American workingman and those of his brother in the
Philippines. An examination of the response of Business and Labor, however, reveals not only the force of economic self-interest but the influence
of division and uncertainty within the Business and Labor communities.
Although such an examination does not disprove the thesis that American
imperialism was the result of the inner necessities of the capitalist system,
it provides a poor exhibit wherewith to prove that thesis.

A majority of the representatives and spokesmen of Business who
offered an opinion concerning McKinley's Philippine policy indicated a
belief in its propriety. Few expressed any great interest in that policy,
however, or in the Philippine-American War. The Philippines was an issue
of major concern for only a few representatives of the business community,
and the initial flurry of excitement respecting the economic advantages of
the islands was not long sustained. When Roosevelt declared the war over
in July 1902, there was only a small U.S. business presence in the islands,
and whatever the long-term ambitions of certain manufacturers and investors respecting the Philippines, they had exhibited by that date more caution than avarice.[3]

Those businessmen who spoke optimistically of the economic oppor-
tunities offered by the Philippines usually emphasized the potential of the
Filipinos as consumers of American produce, shoes, machinery, and tex-
tiles. There was much less talk of the Philippines as a market for surplus
American capital or as a source of raw materials, and little mention of the
possibility of the Philippines serving as the American equivalent of Hong
Kong. Such business organizations as the New York State Chamber of
Commerce were undeniably interested in expanding American trade with
China, but only infrequently did they associate this long-term interest with
the pacification and economic development of the Philippines. As discussion of our Oriental trade had been sustained throughout the previous
decade without reference to the Philippines, so now it evidently had in the
minds of many businessmen no essential relationship to those islands.[4] The

diplomat-publicist John Barrett proclaimed such a relationship as he labored to obtain public support for insular imperialism. He prophesied that the Philippines would not only furnish "the most valuable field of development, exploitation, and investment yet untouched beyond the borders of the United States," but would prove additionally valuable as a vestibule to the untapped markets of China.[5] For the representatives of American finance and industry already involved in the China trade, however, possession of the Philippines did not appear to promise any immediate benefit. When the president of the National Association of Manufacturers and the editor of the New York *Journal of Commerce* made reference to the economic value of the Philippines, they were not employing a code name for the markets of China, and their hopes appeared to rest primarily on the potential of the islands as a market for consumer goods rather than a market for American capital that could not find occupation at home.

Industrial organizations such as the New England Boot and Shoe Association tended to be more optimistic about the economic value of American possession of the Philippines than such mercantile organizations as the Boston Merchants Association. Similarly, those manufacturers whose markets were small or regional were more likely to emphasize the monetary expense of pacification than those manufacturers whose increasing productivity appeared to demand wider markets. The metallurgical industry offered an example of the latter. Naval protection of the Philippines and the construction of railroads in the islands would enhance the effective demand of two of the largest customers of the American iron and steel industry, and most spokesmen for the metallurgical industry advocated the subjugation and retention of the Philippines.

Other businessmen, however, were less certain of the economic advantages of the Philippines and more conscious of the costs of pacification. Of these, Andrew Carnegie was the most famous, but there were others, less rich but equally convinced that colonialism and war were harmful to the national economy. John J. Valentine, Edwin Ginn, Jacob Schiff, James J. Hill, Godfrey L. Cabot, Robert Fulton Cutting, Richard T. Crane, Dana Estes, George Foster Peabody, and Henry Lee Higginson believed that insular imperialism was bad business. All favored the expansion of American commerce, but they saw colonial acquisition and "gunboat diplomacy" as extravagant and dangerous. A nation did not increase its markets by ruling or slaughtering natives; we would be in a better position to command our share of the trade of the Far East if freed of colonial responsibilities. They agreed with the Boston *Traveller* that "we could trade with the Filipinos far better as friendly allies than as hostile subjects," and with the New York *Herald* "that as a mere cold-blooded business proposition we are engaged in a very bad speculation.'' The civil and military administration of the islands would entail a "tremendous drain on our resources," and heavy tax burdens must follow.[6]

For some businessmen, insular imperialism represented bad morals as well as bad economics. They usually avoided formal association with the Anti-Imperialist League, considering it too radical in character or too mugwumpish in membership, but several helped subsidize the distribution of anti-imperialist literature. John J. Valentine assumed personal responsibility for distributing various addresses of the pacifist president of Stanford University, David Starr Jordan. The largest financial contributor to the anti-imperialist movement, however, was Carnegie, and Carnegie may serve as illustration of the attitudes and limitations of the anti-imperialist minority within the business community.

Carnegie was a sincere anti-imperialist, but he tended to oscillate between anger and withdrawal. During the first year of the war he wrote several effective articles for the *North American Review* describing the malign influence of the tropics on white soldiers and the economic disadvantages of colonialism, gunboat diplomacy, and war. The Filipinos should be allowed to prove their capacity for self-government in their own way and by their own standards. He warned America not to imitate the colonial adventures of the European powers. By grabbing tropical colonies we would antagonize Europe, alarm Latin America, and endanger the markets we most needed.[7] Carnegie accepted appointment as an honorary vice president of the Anti-Imperialist League and contributed generously to its treasury. In the summer of 1900, however, he backed off from financing a third-party effort by some of the more single-minded anti-imperialists, and finally announced his support of McKinley in the presidential election. From the beginning, Carnegie preferred to attack the policy of imperialism rather than the Philippine-American War, and during the year 1901 he appeared to lose interest in both. The next spring saw a revival of interest and anger, and now for the first time Carnegie criticized the American soldier. He contributed financially to the investigations of Herbert Welsh, exposing military misconduct in the Philippines, and published an article charging the American army with "the perpetration of such atrocities as have rarely appalled civilized man."[8] Some months later, however, Carnegie expressed renewed confidence in the ability of the Roosevelt administration to correct matters, and informed Welsh that he doubted the wisdom of continuing the atrocity investigation: "We have only to dub ourselves as blackeners of the American troops to render ourselves impotent for all good to the people of the Philippines."[9]

The pendulum indignation of Carnegie was reflected in the more subdued anti-imperialist labors of George Foster Peabody and Edwin Ginn. It was not only their small numbers that restricted the importance of the anti-imperialist minority within the business community but also the sporadic quality of their interest and their reluctance to denounce the war as well as the policy that had engendered it. They offer the historian an indication of the divisions within the business community and an example of the danger of classification by economic stereotypes, but they did not threaten the administration's policy of military subjugation in the Philippines.

The restricted efforts of this minority might have had greater effect had they controlled or influenced a significant portion of the business press. They did not. No important commercial or trade journal took a stand in direct opposition to the administration's Philippine policy. Several editors took a rather neutral stance, but none directly challenged the necessity of the war.

If the business press exhibited little division, neither did it demonstrate much concern, once the first flush of interest in Philippine annexation had passed. Such trade journals as *The Age of Steel*, *The Western Electrician*, and *The Boot and Shoe Recorder* offered editorial comment early in 1899 in behalf of the retention of the islands and the success of the American army, but over the next three years they made infrequent reference to the economic value of the Philippines and rarely mentioned the "insurrection." The editor of *The Age of Steel* was hopeful that when the United States "gets its foot firmly in the colonial boot," it would enjoy "the lion's share of the commerce of Cuba, Porto Rico, and the Philippines," and *The Western Electrician* prophesied that American occupation of the Philippines would be followed by the laying of "5,000 miles of telegraph lines in the archipelago," but the primary concern of both journals was with prices, markets, and labor developments in the United States.[10] The editor of *The Boot and Shoe Recorder of Boston* damned "the obstructionists" who opposed the Treaty of Paris and blamed them for the foolish rebellion of the Filipinos, but as the months went by without bringing any increase in the export of Boston boots to Manila, there were no further references to the Philippines as "one of the richest, natural portions of the earth." If allotment of space is a valid indicator of interest and optimism, both declined as the Philippine-American War continued.

The same pattern holds for *The Railroad Gazette*, though its initial enthusiasm for the Philippines was less pronounced and its loss of interest more gradual. In May 1899, the *Gazette* expressed interest in a rumor that "a syndicate of English and American capitalists" planned to build railroads in the Philippines, and a year later it reported favorably on the proposed construction of a railroad from Dagupan to Baguio in Luzon, but its hopes for a great railroad net covering the archipelago slowly dissipated. The editor worried that the "costly process of subjugating the Philippines" was delaying the establishment of "the machinery of industrial enterprise," and expressed the hope that such enterprise would prove an effective instrument for establishing permanent peace in the islands, but "foreign news" accounted for only a small percentage of the columns of *The Railroad Gazette* and the Philippine-American War received little notice after 1900.[11]

Business papers that sought a more general circulation, such as *The Wall Street Journal*, *The Journal of Commerce*, and *The Commercial Bulletin*, offered comparatively more news of events in the Philippines. In varying degrees they expressed support for the goals and methods of America's Philippine policy, but for none was that policy a matter of primary concern. In the spring of 1899, *The Wall Street Journal* urged General Otis "to follow up his good work" and spoke confidently of the imminence of "a crushing defeat" for Aguinaldo, but it offered no predictions of economic boom in the islands and its editorials on the markets of the Orient and the Boxer Rebellion only occasionally made mention of the Philippines.[12] By 1901 it had adopted a wait-and-see attitude respecting the islands. We should wait until the "insurrection" was over and then decide how best to promote their usefulness. *The Journal of Commerce* of New York[13] and *The Commercial Bulletin* of Boston spoke in similar fashion, but in the case of the latter with much greater confidence in the future prosperity and economic utility of the islands. *The Commercial Bulletin* was edited by Curtis Guild, Jr., a Republican politician and protege of Henry Cabot Lodge, and it was an admitted advocate of insular expansion. Guild was, indeed, one of the few editors to draw an explicit connection between the Philippines and America's ability to "protect the open door policy in Chinese markets." Nor was he reluctant to discuss the war and express the *Bulletin's* total confidence in the conduct and goals of the American army. Aguinaldo's supporters were savages and must be suppressed as we had suppressed Geronimo and Sitting Bull. He hoped General Otis would study the history of the British in the Malay peninsula and their successful labors to chastise bandits and provide protection to a grateful majority of the native population.[14] But even the *Bulletin* seldom gave the Philippines the honor of the lead editorial, and by 1902 Philippine news was used chiefly as filler.

Three tentative conclusions may be offered from this brief examination of the business press: It housed few if any dissenters; its coverage of the war was minimal; its interest in the Philippines was at best secondary after the summer of 1899. When the business press did write of the Philippines, it was in terms of their potential economic value, but those who might have been expected to beat the drums for economic exploitation tapped but softly and sporadically. If McKinley's Philippine policy was an expression of economic imperialism, it failed to generate much enthusiasm among the editors of the business press.

America had its economic imperialists, but the more vocal tended to be neither businessmen nor editors of trade journals but self-appointed advisers and publicists. They were men such as Charles A. Conant, convinced that they knew what the business community should think and the American people as well.

Conant was a contemporary of the British professor J. A. Hobson, and he finds his place in the history of economic thought as an anticipatory echo of Hobson's famous tract on *Imperialism*. Conant, however, was not so much interested in offering a theory on the inspirations of imperialism as in persuading American investors and manufacturers of the economic value of territorial expansion. In the near future the American economy would suffer a glut of capital and goods if it did not now seek new markets for capital investment in the Far East. Capital investment in China and the Pacific was essential for the economic prosperity and social harmony of the American people, and the establishment of colonies would encourage such investment. Colonialism in the Philippines would furnish illustration and precedent.[15] Conant earnestly sought to influence the response of the American business and financial communities to American policy in the Philippines, but the extent of his success remains problematical. He would be quoted by Senator Lodge, but there is no evidence that he was read by the editors of the commercial and trade journals. At least none mentioned him.

A more quoted and important lay adviser to the business community was the secretary of war, Elihu Root. Anxious to revive American faith in the economic advantages of the islands and perhaps to distract attention from the costs of continuing guerrilla warfare, Root issued a special report on economic conditions in the Philippines. Manufacturers and investors were assured that policies of pacification had already brought the Philippines "to the point where they offer a ready and attractive field for investment and enterprise." "The same kind of individual enterprise which has built up our own country" would furnish "the great agency" in assuring contentment, prosperity, and industrial activity in the islands. The War

Department was prepared to offer various kinds of statistical information to interested businessmen, and the army had already done excellent work in such areas as road construction and harbor improvement.[16]

A more concrete form of evidence respecting the response of business to events in the Philippines than the editorials of trade journals and the literary efforts of publicists and government officials would be the extent of business "presence" in the Philippines. There are no satisfactory records of the extent of American manufacturing activity or investment until the second decade of American rule and the reports of Governor General W. Cameron Forbes. Scattered evidence indicates, however, that when the Philippine-American War was declared ended in July 1902, there was only a small amount of American business activity in the islands. Although total trade between the Philippine Islands and the United States increased by almost $21 million between 1899 and 1902, much of this sum was attributable to a single product, hemp. The lugubrious reports and addresses of William Howard Taft, first civil governor of the Philippines, clearly indicate the disappointment of the Philippine Commission at the reluctance of American capital to abandon more accustomed channels and invest in the Philippines.[17] A few mining companies had sent over some engineers, and the Philippine Lumber and Development Company had run a survey with the help of the army, but these efforts were still in the prospectus stage, as were the grandiose plans of A. Burlingame Johnson to develop large sugar plantations and construct an electric light plant on the island of Negros.[18]

The "insurrection" and the counterterror it inspired help explain the reluctance of American business to invest capital or establish branch operations in the Philippine Islands, but it is doubtful that guerrilla warfare alone explains the hesitancy and caution of the business community. Had American capital sought in concert the economic exploitation of the islands, one would expect to find more evidence of pressure on the McKinley-Roosevelt administrations to bring the war to a swift end and more inquiries by manufacturers and investors respecting the assistance they might anticipate from officials in Washington and Manila. One would also expect to see more references to investment opportunities in the financial press. It would seem that those most optimistic about the economic value of the Philippine Islands were Charles Conant, Elihu Root, and Henry Cabot Lodge, not J. P. Morgan, Edward Harriman, or the owners of the textile factories of Massachusetts. American business was slow to risk effort or money in developing the raw materials and markets of the Philippines.

Only a minority of businessmen gave the Philippines much attention, and these tended through the years of the Philippine-American War to pursue a cautious policy until pacification was completed and Congress had clarified its economic policies for the islands. It is probable that they were confused and irritated by the Spooner Act; certainly they would adopt a wait-and-see attitude until Congress made final decision as to the tariff status of the islands.

The Spooner Act of March 1901, or more specifically the Hoar amendment to that act, imposed restrictions on the authority of the Taft Commission to grant franchises and dispose of public-domain lands. Criticized by the Taft Commission,[19] the amendment was disliked but not officially opposed by the McKinley administration. Neither McKinley nor his successor Roosevelt was certain of the best design for economic legislation for the Philippines, and their uncertainty found a parallel in the diverse views of American businessmen. Businessmen who had invested in the domestic tobacco and beet sugar industries were anxious that tariff barriers be erected against competing Filipino products, whereas other businessmen were interested in obtaining cheap raw materials or a preferential position for American goods in the Philippine market. The Philippine Tariff Act of 8 March 1902 illustrated this division. A tariff would be levied against Philippine goods entering American ports, but importers would receive a rebate of 25 percent with an additional rebate granted to American importers of Philippine hemp. American goods entering the Philippines would receive a measure of preference, but that preference would be limited in obedience to our Open Door goals in China and certain provisions of the Treaty of Paris, and all revenues derived from excise and export taxes would be turned over to the Philippine treasury.[20]

The refusal to allow Filipino goods a greater share of the American domestic market probably reflected the influence of economic self-interest, but it did not reflect a policy of colonial exploitation. If there had existed a strong lobby of American investors interested in shaping Philippine policy to their long-term profit, one would expect that they would have demanded a policy of free trade between the islands and the Mother Country. Instead, it was an anti-imperialist of sorts, Jonathan P. Dolliver of Iowa, who tried to exempt Philippine products from the duties of the Dingley Tariff.[21] A confusion of economic interests at home made it impossible for Congress to pursue a concerted program of economic exploitation in the Philippines. The land laws subsequently formulated by the Taft Commission and approved in Washington offer additional illustration. Although they modified the limitations of the Spooner Act, restrictions were still imposed on the size of holdings. If this was contrary to the wishes of some businessmen, it met the desires of others whose primary interest was to protect their domestic investments.[22]

At no point did Big Business offer the administration undivided support for its policies respecting the Philippines in the years 1899–1902.
Although a majority of its representatives favored permanent retention of
the islands, there was a perceptible reduction of interest in the Philippines
and its economic potential as the war continued. The attitudes and opinions
of businessmen, as of most Americans, were influenced by factors of
economic self-interest, but the relevance of the Philippines to their self-
interest was the subject of uncertainty as well as division. If there was a
connection between industrial growth and imperial adventure, it was of
seemingly greater concern to publicists and debating politicians than to
merchants and manufacturers.

Available evidence does not describe a picture of Big Business supporting a policy of conquest and exploitation with single-minded fervor;
neither does it portray Labor as the anti-imperialist champion of the oppressed Filipino. If the chains of industrialism and colonialism were forged
at a single capitalist smithy, most representatives of Labor appeared unaware of the fact.

The figure of Samuel Gompers provides the obvious starting point in
an investigation of the attitudes and motives of Union Labor. Not only was
he president of the American Federation of Labor, but he was as well a
charter vice president of the Anti-Imperialist League and surely the most
frequently quoted of the anti-imperialists within the ranks of Labor. If
Labor opposed McKinley's policy as an expression of its antagonism to
economic imperialism, one would expect to find evidence of such motivation in the words of Gompers and the resolutions of the nation's largest
Labor organization.

Most students of Gompers and the AFL have come to the conclusion
that although Gompers was disturbed by McKinley's experiment in colonialism, his sporadic opposition was inspired by limited fears and a narrow
conception of the welfare of the American workingman.[23] This is a correct
judgment, particularly for the years 1900–1902. Gompers' anti-imperialism
peaked early, and the man who was prepared in March 1899 to denounce
standing armies as a tool of oppression was ready by 1902 to accept the
permanent retention of the islands so long as barriers against Oriental
immigration were not endangered.

Gompers' boldest words in opposition to the Philippine-American
War were offered at the Tremont Temple in Boston on 20 March 1899 at a
meeting arranged by Erving Winslow and the Anti-Imerialist League. In
this speech he excoriated the administration for "waging war upon the
only Asiatic people who ever tried to establish a republican form of gov-

ernment.'' He pointed to the dangers that a large standing army posed to workingmen at home, and he risked the charge of treason by praising the courage of the Filipinos and suggesting that at some time in the future the claims of national patriotism would have to accommodate themselves to the ideal of international brotherhood:

> If international peace cannot be secured by the intelligence of those in authority, then I look forward to the time when the workers will settle this question [of how to abolish war] by the dock laborers refusing to handle materials that are to be used to destroy their fellow men, and the seamen of the world . . . while willing to risk their lives in conducting the commerce of nations, absolutely refusing to strike down their fellow men, even though they may be employed by a foreign power.[24]

This speech was given when the Philippine-American War was less than two months old, and Gompers would never again offer so sharp a dissent. The next year would see him decline various invitations to speak at meetings sponsored by the Anti-Imperialist League and then disappoint Erving Winslow by refusing to give his support in August 1900 to the Liberty Congress. In all likelihood, Gompers voted for William Jennings Bryan and approved the Philippine plank of the Democratic party in the election of 1900, but he refused to give either his formal endorsement. The reluctance of the AFL to be linked with any party or candidate and Gompers' philosophy of ''unionism pure and simple'' help explain this refusal, but it also reflected his erratic retreat from dissent to accommodation. By 1902 the retreat was complete. No longer did the *American Federationist*, the official organ of the AFL, denounce imperialism; rather it was content to warn its readers to resist such possible by-products of our Philippine policy as the free import of sweatshop Filipino goods and the removal of barriers against coolie immigrants.[25]

Gompers' identification with the general membership of the AFL was most pronounced when his arguments were most selfish. Denunciations of McKinley's Philippine policy generated considerable division within the AFL, but no one ever rose at an AFL convention to speak in behalf of the Oriental immigrant. Within the AFL, the unions initially most prepared to support Gompers in his opposition to McKinley's colonial policy were his own Cigarmakers' International Union and the unions of the Seamen, Carpenters, and Boot and Shoe Workers. Their greatest success came with the AFL convention in Detroit in December 1899, when they pushed through a resolution in behalf of Philippine independence. This resolution marked the height of anti-imperialist sentiment in the AFL, and it passed only after sharp debate. Within the AFL there were several unions whose leaders supported McKinley's Philippine policy, and the tradition of union autonomy within the AFL helped strengthen the effectiveness of their opposition to resolutions in behalf of Filipino freedom. It is less surprising that no future AFL national convention called for Philippine independence than that the Cigarmakers and their allies were successful in December 1899.[26]

With the summer of 1900, the AFL no longer emphasized the issue of imperialism and gave little attention to the Philippine-American War. Resolutions by the AFL executive council and the annual conventions were confined to possible consequences of Philippine annexation for the economic welfare of the union laborer. There was no public recantation by the anti-imperialists within the AFL, but they were reluctant to risk disunity or the distractions of political involvement.

The division within the AFL conventions reflected a broader division among leaders of "the working and producing classes." John W. Parsons, Henry Lloyd, John Hicks, Andrew Furuseth, George F. McNeill, and T. J. Elderikin were self-declared enemies of colonial rule, but their right to speak for Labor was challenged by such union men as Samuel B. Donnelly and James Campbell. Donnelly, a prominent member of the International Typographical Union, was a declared champion of commercial expansion, and Campbell was a spokesman for the Glass Workers Union, which generally supported administration policy in the Philippines. Campbell extolled the fact that an increasing number of glass bottles were being exported to the Philippines now that they were an American possession, and suggested that Gompers and the anti-imperialists undervalued the national loyalty of the American workingman: "The laboring man is patriotic, and he does not forget . . . [that] the laboring men constitute the great body of the army which will not forsake the flag and turn traitor in the hour of extremity."[27] The anti-imperialists, however, were a majority among Labor spokesmen. The declining Knights of Labor passed resolutions in opposition to overseas expansion, and its Grand Master Workman, John W. Hayes, was a vice president of the Washington Anti-Imperialist League.[28] Henry George warned the workingmen of New York City against colonial adventures as a distraction to domestic battles, and Patrick Collins in Boston and Patrick Ford in Washington made earnest efforts to link the labor movement and the cause of anti-imperialism.

The Labor press offered a similar ratio between opponents and supporters of McKinley's Philippine policy, and bore witness that the narrowing of concern by Gompers and the AFL as the Philippine-American War continued was typical of many groups within the ranks of Labor.

Editors of union newspapers naturally tended to reflect the anti-imperialist or expansionist sentiments of the union's leadership. The *Cigar Makers' Journal* was quick to denounce the McKinley administration for "ruthlessly waging war on the Filipinos,"[29] whereas editors of the papers of the Typographers, Railroad Trainmen, and Glass Workers initially applauded American occupation of the Philippines. Of the anti-imperialist newspapers, the *National Labor Standard*, the *Journal of the Knights of Labor*, and the *Coast Seamen's Journal* offered the broadest and boldest attack. The editor of the *National Labor Standard* took a position on most issues to the left of the AFL and the *American Federationist*, and his criticisms of colonialism were both more blunt and of longer duration. McKinley's Philippine policy was judged a conspiracy against the workingman, designed to benefit a small body of capitalists at the expense of the tax-paying public and the American workingman. It could only mean a flood of cheap Asiatic goods into the American home market or the removal of American factories to the islands and the reduction of work opportunities at home. Permanent pacification of the islands would require a military force of 40,000 men, and intelligent workingmen must oppose an expanded army. It could be used to thwart the rights of Labor to organize and strike.[30] Editorials in the *Journal of the Knights of Labor* and the *Coast Seamen's Journal* echoed this thesis, at least in the early years of the war. The people of America should not have "an India saddled upon them" in order that our captains of industry might have more territory "to rule and plunder." During the campaign of 1900, both papers called for the defeat of McKinley and imperialism.[31]

But even the most anti-imperialist of labor papers tended to lose interest in the issue of the Philippines after the election of 1900 and to limit their opposition to colonial legislation harmful to the economic interests of union labor. Although the *National Labor Standard* would continue to offer periodic blasts against militarism, most editors were willing by 1902 to confine their anti-imperialism to warnings against coolie immigrants. In the spring of that year a few labor journals offered comment on military atrocities and their investigation, but they gave more space to congressional hearings on Chinese exclusion than to pacification campaigns in Samar and Batangas. The *American Federationist* completely ignored the issue of Philippine atrocities but devoted forty columns to the congressional bill to reenact Chinese exclusion.[32]

If one describes the response of Labor to the administration's Philippine policy by the simplistic categories of "pro" and "anti," there is no reason to question the usual judgment that a majority of Labor leaders and unions were on the anti-imperialist side. At no time, however, was there a majority in open dissent to the Philippine-American War, and after the election of 1900 the anti-imperialism of many union officials and newspapers sharply diminished. Having always been inspired more by fears for the domestic welfare of the workingman than a sense of international brotherhood, such Labor leaders as Sam Gompers were by 1901 increasingly susceptible to administration promises that American possession of the Philippines would not endanger existing barriers against sweatshop goods, Oriental immigration, and contract labor. By 1902 anti-imperialism in the ranks of Labor had been accommodated. It appeared not greatly to matter whether the United States kept the islands so long as congressional barriers were maintained against Asiatic goods and immigrants.[33] One must conclude that if the response of Union Labor to U.S. policy in the Philippines was influenced by the force of economic self-interest, it defined that interest narrowly. The opposition of Labor was neither uniform nor constant, and its primary target was not monopoly capitalism nor the Philippine-American War but the Oriental immigrant who might serve the purposes of the anti-union manufacturer to lower wages, break strikes, and thwart union organization.[34]

An analysis of the response of Business and Labor to American colonialism and the Philippine-American War does not disprove the thesis that American imperialism was inspired by the fears of manufacturers, bankers, and investors that the United States would suffer economic glut and social dissension were she to deny herself the opportunity of colonial expansion. Such an analysis does, however, raise serious doubts as to the validity of this thesis.

If America's Philippine policy was primarily the product of monopoly capitalism, one would expect that there would have been more support and unity within the ranks of Big Business and more and stronger opposition on the part of the spokesmen of Organized Labor. Admittedly, it is foolish to expect to find total unity within any group on a public issue, but the point to emphasize is that there was sufficient division within both Business and Labor to lessen the possibility that any subset in either group could effectively dictate the Philippine policy of the U.S. government.

Although a majority of bankers and manufacturers appear to have supported the policy of the administration and a majority of union leaders probably opposed it, there was considerable uncertainty in the ranks of both, and a perceptible decline of attention and concern during the years 1899–1902. Economic self-interest undoubtedly played a part in determining the response of businessmen and union officials, but interpretations of that self-interest were particular and varied. To describe the response of Business and Labor as a struggle between two armies waging war over a policy of economic imperialism implies a class solidarity false to the facts of American history.

CHAPTER VI

The Response of Organized Religion and the Missionary Impulse

No more than businessmen and union members did priests and pastors respond to the Philippine-American War with a single voice. There were differences between the Catholic and Protestant clergy, and within the Protestant fold there were wafflers as well as advocates and a small band of angry dissenters. On balance, however, organized religion rallied to the support of colonialism, prepared to subordinate the unattractive features of war and emphasize the opportunities for service. The most important stimulus for many churchmen and lay leaders was the missionary impulse; the single most dominant mood was that of determined optimism.

It would have been understandable had the Catholic church in the United States taken a position of opposition to McKinley's Philippine policy. Most Filipinos were Roman Catholic in faith, and American reconstruction of their political, social, and educational systems would reduce the authority of the Philippine Catholic church, emphasize the separation of church and state, and promote secularization. The Roman Catholic priest in America could not view the Philippines as a great field for religious conversion, and might be expected to harbor a natural suspicion against the ambition of Protestant missionaries to accompany the triumphs of General Otis with victories of their own. There were contrary influences at work, however, sufficient not only to limit Catholic opposition but to furnish certain Catholic leaders with their own version of the missionary impulse.

The 1880s and 1890s had seen the Catholic hierarchy in the United States fighting nativism and the American Protective Association and demanding recognition of the Catholic church as a loyal American institution. James Cardinal Gibbons and other spokesmen publicly endorsed the constitutional requirement of the separation of church and state. Loyalty to Rome, they insisted, did not imply disloyalty to the Founding Fathers. For some members of the hierarchy, patriotism found support in professional ambition. American possession of the Philippines could mean the replacement of Spanish clerics with American priests, and as the influence of the United States increased in the council of nations so there would be a corresponding increase in the influence of the American church in the councils of Catholicism. Both the Filipinos and the Curiate could only benefit from an injection of American vitality and dedication. Archbishop John Ireland as well as Mr. Dooley's ''Hennessy'' favored the expansionist course of the administration. It would enhance the nation's wealth and prestige, and increase the opportunities available to the American priesthood as well as the Catholic entrepreneur. At least this would be the case if American Catholics kept a sharp watch against the monopolistic designs of Protestant missionaries in the new colonial empire.

Catholic advocates of McKinley's Philippine policy were subject to rather special worries. Not only were there anti-imperialists within the priesthood and laity, but the American Catholic Church had reason to be suspicious of Protestant exclusiveness and the policies of certain civilian and military officials. Criticism of the Spanish friars, secularization of Filipino schools, and desecration of Philippine churches made it difficult for such expansionists as Archbishop Ireland to sustain a note of patriotic optimism.

Initially the Catholic press had showed little concern for the difficulties of the Spanish friars in the Philippines, but when various Protestant journals began to denounce ''the greedy friars'' and call for their removal, *The Pilot* and other Catholic publications began to view the friars as underdogs who deserved to be championed by their coreligionists.[1] They pointed out that the eighth, ninth, and tenth articles of the Treaty of Paris specifically protected the religious and property rights of all persons and corporations in the islands. In obedience to those articles the Franciscan and Dominican orders should be restored to their former lands. The defense offered by *The Pilot* and the *Ave Maria* was vigorous but brief. Once the American government indicated its intentions to negotiate with the Vatican and purchase the land claims of the friars, Catholic editors lost interest in ''these forgotten civilizers.'' Their concern had in any case centered upon the property rights of the friars, not their political authority.

Catholics divided as to how completely church and state should be separated in the Philippines, but most recognized the necessity of some measure of separation under American rule. No Catholic prelate or editor suggested that the Catholic church in the Philippines should enjoy undiminished political authority. Where secularization became a matter of controversy was in the area associated with the labors of Dr. Fred Atkinson. Atkinson was appointed superintendent of schools for the Philippine Islands and was entrusted by the Taft Commission with the task of constructing a system of public education. Public education in the eyes of Atkinson and Taft was secular education, and by the summer of 1901 Atkinson had issued regulations prohibiting religious instruction in the Philippine schools and suggesting the removal of crucifixes and other religious ornaments from school walls. *The Catholic Universe* of Cleveland and the New York *Freeman's Journal* vied with each other in denouncing Atkinson, his regulations, and the restriction of teaching appointments to Protestant soldiers and civilians. When Catholics in uniform were dying to make good the claim of American sovereignty in the Philippines, it was insulting as well as stupid for an ambitious bureaucrat to determine policy by his own religious bias. Even after Atkinson gave way and sought to recruit Catholic teachers and allow religious instruction in Philippine schools on a voluntary and limited basis, the *Freeman's Journal* continued to warn the administration that Catholic support for colonial expansion was dependent on religious equality and fair play.

The same warnings were offered whenever official policy appeared guilty of favoritism to Protestant missionaries. In somewhat contradictory fashion, Catholic editors declared that Protestant missionary effort had no conceivable chance of success and forecast dire results for the religious health of the Filipinos and the success of the pacification program were it to succeed. The true path of pacification was to assure the Filipinos that they would be left undisturbed in their Catholic faith. Many echoed the sentiments expressed by Archbishop Ireland to the Protestant readers of *The Outlook*: "I want to see American rule made possible in those islands. Do your Protestant missionaries realize that they are doing the greatest harm to America by making her flag unpopular? . . . Give the Catholic Filipinos at least a chance to know us as we really are; that we are not out there to stir up religious as well as political hate."[2] But others were less interested in illustrating the "impolitic" nature of Protestant evangelism than in castigating signs of official partiality in its behalf. When Jacob Gould Schurman returned to the United States and publicly expressed his faith in the political propriety of Protestant missionary efforts and suggested that their effectiveness would be improved if the Protestant sects formed an ecumenical union in the Philippines, the *Catholic Universe* entitled its lead editorial, "Protestant Impudence and Gall": "Who is going to give us the best Protestantism? Is McKinley's Philippine commission empowered to recognize and name this new state church . . . or is it to be a religion by selection? . . . What is to predominate? The immersion tub of the Baptists, the amen corner of the Methodists, the rationalistic tendency of the Presbyterians, or that composite entity called Episcopalianism?''[3]

There was more of scorn than anger in Catholic response to Protestant missionary efforts, and that scorn was directed against particular officials and missionaries, not against the goals of military pacification. Scorn became anger only when rumors began to circulate that American officers and soldiers were guilty of desecrating and despoiling Catholic churches in the Philippines. On this issue some Catholic spokesmen were prepared to criticize the war.

There was probably less stealing of crucifixes, chalices, and vestments by souvenir-hungry soldiers and less occupation of Catholic churches for military observation posts than was reported in the excited editorials of the Boston *Pilot*, but instances of vandalism were more numerous than Generals Otis and MacArthur would admit. Impatient with the censorship of military officials in Manila, many Catholic editors would exaggerate on the side of the prosecution. Their editorials stirred the Metropolitan Truth Society and the Catholic Young Men's National Union to send formal protests to the president, demanding that he give his immediate attention to the matter and punish the guilty without fail.[4] It was not an editorial, however, but a photograph that caused the greatest stir. *Collier's Weekly*, in its issue of 9 September 1899, featured a full-page photograph showing the interior of a church in Luzon that had been converted into a field telegraph station. Wires ran from altar to nave, military supplies were stacked in the chancel, an officer lolled in the background puffing at a cigarette. For the editor of the San Francisco *Monitor*, the photograph was ''an unimpeachable witness'' of desecration and prejudice; the Holy Name Society sent a petition to the secretary of war signed by several thousand members; and the *Freeman's Journal* demanded to know whether the war against the Filipinos was about to be ''converted by the Protestant bigots into a war against the Catholic church.''[5]

Catholic anger was mitigated after a time, however, by assurances from the War Department and indirect promises of scrupulous respect for Catholic church property in the future. As with other issues of worry to Catholic spokesmen in America—the treatment of the friars, the secularization of schools, the official encouragement of Protestant missionaries—the issue of church desecration was, for a majority, cause for disgruntlement, not dissent. It simply made neutrality or support more difficult.

There were various factors at work to limit Catholic opposition and prevent disgruntlement from achieving the status of dissent. For one, there was the fact that not only were certain Catholic leaders favorable to expansion but they were politically sympathetic to the Republican administration.[6] Others were determined that the Faith not be weakened by political disputes and partisan division. Cardinal Gibbons feared lest the issue of colonialism assume a sectarian character, and did not wish to see the Church take an official stand in support or opposition to American policy in the Philippines. Were it to do so, division within the hierarchy between the followers of Ireland and the supporters of the Democratic anti-imperialist Bishop Bernard J. McQuaid would only increase.[7] Gibbons probably inclined toward Ireland's belief that the Catholic church in America should bear sympathetic witness to the new ambitions of the nation—"Our national pride is armed, and we want to be a power *in toto orbe terrarum*"— but he appreciated that a fair-sized minority of priests shared McQuaid's conviction that God and safety would best be served if the United States limited its international ambitions.[8]

A more important restraining influence than the fear of accentuating political and ideological divisions among Catholic prelates was the fear of identifying Catholicism with the suspect patriotism of the Anti-Imperialist League. A few Catholic laymen such as Patrick Ford and Patrick Collins were members of the League, and the anti-imperialist bishop from Peoria, John L. Spalding, was so bold as to speak at an anti-imperialist meeting,[9] but for many Catholic priests and editors the leadership of the Anti-Imperialist League hinted of un-American radicalism. So long as the Anti-Imperialist League was the chief organ for expressing opposition to the policy of colonialism, they would not allow their suspicions of certain consequences of colonialism to escalate into dissent.

This was true not only because Catholic spokesmen placed a high premium on public recognition of the Church as a loyal American institution but because of the nature of Catholic opposition. Catholic antagonism was limited to such targets as secularism, evangelism, and Protestant bigotry. It was not directed against militarism, colonialism, and war. Although various Catholic prelates and editors were angered by the conduct of particular American officials, there was little sympathy expressed for the insurgents or their goal of national self-determination. They would attack certain features of our Philippine policy; they never thought to demand withdrawal of the American army or a negotiated settlement with Aguinaldo.

Even when the Protestant missionaries were fervently denounced, it was frequently on the score that they were obstacles to programs of pacification. Father Joseph Algué, a Jesuit priest, stressed the "dangerous and impolitic nature" of Protestant evangelism and its effect of making more difficult the task of the American soldier and administrator. Did not Americans realize that in the Philippines some of the most loyal supporters of "the new order of things" were prominent and devout Catholic laymen? The American priest was the truest and best ally of "the new order."[10] Father Algué offers an excellent example of the somewhat troubled Catholic version of the missionary impulse.

Protestant clergymen and editors offer a greater range of opinion than their Catholic counterparts. There were Social Darwinists convinced that the Filipinos must be crushed for the sake of political and social progress, and there were moderate supporters of colonialism, unhappy neutrals, and, finally, a small band of ministers who denounced the war as well as expansion. Diversity of response was exhibited not only within but between the Protestant sects. At the risk of oversimplification, one can describe a pattern where support for colonialism and the Philippine-American War roughly corresponds with the strength of Calvinist doctrine in the sect's theology. The Presbyterian and Congregational churches tended to be staunch supporters of the administration's Philippine policy, whereas Unitarians, Universalists, and Friends leaned toward dissent. There was division within the Baptist churches, although a majority of the Northern Baptists appeared to favor expansion and the stern suppression of the "rebellion," and even greater division and uncertainty within the Episcopal church. The Methodists refuse to fit the pattern. They did not subscribe to Calvin, but most Methodist pastors and editors took pride in their coreligionist McKinley and supported his diplomatic and military policies.

An examination of fifteen Protestant journals[11] and the sermons and addresses of two score of Protestant ministers would indicate that for all the diversity of response, the majority attitude was one of determined optimism. The carnage of war must be a source of sorrow, but Americans should take heart in the thought that in the long run American missionaries and American institutions must promote the well-being of the Filipino. Political and spiritual enlightenment would succeed military pacification.

This was a theme that found supporters among the opponents as well as the advocates of insular imperialism. Among preachers of the Social Gospel, both the anti-imperialist Walter Rauschenbusch and Washington Gladden, an advocate of territorial expansion, held high hopes for American missionary endeavors in the Philippines. As Episcopal Bishop William Huntington saw in Christian evangelism the saving grace of an unwise policy, Methodist Bishops Frank W. Warne, John F. Hurst, and James M. Thoburn believed the American missionary provided conclusive proof of the rightness of American policy in the Philippines.

Some anti-imperialist ministers, of course, found no consolation in the opportunities that would be afforded Protestant evangelism by American sovereignty in the Philippine Islands. They accused their colleagues of wishing "a mixed policy of guns and Holy Ghost" and bade them remember that the Kingdom of Heaven was "to come as a grain of mustard seed and not as a 13-inch shell."[12] These men formed a small but highly articulate band of dissenters, determined opponents of the war as well as the imperialist policy "which is its natural father."[13] It was their belief that we had no right to be in the Philippines and our presence there could not be of service to the Filipinos. The fruits of tyranny would not be the elevation of the Filipino but the brutalization of our own people. Our proper mission was to bear peaceful witness to the virtues of democracy and Protestant Christianity, not to "thrust forward, sword in hand, into the arena of imperial conflict." It was the wish of the Creator that "each nation or race of men work out their destiny for themselves." To associate evangelism with military conquest was to "exchange the standards of Mohammed for those of Jesus Christ."[14]

These clerical dissenters never formed a society or caucus, but certain of them occasionally joined in meetings of protest. One of the better publicized meetings was that held in Tremont Temple, Boston, on 22 May 1902, when nine ministers and one rabbi offered successive denunciations of the conduct of the American army in the Philippines.[15] Among the speakers was Leighton Parks, the most zealous ministerial critic of the tactics of military pacification. In one sermon, Parks had asked the congregation at Boston's Emmanuel Church—many of them descendants of the Minute Men—to compare the conduct of certain American officers in the Philippines with that of General Gage in 1775. Gage had wanted to know where the arms and powder were stored at Concord, but he had not tortured the Patriots of the village in an effort to extort that information. Parks' listeners should not seek to hide behind the false doctrine of military necessity. Every citizen was responsible for what was being done in the name of America in the Philippines. "For God will ask of every one of us, 'What did you do and say and pray in that time of national humiliation?' "[16]

Most Protestant leaders would have considered such a question erroneous as well as rhetorical. American sovereignty in the Philippines offered not humiliation but opportunity. If we failed to follow conquest with redemption, then shame would be our portion, but there was no reason to predict such failure. The editors of *The Outlook* and *The Advance* were convinced that where duty was obeyed there could be no sin. Their confidence was sincere if carefully cultivated, and it was representative of the response of a majority of Protestant journalists and clergymen.

Lyman Abbott, editor of *The Outlook*, saw that journal as an instrument for promoting and propagating Christian solutions to the domestic and foreign problems facing America.

Abbott's admiration was confined to those who would combine the obligations of American nationalism and the Social Gospel. A friend and admirer of McKinley and Roosevelt, Abbott was not a jingoist nor, by his own definition, an imperialist. He believed that America must be sovereign in the Philippines not because we hungered for power but because we heard the call of duty. We had a Christian obligation to rule, for the only alternative to American sovereignty in the islands was civil war and anarchy, followed by European intervention. We must subdue the insurgent minority in order that we might develop the Filipino capacity for self-government and, in the process, free them from ignorance and superstition. Our policy was not one of imperialism but emancipation. We were a race of "discoverers, explorers, settlers, organizers," and we must exercise our God-given abilities and do for the Filipinos what they could never do for themselves. Those who called themselves anti-imperialists foolishly refused to recognize the fact that "the present war was necessary to establish the first principle, that we could not relinquish to the Tagals the responsibility of a government which events had put in our hands."

Abbott found it difficult to see why Aguinaldo could be so stubborn when America's benevolent intent was so obvious. If certain of the techniques of pacification appeared severe, Americans could already take pride in the valuable labors of the Young Men's Christian's Association in Manila, the "marked energy" of the Society of Christian Endeavor, and the dedicated efforts of Dr. Fred Atkinson to free education in the Philippines from religious prejudice and so assure the "improvement of the Filipino race." Religious liberty and the English language would prove the most effective tools of pacification.[17]

The Chicago *Advance*, the most prominent Congregationalist journal west of New England, expressed a similar confidence in the ability of America to educate and elevate the Filipinos, but the editor of *The Advance* put primary emphasis on the contribution of the American missionary and found it more difficult to ignore the casualty figures of the Philippine-American War. He expressed disappointment that the Schurman Commission did not include at least one missionary, and chided American military officials in Manila for giving insufficient support to our pioneer clerical and medical missionaries. The war itself was to be laid to the door of Aguinaldo, but *The Advance* could take no pride in reports of heavy Filipino casualties at Caloocan and Malolos and it informed its readers not to take pleasure in the "hurrahing" of Cecil Rhodes. That rambunctious imperialist was not a good guide for the conduct of America, and we should be careful not to "belie our fair promises" by leaving the natives to "the exploitation of politicians and capitalists." In the fall of 1900, *The Advance* exhibited a strengthened conviction in the necessity of the war as the Boxer Rebellion erupted in China and Western diplomats and missionaries were besieged in Peking. "A show of force is the only argument which appeals to an Oriental mind." The editor would chastise the administration for its failure to close the saloons in Manila; he would denounce "the barbaric order" of General Smith during the Samar campaign, but these were the errors of individuals. The goals of our Philippine policy were righteous and that policy could only work for the long-run benefit of the native population. When the war was declared ended on 4 July 1902, *The Advance* informed the Filipinos that they were now assured "the clemency, as they were already assured of the determination, of this nation."[18]

The missionary impulse helped determine the response of many Protestant ministers and editors. The Rev. Randolph H. McKim proclaimed his confidence that the future would witness "a religious as well as a political reconstruction" in the Philippines, and Dr. Alice Condict, a medical missionary, assured her countrymen that American evangelism would serve as a "transfusion" and put "warm blood into the veins" of the spiritually anemic Orientals. Dr. Condict and Mr. McKim separately voiced their conviction that the hand of Providence was visible in the establishment of "The Evangelic Union of the Philippine Islands." Initially composed of fifty-four missionaries, that Union provided inspiration for a score of editorials in the Protestant press.[19]

The Methodist press was particularly vocal in acknowledging the missionary impulse and expressing confidence that the missionary would prove the truest expression of American benevolence. *The Christian Advocate* saw the labors of the "Protestant ambassadors of Christ" providing redemption not only for the uncivilized Filipinos but for the occasional sins of the American soldier. The *Advocate* offered almost unlimited space to Dr. Homer C. Stuntz, the self-appointed propagandist for Methodist missionaries in Luzon, and whenever its editors were threatened with discouragement as a result of the war's duration or reports of the use of the water cure, they took hope from the prophecies of Dr. Stuntz. Dr. Stuntz predicted that Northwestern University would soon have a worthy rival in Manila—he hoped that it would be named McKinley College—and he explained to the readers of the *Advocate* that American possession of the Philippines was essential not only to missionary endeavors in that archipelago but to those of our missionaries in China as well. In the Philippines the American missionary and the American administrator were partners in "a great experiment" to educate the natives to an understanding of religious and political values essential to their elevation. Placed against this prospect, a few instances of military severity should not receive undue attention. The water cure was, in any case, given only to Filipino captives who had military information essential to the safety of our soldiers.[20]

For Protestant expansionists, evangelical opportunity not only overshadowed the techniques of military pacification but mitigated the effect of reports of immorality among the American army of liberation. The licensed brothels of Manila threatened to diminish the pride of church-going Americans in our colonial adventure, and for a time it appeared that moral outrage might prove stronger than the missionary impulse. It was only when evangelism was publicized as the redeemer of sin as well as the extirpator of foreign superstition that this danger was overcome.

The first strictures of the religious press were not directed against prostitution in Manila but against polygamy in Mindanao, and particularly the treaty of General John C. Bates with the Sultan of Sulu. That treaty, by promising to respect the religious customs of the Moslem population in the southern islands, seemed to give tacit approval to the accustomed privilege of Moslem leaders to enjoy several wives and enslave certain enemies. At least this was the interpretation given by *The Christian Work* of New York and *The Standard* of Chicago, which proclaimed the treaty to be in direct conflict with the Thirteenth Amendment to the Constitution.[21] *The Watchman*, a Baptist weekly published in Boston, was equally censorious and called upon the administration to repudiate General Bates and his treaty.[22] Before they could mount a major attack in behalf of the identity of patriotism and monogamy, the attention of these journals was deflected toward a more accustomed target, the army canteen. This beer-serving institution had long been denounced by the American Temperance Society, and when it was transferred to the Philippines it gained additional enemies. The editor of *The Advance* was particularly concerned with its effect on the volunteer soldiers; it would "rob them of their most valuable possession, their manhood."[23] Agitation by the Temperance lobby brought about the suspension of the army canteen in the Philippines, a result most satisfying to prohibitionist editors in America and to saloon-keepers in Manila.

A long report in *The Independent* by Harold Martin, a correspondent for the Associated Press, alerted the public to "the shameful spread of the saloon" in our new colonial possessions. According to Martin, there were hundreds of these "institutions of civilization" in Manila and its environs by the summer of 1900. They had "wreaked havoc among the 60,000

American soldiers that at one time or another . . . have been quartered about Manila,'' and they were beginning to corrupt the traditionally temperate Filipinos as well.[24] Expansionist and anti-imperialist clergymen now joined hands to demand action by the administration, and editorials in the religious press excoriated ''the liquor business under American auspices in Manila.'' Josiah Strong, the famous ministerial exponent of Social Darwinism, was particularly vehement. Our mission was to redeem the Filipinos; the saloon could but corrupt them: ''We are altogether responsible for whatever ravages imported drink may make among the natives of our dependencies. We shall be held responsible by the world conscience, and we must hold ourselves responsible.''[25]

Moral outrage did not reach its peak until reports reached America suggesting that many American soldiers suffered ''shameful maladies.'' Chaplain Peter MacQueen informed a U.S. senator that a recent month had seen 2,700 new cases of venereal disease and that ''there was not standing room in the prostitution houses of Manila.''[26] Most clerical editors were too respectful of the sensitivities of their audience to go into the sordid details; but there were acceptable code terms, and allusions to ''bodies damaged for life'' were understood even by the most ascetic.[27] The pacifist editor of The Woman's Journal insisted that ''herding men together in standing armies'' always produced ''frightful results,'' and expressed the hope that reports of vice in Manila would further the cause of women's suffrage in America: ''When women are aware of what militarism implies of danger to manhood, to womanhood, and to the American home, they will demand the ballot in order to put a stop to war altogether.''[28] When these moral guardians received news of efforts by the Army Medical Corps to reduce the danger of venereal disease among the troops by means of licensed brothels and medical certification of their inhabitants, they were not only unappeased but outraged. Vice regulated was vice authorized. A photograph of two licensed brothels in Manila flying the Stars and Stripes was the object of particular excitement, and several copies were sent to the War Department accompanied by denunciations of those who would simultaneously insult chastity and patriotism.[29] So great was the pressure directed against the War Department that the inspection of prostitutes by army surgeons was henceforth forbidden, and ''official brothels'' were stripped of their rank.

The action of the government had a conciliatory effect, and expressions of editorial anger were succeeded by renewed declarations of evangelical confidence. Optimism appeared more necessary and was consequently more determined. There were moral dangers lurking in the tropics, but this was all the more reason to support the endeavors of true men of God—the upright administrator, the conscientious civil servant, the teacher, and the missionary.

The publicity given military atrocities in the spring of 1902 should have served as a further test of faith and optimism, but it was a test that many chose to avoid. The majority response of Protestant leaders to reports of military atrocities was a mixture of doubt and apathy. These reports gained general currency only when the end of the war was in sight and the War Department offered assurances that such incidents were but rare exceptions to the generally humane conduct of our brave soldiers. Emotional fatigue encouraged acceptance of those assurances, as did a well-practiced determination to accentuate the positive features of American colonialism. Herbert Welsh, the anti-imperialist investigator from Philadelphia, should not have been surprised when a majority of Episcopal bishops chose to ignore his appeal for a petition to Congress and Lyman Abbott politely refused him space in the pages of *The Outlook*.[30] Abbott and his religious compatriots made no effort to defend the water torture, but they could not be expected to publicize it, convinced as they were that instances of military misconduct would be more than compensated by the exercise of evangelical duty and the blessings of American rule.

No more did Catholic priests and editors emphasize the issue of military atrocities. By 1902 they had fixed their positions respecting the dangers and opportunities offered by American conquest of the Philippine Islands. Catholic and Protestant churchmen divided on many counts, but a majority of both were determined to advance their faith by assuming a posture of sympathetic support for American colonial rule in the Philippines. Optimism for the future proved stronger than uneasiness with the present. There were Catholic leaders opposed to insular imperialism and a band of anti-imperialist Protestant ministers prepared to declare the Philippine-American War wicked as well as unnecessary. On balance, however, organized religion supported the war and American sovereignty in the Philippines. The war's end was greeted with relief but without shame. The prophecy of the editor of *The Watchman* expressed a stubborn confidence shared by many: "We shall now enter upon that era of making our presence in the islands a blessing, to which we have all looked forward through these weary years of bloodshed."[31]

CHAPTER VII

The Influence of Racism and the Response of the Black American

Following his election to the Senate by the Indiana state legislature in June 1899, Albert J. Beveridge made a visit to the Philippines, where the ardent young imperialist discussed the progress of the war with the military high command in Manila and enjoyed several expeditions "into the field." Upon his return, he reported to the readers of the *Saturday Evening Post* that the morale of the American soldier was high and his valor and bravery all that could be desired. He reported further his pleasure in the "remarkable and striking ethnological fact" that "the Saxon type" was dominant "throughout our active fighting force":

> Everywhere the pale blue or gray eye, everywhere the fair skin, everywhere the tawny hair and beard. . . . These thoroughbred soldiers from the plantations of the South, from the plains and valleys and farms of the west, look the thoroughbred, physically considered. The fine line is everywhere. The nose is straight, the mouth is sensitive and delicate. There are very few bulldog jaws. There is, instead, the steel-trap jaw of the lion. The whole face and figure is the face and figure of the thoroughbred fighter, who has always been the fine-featured, delicate-nostriled, thin-eared, and generally clean-cut featured man.[1]

Admiration for the fair skin of the thoroughbred Saxon implies, of course, a corollary sentiment—scorn for the dark-skinned native who might lack delicate nostrils and who surely could not exhibit a tawny beard. For Beveridge and many Americans this failure stood as a symbol of innate inferiority. Filipinos were not only different, they were "brown men," and so, inferior. Colorphobia was a disease of epidemic proportions in the United States, and it could not help but influence the attitudes of many Americans toward the Filipino and thus their attitudes toward his subjugation. The Filipino was both a "monkey man" and a "nigger." In the cartoons of the day Aguinaldo and the insurgents were sometimes shown as wild-eyed cannibals, but more usually as shrunken versions of Mr. Bones.[2] Whether there was a bolo in his teeth or pickaninny ribbons in his hair, Aguinaldo was always dirty; for cleanliness was an attribute reserved for the advanced and progressive Caucasian race:

> O, Aguinaldo leads a sloppy life,
> He eats potatoes with his knife,
> And once a year he takes a scrub,
> And leaves the water in the tub.[3]

A belief in the innate incapacity of colored races had inspired support for acquisition of the Philippine Islands, and the subsequent "insurrection" of the Filipinos was seen as confirmation of their need for American rule and tutelage. For *The New York Times*, Aguinaldo's "insane attack" and "stupendous folly" offered conclusive proof that the Filipinos were undisciplined children; to give them political power was "to give a dynamite cartridge to a baby for a plaything."[4] Rebellion was a sign of instability, stupidity, and political immaturity—at least when it was little brown men who rebelled.

There were many influences at work to persuade Americans to accept this tautology. Not only had the 1890s witnessed the publication of a number of works on "the science of race," but there was the example of the British and the wish of certain Americans to copy and succeed their British cousins. What little Americans knew about the Filipinos and their aptitudes came chiefly from British sources. John Foreman and other British travel writers had laid great stress on the tribal divisions of the Filipinos as well as their childishness.[5] Such American writers as John Barrett and Charles Denby picked up the theme and emphasized as well the "tropical nature" of the Filipinos. Honesty was as foreign to their natures as diligence, and their slyness and sloth were typical of races debilitated by the climate of the tropics. Not all "authorities" were prepared to agree with Arthur Stanley Riggs that the Filipinos were "degenerate scion of ancient Malay pirates [facing] . . . a racial sunset," but it was generally accepted that by heredity, environment, and history the Filipinos were a handicapped race. They were Orientals, they lived in the tropics, and their previous experience with Western ways had been confined to Spanish superstition and tyranny.[6]

The arguments of these self-appointed scholars achieved official confirmation with the well-publicized preliminary report of the Schurman Commission.[7] The McKinley administration saw that this report was published prior to the congressional elections of 1899, and it was offered as the judgment of men both expert and objective. The commissioners insisted that the population of the Philippines was a conglomerate of the Negrito, Oriental, and Indonesian races, with the Malays themselves divided into many quarrelling tribes. There was no Filipino nation and indeed no Filipino community. Aguinaldo was the ambitious chieftain of a single tribe. The "government" that he had headed in the summer and fall of 1898 had served "only for plundering the people under the pretext of levying 'war contributions.'"[8] Under American direction and guidance, the Filipinos could be expected to develop a measure of political capacity, but for the moment they were a collection of races and tribes incapable of self-government. They lacked self-control, organizational ability, and acquaintance with the processes of law.[9]

Official pronouncements always spoke of incapacity, never of inferiority. But in the popular mind there was no appreciable distinction. Americans admired those who were efficient, progressive, and technologically competent.[10] People who were incapable were inferior. They were like children, who should take orders from their parents, or like "niggers," who were expected to obey the instructions of white men.

The stereotype of the Filipino held by many Americans combined the supposed characteristics of the untrained child and the rascally Sambo. It can only be understood when placed against the history of black-white relations in America and the association of slavery and color in America's own past. Colored men in America were "niggers" and so, too, were the men of color of the Philippines. It was the not coincidental misfortune of the Filipino to fall under American jurisdiction at the very time when the American black man was suffering the climax of official segregation and statutory discrimination in the South and a reduction in political recognition and respect in all sections of the country. If the American-born black man was judged incapable and so inferior, how much more "the Filipino nigger," for he was stunted, foreign, and rebellious.

The ridiculous can occasionally be illustrative, at least for the tenets of white supremacy. On the inside cover of *McClure's Magazine* in October 1899, there was an advertisement for Pears' Soap featuring a resplendently uniformed Admiral George Dewey bending over a washbowl. His attitude was to be associated with the civilizing duty of advanced nations: "The first step towards lightening The White Man's Burden is through teaching the virtues of cleanliness. Pears' Soap is a potent factor in brightening the dark corners of the earth, as civilization advances, while amongst the cultured of all nations it holds the highest place. . . . "

For some Americans inherited beliefs in the innate inferiority of men of color was strengthened by their adoption of the theories of Social Dar-

winism. The more serious students of this pseudoscience did not distinguish men by the color of their skins, but their classification of advanced
and backward peoples could be joined to colorphobia with a consequent
strengthening of the racism implicit in both.

Theodore Roosevelt can serve as example of an American whose
support for imperialism in the Pacific was encouraged by a readiness to
apply Social Darwinian notions of "fitness" to the sphere of international
relations. Roosevelt blended those notions with his own version of romantic nationalism and would have denied that the composition could be labeled "racist," but it may.

Roosevelt had no use for Beveridge's gushing admiration for those
with tawny beards and delicate nostrils, but he was convinced that the
progress of the world depended on the masterful leadership of the virile
and advanced people and equally convinced that, over the course of a long
historical development, the Anglo-Saxon peoples had created political and
social institutions that could help direct the less developed peoples into the
march of civilization and progress.[11] There was no eternal fixity in the
status of the various races, but those who were at present "backward"
must accept the leadership of the "advanced." If they did not they had to
be coerced, as the British had coerced the Kaffirs and as we now had to
coerce the Filipinos. We could not allow the ignorance of a few Tagal
bandits to destroy the opportunity given us to bring order, civilization, and
progress to the Philippines. Certain peoples had to be governed without
their consent when rights and interests broader than their own demanded
precedence. His friend Captain Mahan was quite right. The Filipinos had
no right at present "to administer the country which they happen to be
occupying." The right of self-government implied "a political fitness and
a fair probability of political propriety of action."[12]

Under the pressure of the campaign of 1900, Roosevelt would declare
that the Filipinos were as savage and irrational as the Apaches who had
taken to the warpath under Geronimo and, with a blithe disregard for
ethnological consistency, would refer to Aguinaldo as "the Oceola of the
Phillipines" and "a renegade Pawnee."[13] But in calmer moments he saw
the Filipinos not as a band of savages but as an untutored race whose
vitality had been sapped by the tropics. Under American tutelage, they
might some day attain to the level of a civilized people. It was only the
civilized, of course, who could profit from liberty and self-government.
Roosevelt agreed with Whitelaw Reid that "if men will not govern themselves with respect for civilization and its agencies, then, when they get in
the way, they must be governed." This had always been the way "when

the world was not retrograding,'' and it was not to be expected that progress could be assured "without some blood having been shed."[14]

Men such as Reid and Roosevelt found justification for their simplistic version of Social Darwinian theory not only in the lessons taught by their British cousins but in the frontier thesis of Frederick Jackson Turner. As American civilization had evolved through successive cycles of westward settlement and been tempered by the experience of succeeding generations of pioneer farmers, so America had now a special responsibility and need to march westward across the Pacific. Our national experience offered proof of the identification of expansion and strength, and unless this country followed the trek to the tropics its individualistic tradition could wither and die.[15]

Most Social Darwinists did not begin by emphasizing color, but in their emphasis on the "superior fitness" of certain peoples and their conviction that the Anglo-Saxon was the most fit to bring progress to the dark places of the earth, they became as scornful of "tropical peoples" as any Mississippi redneck. William Allen White might deplore lynchings in the Deep South, but he informed readers of the *Emporia Gazette* that "only the Anglo-Saxons can govern themselves." It was their manifest destiny "to go forth as a world conqueror."[16] The Negro at home was society's ward, worthy of benevolence because incapable. The Filipino abroad was a ward as well, but rather more backward and certainly more obstreperous. For him the rod must not be spared; the ignorant must be coerced in order to be schooled.

The influence of Social Darwinism was not confined to the ranks of the imperialists. Many anti-imperialists divided humanity into "advanced" and "backward" peoples, and a few characterized the Filipinos as "savages." Racism was sufficiently widespread in the thinking of white Americans in the 1890s that no group in the debate over colonialism and the Philippine-American War totally escaped. There was less racism in the anti-imperialist ranks, however, and its motivation and rhetoric were rather different.

Southern anti-imperialists such as Senators Tillman and Carmack probably uttered as many slurs against "inferior races" as their expansionist counterparts, but most anti-imperialists who warned against the danger of embracing the Filipino within the American political system emphasized the cultural differences of the Filipino rather than his genetic inferiority. They were inspired to emphasize those differences by their desire to persuade their countrymen that institutions designed for American citizens would be endangered by their extension to colonial vassals. There was an element of ethnocentrism in the attitude of men such as Senator Hoar and Edward Atkinson, and a note of *noblesse oblige* as well, but these men did not emphasize the color of the Filipino's skin in the manner of Charles Denby and John Barrett. A distinction should be made, moreover, between the comments of various anti-imperialist spokesmen before February 1899 and those made after that date. Hoping to prevent acquisition of the islands, many anti-imperialists emphasized the unassimilable qualities of the Filipinos during the debate over the Treaty of Paris. Once the "insurrection" began, however, the literature of the Anti-Imperialist League tended to emphasize the rights of the Filipinos more than their differentness. If there was a patronizing tone in the comments of Erving Winslow, E. L. Godkin, and Carl Schurz, their chief theme was that the Filipino should be allowed the opportunity to prove his capacity for self-government. America forever debauched its ideals when it dealt with any group to whom it refused to give full citizenship. We had failed with the Indian and the Negro; there was no reason to believe we would do better by the Filipino.[17]

Though the anti-imperialists found it difficult to judge the Filipino as intelligent as his American friends, they were nonetheless disturbed by the racism of the advocates of colonial expansion. The numerous parodies of Kipling's "White Man's Burden" always contained verses scornful of those who saw the Filipino as "half devil and half child."[18] For a few anti-imperialists, indeed, one of the most distasteful features of the experiment in imperialism was its probable impact on the American Negro. Moorfield Storey, Samuel Bowles, Jr., William Lloyd Garrison, Jr., Gamaliel Bradford, and George F. Hoar were men proud of their descent from abolitionists and Free Soilers, and each expressed his fear that tyranny over colored peoples abroad would increase racial animosities at home and lead to the further subjugation of the American Negro. Senator Hoar saw a parallel between the new wave of lynchings in the South and our "lynching of a people" in the Philippines, and instructed his Republican colleagues that those who insisted upon the incapacity of the Filipinos no longer dared to question Negro disfranchisement in the South.[19] Bowles, editor of the Springfield (Mass.) *Republican*, made the same point and informed his readers that "the contempt we have shown for the rights and protests of the natives of the Philippines . . . the killing of them by the thousands and the looting of their homes" was certainly not calculated "to increase the southern white's regard for the negro as a fellow-being of like feelings and claims to life and liberty as himself."[20]

A minority of white anti-imperialists saw a connection between the exhibition of racial contempt abroad and the present and future status of the American Negro at home. Did the American Negro recognize such a connection? Did he oppose colonialism and American subjugation of the Filipino because he judged administration policy in the Philippines harmful to the political rights and human dignity of the black man in America, or were the appeals of nationalism stronger than sentiments of racial empathy? Was there, indeed, anything identifiable as a separate black response to the Philippine-American War?

The majority of black Americans at the turn of the century lived in the rural South, and it is unlikely that most impoverished and illiterate share-croppers had opinions on American foreign policy. Consequently, the black response to insular imperialism and the Philippine-American War must be pieced together from random bits of evidence indicating the opinions of Negro editors, churchmen, professional men, and soldiers. These pieces are not as numerous as one would wish, nor are they easily fashioned into a consistent pattern. They offer not definite answers so much as clues to the response of Black America.

The black press provides examples of editors who entertained a con-scious racial identification with "the colored peoples of the Philippines" and others who saw the Filipino as a foreigner with no claims on the sympathy of the American Negro, but the majority response of the black press was clearly anti-imperialist in tone.[21] Certain of the older and better established Negro papers, such as the Philadelphia *Defender*, the Rich-mond *Planet*, and the Salt Lake City/Chicago *Broad Ax*, were strong opponents of McKinley's diplomatic and military policies in the Philip-pines.[22] The editor of the *Broad Ax* saw the war as one designed "to satisfy the robbers, murderers, and unscrupulous monopolists, who are ever crying for more blood," and H. C. Astwood, editor of the Philadel-phia *Defender*, saw our slaughter of the Filipinos as "one of the most unrighteous acts ever perpetrated by any government."[23] Some papers expressed open sympathy for the Filipino and identified his struggle for liberty with that of the American Negro, but they were usually reluctant to speak out against Negro enlistments or to withhold praise from the exploits of black volunteers.[24] Anti-imperialist editors gained unanimity only in their condemnation of colonial adventures as dangerous distraction to the correction of domestic injustice and their conviction that a government that dealt unjustly with its own "dark-skinned peoples" could do no better for those in foreign lands. Those papers that did acknowledge a sense of racial kinship with the Filipinos appeared confused as to the nature of that kinship. For some, kinship was limited to the position of "the Malays" as fellow victims of white domination, but other anti-imperialist black editors were as ready as Mrs. Jefferson Davis to identify the Filipino as a Negro. The editor of *The American Citizen* of Kansas City expressed the hope that black troops would not be utilized in the Philippines, for this would be "a pitting of Negro against Negro."[25]

The Cleveland *Gazette* offered an example of a newspaper convinced that McKinley's Philippine policy was harmful to the interests of black Americans but uncertain of its reasons and ambivalent in its criticism. Having supported the Spanish-American War, it attacked the administration for its failure to give American Negroes equal opportunities in Cuba or to take any action against the rising incidence of lynching and racial crimes in the United States. The *Gazette* offered no criticism of territorial expansion per se, but denounced "imperialism," which it identified with white domination of "colored peoples." The black soldier should not be ordered to the Philippines, and the administration was damned for its failure to praise the valor of the uniformed Negro in Luzon. The Filipinos were to be pitied for their subjugation to Anglo-Saxon white supremacists, and they had fewer claims on the sympathy of white Americans than did their black countrymen. The *Gazette* distrusted the foreign policy of William McKinley, but its anger was directed primarily against McKinley's failure to correct domestic injustice.[26]

Not only was there confusion in the motives and arguments of the anti-imperialists, but the black press offered examples of editors apparently unconcerned with insular imperialism and its impact on the American Negro and editors convinced that the Philippine-American War was both rightful and of potential benefit for the American Negro. George L. Knox, editor of the Indianapolis *Freeman*, believed that the war would offer Negroes the opportunity to serve with distinction and obtain thereby greater respect and recognition at home. The islands, moreover, could provide economic opportunities for the Negro veteran and Negro entrepreneur.[27] The Republican affiliation of such papers as the *Freeman* and the Richmond *St. Luke Herald* undoubtedly encouraged them to take a favorable view of the colonial policy of William McKinley, but they were not alone in emphasizing the value of Negro patriotism and gallantry as correctives to racial prejudice. *The Savannah Tribune* hoped that a display of Negro valor would assist the Negro in his struggle for the rights of first-class citizenship, and the shift of the Washington *Bee* and the New York *Age* from a position of opposition to one of fluctuating support for the war was, in part, the result of their determination to emphasize the capacity of the black American to fulfill all the obligations of citizenship including that of military service. Thomas Fortune, editor of the *Age*, had convinced himself by 1901 "that the more dark peoples that we have under our flag," the more "outlets" there would be for the American Negro.[28]

The performance of the Twenty-fourth Infantry Regiment in Cuba during the war with Spain had been a source of pride for all Negro editors, and even those who opposed American policy in the Philippines were not prepared to criticize the participation of black soldiers in the campaigns in Luzon. E. E. Cooper, editor of a Washington weekly, insisted that however small the sympathy of the Negro for the war, "he was first of all an American and would fight beside his white brother wherever it was necessary."[29] The valor of the black soldier stood witness to the capacity as well as the patriotism of the American Negro. *The Colored American Magazine* saw the anomaly of black soldiers fighting to give America the privilege of bearing the white man's burden in the Philippines, but insisted that American Negroes had but one country. "Our racial sympathies would naturally be with the Filipinos . . . but we cannot for the sake of sentiment turn our back on our own country."[30]

Black journalists such as J. Gordon Street of the Boston *Courant* and William Monroe Trotter of the Boston *Guardian* saw the war as yet another example of white racism, but they appeared uncertain of its impact on the status of the American Negro and were more consistent in their demand for equal treatment for the black soldier than for the right of the Filipino to national self-determination.[31] A demonstration of the ability of the Filipinos to govern themselves might assist the American Negro to secure his rights under the Fourteenth and Fifteenth Amendments. Of more immediate importance, however, was the struggle against racism in the army and the demand that Negro soldiers serve under Negro officers.

A majority of black ministers were suspicious of the war and its racist overtones, but there were more expansionists to be found among black churchmen than black journalists. The African Methodist Episcopal Church was deeply divided. If the editor of *The Christian Recorder*, its official organ, was sympathetic to the Filipinos' struggle for freedom, Bishop W. J. Gaines declared his willingness to exchange his cassock for a uniform, go over to the Philippines, and "help finish the job." Gaines mentioned the opportunities for missionary endeavor that American rule would provide and suggested that because the Filipinos "are like us a colored people," there would be particular opportunities for the Negro minister and colonist. This theme was also urged by the black chaplain of the Ninth U.S. Cavalry. A Methodist and an expansionist, Chaplain George W. Prioleau wrote frequently to *The Colored American* of Washington urging its readers to support the policy of the McKinley administration. The Filipinos knew nothing "about commercial and agricultural business and a very little about government," and we could not allow their "indolence and laziness to retard American progress."[32]

The judgments of Bishop Gaines and Chaplain Prioleau were hotly contested by other black church leaders. Bishop Henry M. Turner led an anti-imperialist faction in the African Methodist Episcopal Church, proclaiming that America was engaged in an "unholy war of conquest . . . [against] a feeble band of sable patriots," and Bishop Alexander Walters, president of the national Afro-American Council, insisted that America was so "impregnated with colorphobia" that it was particularly ill-prepared "to carry on the work of expansion . . . among the dark races of the earth." For a nation "so enamored of Anglo-Saxon superiority" as the United States to assume the task of improving "our little brown brother" was logic gone mad.[33] A ministerial correspondent of *The Christian Recorder* declared that the Filipinos were "foreign members of [our] own household," and the clerical editor of the Helena *Reporter* publicly advised Negro soldiers "not to fight against the brave Filipinos." The Rev. W. A. Holmes characterized the war as an effort by the white American to inflict on the inhabitants of the Philippines "color-phobia, jimcrow cars, disfranchisement, lynchers, and everything that prejudice can do to blight the manhood of the darker races." The government's treatment of the "brown peoples" of the Philippines was a logical extension of its policy toward Black Americans.[34] One black minister, William H. Scott of Woburn, Massachusetts, was so convinced of the racist error of American Philippine policy that he volunteered to tour the Northeast for the Anti-Imperialist League during the summer and fall of 1900, denouncing the war and urging black citizens to express their opposition to imperialism by ignoring their ties with the Republican party and voting for Bryan.[35]

Black citizens of Boston held a meeting in Faneuil Hall, in October 1900, and passed resolutions in behalf of Filipino freedom and the candidacy of Bryan, but neither that meeting nor the support given McKinley by a majority of the black electorate in the balloting of 6 November furnishes a satisfactory measurement of the political response of Black America to the Philippine-American War. Despite the travels of William H. Scott and the contrary efforts of J. E. Bruce, a Negro newspaperman employed by the National Republican Committee, it is doubtful that the issue of colonialism determined the presidential choice of many black voters. A majority of registered black voters chose the Republican ticket in 1900 because they were persuaded by reason and habit that the G.O.P. was less unsympathetic to Negro rights and Negro enfranchisement than the national Democratic party.[36]

During the campaign the handful of black officeholders in Washington had assured Republican managers of their own loyalty and their belief that most American Negroes were prepared to trust the party of Lincoln to do justice abroad as well as at home.[37] More important, however, than the self-serving labors of the Recorder of Deeds and the Stamp Clerk in neutralizing the impact of McKinley's colonial policy on the black vote in 1900 was the stance of Booker T. Washington. Washington's "Atlanta Compromise" not only deemphasized the political participation of the American Negro but discouraged ideological identification as well. More militant leaders, such as W. E. B. DuBois, were prepared to advocate political action, but they found it difficult to see in William Jennings Bryan a champion of "colored peoples" or in the party of Benjamin Tillman a source of hope. It was an opinion shared by many Negro professional men of the anti-imperialist persuasion.

One of the most articulate black anti-imperialists was Kelly Miller, a professor of mathematics at Howard University. Miller contributed articles to the Washington *Bee* and other black journals proclaiming the necessary association of the doctrines of human equality and national self-determination. For the New England Anti-Imperialist League he wrote a pamphlet that sought to relate the rising incidence of lynchings in the southern states to the apathy of American whites toward the slaughter of Filipinos in Luzon. Each was an expression of white racism, and all persons interested in the welfare of the "colored men in America" must oppose the unrighteous subjugation of the Filipino.[38]

Similar opinions were expressed by Frederick McGhee, a Negro lawyer in St. Paul, Archibald H. Grimke, and Lewis H. Douglass, son of Frederick Douglass and a frequent contributor to the New York *Age*. Douglass insisted that the policy of "benevolent assimilation" was pure hypocrisy, and that only the most self-deluded black American could believe that the government would "act more justly ten thousand miles away than it can at home."[39] Clifford Plummer, a Boston attorney and secretary of the National Colored Protective League, also stressed the connection between the worsening condition of the blacks at home and McKinley's war in the Philippines. Insisting that "American Negroes and the poor blacks of the Philippines" were both fighting for independence, he was one of the few black leaders ready to suggest that Negro troops were fighting on the wrong side in the Philippines.[40] Plummer, with the encouragement of Erving Winslow, attempted to organize a "Colored Auxiliary of the Anti-Imperialist League." The attempt never got off the ground,[41] but it is interesting as indicating a major obstacle to cooperation between Negro opponents of colonialism and the leadership of the Anti-Imperialist League.

It was both paradoxical and self-defeating to suggest that a "colored auxiliary" be formed to denounce the racism implicit in the Philippine policy of the administration.

The black soldier served in what was the equivalent of a "colored auxiliary." The Twenty-fourth and Twenty-fifth U.S. Infantry and the Ninth and Tenth U.S. Cavalry were the black regiments of the regular army. Led by white officers, all saw service in the war, as did the Forty-eighth and Forty-ninth Volunteer Infantry. The latter were recruited specifically for service in the Philippine-American War and included a few black officers, though none above the rank of captain. These six black regiments had a slightly higher desertion rate than other regiments serving in the Philippines,[42] but scattered correspondence and records indicate no serious morale problem. It does not appear that many black soldiers suffered psychological anxiety when engaged in a colonial war against "a people of color." Some were unhappy about their role as instruments of white colonialism, and several wrote to parents and Negro editors expressing their anger at the way in which white soldiers referred to the Filipinos as "niggers."[43] But others were hopeful that the overseas service of the Negro soldier might lessen the discrimination suffered by the black man at home, and still others were ready to refer to the Filipino as a "gu-gu" and complain of his refusal to fight in the open.[44] For many southern Negroes, army service offered more of an escape than a psychic dilemma, and the Forty-eighth and Forty-ninth Volunteer Regiments were quickly raised.

As respects the response of the black soldier, one may make the initial judgment that national identification was stronger than racial sympathy. If the black soldier entertained no colorphobia toward the Filipino, he could still entertain the prejudices of the warrior for the civilian. For him the Filipino might be less foreign, but he was still not to be confused with an American of any race or color. For most black soldiers duty lay in obedience to orders. Sgt. M. W. Sadler of Company K, Twenty-fifth U.S. Infantry, probably spoke for many when he informed the readers of the Indianapolis *Freeman*: "Whether it is right to reduce these people to submission is not a question for the soldier to decide. Our oath of allegiance knows neither race [nor] color. . . . "[45] A single ambush had convinced another member of Company K that, whatever his color, the Filipino was an enemy. Three of his black comrades had fallen victim to "the enemies' butchery." Their bodies had been "incased in the Stars and Stripes . . . [and] shipped to the land they so dearly loved."[46]

Those Negroes who did desert appear to have done so more from irritation with such stiff-necked white officers as Colonel A. S. Burt, commanding officer of the Twenty-fifth Regiment, than from a sympathetic identification with the Filipinos and their battle for national independence. Only nine black soldiers joined the insurgents. The most famous of these "renegades" was David Fagan, a corporal of the Twenty-fourth U.S. Infantry Regiment, who joined the guerrillas under General Lacuna and was commissioned a captain in the insurgent army. Taking a Filipino common-law wife, Fagan adopted the Filipino cause as his own. Next to Aguinaldo, he was the most despised insurgent in the eyes of the American officer corps in Luzon, and a high price was put on his head.[47]

One of the more dramatic incidents of the war saw a skirmish between a Filipino ambushing party led by Captain Fagan and a detachment of Negro soldiers of the Twenty-fourth Regiment doing garrison duty at the town of Magalang in central Luzon. After Fagan had surprised and killed a handful of troopers escorting the mule wagons, he set up an ambush to meet the rescuing scouts. As the latter were about to be cut down, reenforcements arrived on both sides, and what had begun as a private vendetta developed into a full-fledged battle. In that battle the Negro soldiers of the Twenty-fourth, stung by the taunts of Fagan, fought with a grim determination that won the commendation of their white officers. One of Funston's Scouts later remembered with particular favor Sergeant Washington, "a white-haired negro grown old in his Uncle Sam's army." Though injured, Washington refused to retire from the scene of battle and "stood there flat-footed, cursing and taunting the gugus, fighting like a madman."[48] The figures of Captain Fagan and Sergeant Washington mark the outer parameters of the response of the black soldier in the Philippine-American War.

Certain American officers and officials worried over that response, especially after documents were captured containing appeals from various insurgent generals "To the Colored American Soldier." The latter should leave the army where he suffered racial prejudice and join the Philippine army where he would receive rank and honor.[49] When worries over mass desertions proved to be groundless, they were succeeded by worries over the demoralizing effect of Negro fraternization with Filipino civilians. Having earlier advocated the use of black troops because they were "naturally fitted" for a tropical climate, various officers now complained that the Negroes were too adaptable and "lacked the necessary moral stamina." William Howard Taft echoed this theme as he complained to the Secretary of War that Negro troops "get along too well with the native women." Taft declared that each black soldier had a native mistress and that this created "a good deal of demoralization in the towns where they are stationed."[50] It was probably on the advice of Taft as well as General Adna Chaffee that the War Department arranged the return of the black regiments in 1902, ahead of the regular pattern of rotation. Prior to their return, no member of any of these six regiments was ever put on special duty as a member of the Manila police force or allowed to serve with the Filipino constabulary.[51]

The discrimination suffered by the black soldier during the Philippine-American War makes all the more dubious the efforts of certain Americans at the war's end to push various schemes of Negro colonization in the islands. Senators Tillman and Morgan were undoubtedly moved by a wish to reduce the black population in South Carolina and Alabama, but self-declared "friends of the American colored man" also spoke of the need for "the capable Negro" to play a role in bringing American institutions to the Philippines. The Filipinos desired "occidentalism" but wished to receive it "through hands of a like complexion to theirs." W. S. Scarborough, a black scholar, was indeed convinced that American "men and women of color" would be of "inestimable value" in helping to lead the Filipinos "out to the light and on to strength."[52]

Whatever the motives of their advocates, proposals for colonization in the Philippines met a very mixed reaction from black veterans and black editors. Some members of the Forty-eighth and Forty-ninth Volunteer Regiments elected to be discharged in the islands and to take up residence there, but they were few in number. Captain John L. Waller, a well-known spokesman for black veterans, compared the proposals of Tillman and Scarborough to the African colonization schemes of Henry Clay sixty years before, and most black soldiers welcomed the prospect of returning to their own country, where injustice and prejudice had the attribute of familiarity. Black editors expressed somewhat greater enthusiasm, but their interest in Negro colonization and entrepreneurial opportunities in the Philippines was not of long duration. By 1903, they were offering editorial praise to the black members of the Union League of Bedford, Massachusetts, which had passed a formal resolution advising Negroes to remain at home and fight for their rights as American citizens.

So fragmentary is the evidence respecting the opinions of the various parts and pieces of the black community that dogmatism is a luxury denied the student of its response to the Philippine-American War. It seems clear, however, that the black soldier both during and after the war felt less identification and sympathy with the Filipino than did the black civilian. Among black civilians, editors tended to be more anti-imperialist than churchmen, and black professional men, even when ready to identify the war with white racism, found it difficult to cooperate with the Anti-Imperialist League or accept the emphases of its rhetoric. The issues of colonialism and military pacification in the Philippines changed the votes or party affiliation of few American Negroes. Those who felt a sense of kinship with the Filipino offered him their emotional sympathies, but either from social fear or political impotence were unable to do much more. They seemed uncertain as to the relationship of colonialism abroad and Jim Crow prejudice at home and uncertain respecting the consequences of military victory in the Pacific for the status of the black man in Charleston or New York City.

Many Negroes appeared unconcerned with the adventures of American diplomacy; a few were convinced expansionists; and black anti-imperialists tended to oppose the administration's foreign policy more on the grounds that it was a dissipation of energies that should be directed to the correction of domestic injustice than from a conviction that it posed a direct and immediate danger for the American Negro. A minority did proclaim that such a danger existed—a minority intellectually independent of the handful of white anti-imperialists who held this belief—and they usually expressed a strong sense of racial identification with the Filipinos. Others sympathized with the Filipino only because he was an underdog or victim. Some, in brief, were troubled by the conflicting pulls of color and nationality, but many were not.

Few black Americans found any great joy in colonialism, but the association of patriotism and the rights of citizenship placed limits on expressions of dissent and opposition. Clifford Plummer and a few other black anti-imperialists might exceed those limits, but it is difficult to avoid the conclusion that though there were many blacks who were unenthusiastic about imperialism and quite a number who were opposed to the war it generated, few blacks figured importantly in the anti-imperialist movement. White racism restricted the instruments available to black opponents of America's Philippine policy.

The response of black Americans to colonialism and the Philippines was probably less tinctured by racist preconceptions than that of most white Americans. As Social Darwinist notions of racial fitness and inferiority helped persuade white America to take the course of colonialism and our experience in the Philippines accentuated feelings of white superiority, so questions of discrimination and color influenced the response of black Americans. But it was their own problems rather than an imagined parallelism of Afro-American and Tagalog that shaped the attitudes of the more concerned and articulate black editors, preachers, lawyers, and soldiers. Whereas the response of many white Americans was molded by the seductive illogic of "racial science" and the misapplied example of the British, the response of black Americans was primarily the product of their personal fears and discontents as victims of an increasingly racist society. Domestic wrongs and aspirations were the primary determinant. Some black Americans saw the Philippine-American War as a source of personal opportunity, others as a racist conspiracy, but for most it was a harmful and costly distraction.

CHAPTER VIII

Scholars and Writers

Public opinion analysts attempt to isolate and compare the elites and subgroups that compose the articulate public. In their labors they often combine the literary and academic "communities," probably in the belief that both share if not the life of the mind at least the use of the pen. Toward the Philippine-American War these communities also shared an attitude of disappointment and disgust. They form the single segment of the American public where majority opinion was clearly opposed to the acquisition and conquest of the Philippine Islands. Other groups offered many individual examples of dissent, and a majority of union leaders and black journalists and ministers offered occasional opposition, but the scholars and writers alone provide an example of majority sentiment in consistent opposition. That opposition was in the end ineffectual, but so, too, was it frequently eloquent and occasionally courageous.

On the American campus, opposition was not confined to faculty row but in several instances found residence in the office of the president. Henry Wade Rogers denounced the nation's Philippine policy publicly and often. He was in consequence encouraged to resign as president of Northwestern University. The trustees of that Methodist institution judged it unseemly that a college president serve as an officer of the American Anti-Imperialist League and attack the diplomatic goals of William McKinley, the champion of Methodist missionary endeavor. The anti-imperialist sentiments of E. Benjamin Andrews, president of Brown University, Daniel Coit Gilman of Johns Hopkins, G. Stanley Hall of Clark University, James Burrill Angell of Michigan, and Edwin A. Alderman of the University of North Carolina were reserved primarily for private correspondence and inspired less ire from trustees or alumni, whereas the criticism offered by Charles W. Eliot of Harvard was sufficiently avuncular to assure that there would be no diminishment of his increasing authority as an educational statesman. His carefully phrased admonitions against censorship in Manila and the waste of national treasure in "a cruel war" won the approval of

Moorfield Storey, but on balance Eliot was more prepared to advise than to dissent.[1]

A more outspoken opponent of insular imperialism and the Philippine-American War was the president of Stanford University, David Starr Jordan. A vice president of the Anti-Imperialist League and a prolific writer, Jordan gained national attention with his widely distributed speeches denouncing the military and diplomatic policies of the McKinley administration. Though a believer in Anglo-Saxon superiority and the beneficial extension of American influence, Jordan decried gunboat diplomacy, acquisition of overseas territory, and the barbarity of war. Colonialism was slavery in another guise; it could only corrupt our democratic institutions at home while assuring rebellion abroad. The Filipinos were not rebels against "law and order" but against "alien control." "It was our fault and ours alone that this war began''; it was "our crime" that it continued. Withdrawal from the Philippines would not lessen our diplomatic authority and influence; rather it was our present conduct that was the source of distress to our "genuine friends" in other lands.[2]

The only college president more quoted than Jordan was the chairman of McKinley's first Philippine Commission, Jacob Gould Schurman, president of Cornell University. Schurman was the only college president identified in the public mind with support of administration policy.[3] Schurman has been called by one student of his career a "reluctant expansionist," and perhaps he was.[4] More certainly, he was a man who oscillated between an admiration for the aims of American policy and uncertainty as to its practical consequences, and the short period when he enjoyed a measure of influence was the period when he was most admiring and least uncertain. It was not until the election of 1900 had passed and the war had entered its third year that Schurman began to express doubts about the benefits of American rule, and it was not until the spring of 1902 that he publicly declared his wish that American policy recognize the goal of Philippine independence. Then, in an attempt to lend consistency to his views, Schurman sought to make the Philippine-American War the crucible of Filipino nationalism. The Philippine republic of Aguinaldo had been made only of straw, but three years of struggle and fighting had produced among the Filipinos "a people" and "a universal passion" for immediate independence.[5]

Schurman's conversion came too late for him to receive commendation from the anti-imperialists of the academic community; nor had he earlier been recognized as its spokesman by the minority of professorial expansionists. Those academics who were prepared openly to proclaim their admiration for American policy in the Philippines saw Dean C. Worcester, professor of geology at the University of Michigan and a diligent member of both the Schurman and Taft Commissions, as a more forthright champion and a better stylist.[6] It was British writers, such as Benjamin Kidd, whom they most usually quoted, however, for it was British example they most admired. When Professor Franklin Henry Giddings of Columbia University announced his acceptance of American colonialism, he took care to express allegiance not only to the moral philosophy of Utilitarianism but to "Mr. Kidd's significant contribution to political economy," *The Control of the Tropics*. Kidd had traced the civilizing mission pursued by Britain over the past century and had demonstrated that the major question of the next century was whether world politics would be dominated by Anglo-Saxon peoples "in the interest of an English civilization, with its principles of freedom, self-government, and opportunity for all; or by the Russian-Chinese combination, with its policy of exclusiveness and its tradition of irresponsible authority."[7]

Giddings, however, was in a minority among the faculty of Columbia and within the academic community at large. Among faculty members who took a stand on public issues, imperialism and the Philippine-American War were generally deplored. Charles Eliot Norton and William Graham Sumner served as spokesmen for the professorial anti-imperialists at Harvard and Yale. A similar role was assumed by Felix Adler at Chicago University, J. Neal Steere at the University of Michigan, Frederick W. Starr at Columbia, J. Scott Clark at Northwestern, Melville B. Anderson at Stanford, I. J. McGinity at Cornell, and Arthur Latham Perry at Williams. Between one campus and another there were obvious differences. Most campuses in the South were comparatively quiescent, those of Harvard, Stanford, and Chicago, the most vocal on the war and the conquest of the Philippines. The University of Chicago had perhaps the greatest ratio of active anti-imperialists on its faculty—in addition to Adler there were Hermann von Holst, Adolph Cohn, A. A. Berle, James Lawrence Laughlin, and more than thirty other dissidents[8]—but rare was the campus that did not offer some examples of professorial opposition.

Dissent, however, was usually limited to the signing of petitions, talks before local community groups, and conversation in the faculty club dining hall. Probably no more than half of the professorial dissenters formally joined a branch of the Anti-Imperialist League; nor were there any efforts to form separate organizations for campus or guild. The instrumentalities of the teach-in and the full-page advertisement in *The New York Times* played no part in professorial dissent during the Philippine-American War. No more did professorial anti-imperialists try to use their professional societies to pass resolutions and manifestos. Even the more angry and determined academics were prepared to fight imperialism and war exclusively in their role as private citizens and within the customary channels of public debate. The expository essay was the most accustomed channel and so the most congenial.

The American professoriat at the end of the nineteenth century was, of course, a fairly homogenous group. Most were products of social advantage and the upper middle class. It was not to be expected that they would proselytize their views among the laboring poor or use the lectern in an effort to incite civil disobedience. Radical neither in temperament nor in social-economic philosophy, they were not enemies of the political and economic establishments. They were, however, men capable of moral outrage and a sense of superiority. Often they viewed the ills of the present with a sense of nostalgia for a purer past, a past where there was less of jingoism and money-grubbing and more attention paid to the counsel of superior intellect.

This was particularly true of those anti-imperialist professors represented by Charles Eliot Norton, self-proclaimed "apostle of beauty" and professor of fine arts at Harvard University. Norton was one of the few who had opposed the war with Spain, insisting that it was a war unnecessary in origin and dangerous in result. The adulation accorded Dewey reminded him of that granted a football hero—and football was perhaps the only thing more brutal than war—and he viewed McKinley as representative of everything cheap and false in American culture. Theodore Roosevelt, for all his dangerous faults, had "at least the instincts . . . of a gentleman," but McKinley was a "smug, canting, self-righteous servant of the Devil." McKinley was leading the nation willy-nilly in the direction of militarism, financial bankruptcy, and the corrupting morass of European power politics.[9]

As an admirer of British society and culture, Norton found some difficulty in warning America not to be misled into the imperial ways of Britain. Though convinced that the superiority of the British civil service was due in part to the demands of colonial administration, he concluded that the political and social structure of the United States was so different from that of Britain that this nation would derive from colonialism only its dangers and none of its benefits. It would serve to corrupt American youth, not stimulate a sense of public duty; it would be only another theater for venality, greed, and boodle. If America wished to take the advice of Britons, it should not listen to the siren calls of Joseph Chamberlain, but to those anti-imperialist Englishmen who were protesting the bloody and unrighteous Boer War.[10]

Norton wished American foreign policy to be more mindful of the warnings of Washington's Farewell Address, and a similar note of isolationism and traditionalism was sounded by other gowned Jeremiahs. Professor Thomas E. Will of Ruskin College in Trenton and Professor George P. Fisher of Yale denounced insular imperialism as a "reversal" of American policy, and James Lawrence Laughlin of Chicago wrote a "Liberty Tract" for the American Anti-Imperialist League in which he sought to prove that McKinley's diplomatic and military policy in the Philippines was contrary to the U.S. Constitution and the credo of American patriotism.[11]

Many of the professorial anti-imperialists, such as David Ames Welles of the Massachusetts Institute for Technology, were laissez-faire liberals and some were self-proclaimed Social Darwinists. The latter, represented by William Graham Sumner, John W. Burgess, and John Fiske, saw themselves as exemplars of a "pure" version of Social Darwinism, one uninfected by the romantic nationalism of such popularizers as Roosevelt and Whitelaw Reid. As Burgess and Fiske explained it, the superior fitness of certain national species would result in their natural growth and expansion, but imperialism was the product of military force and political manipulation and formed no true part of the laws of social evolution. "Undeveloped races" could progress only by means of the slow process of normal evolution. Their progress could not be hurried by external coercion or indoctrination.[12]

Stronger than the themes of isolationism, traditionalism, or doctrinal purity, however, was the note of moralism. Professorial critics tended to see American policy as immoral as well as unwise. In his widely circulated Phi Beta Kappa address, "The Conquest of the United States by Spain," Sumner insisted that we would "suffer morally" by forsaking the ideals of the Founding Fathers. We would fall prey to "the same vanity and self-conceit" that had brought defeat and ruin to Spain; as we became mercantilist tyrants, suppressing endless rebellions and "slaughtering thousands of Asiatics under a calculated misinterpretation of our civilizing mission."[13] Professor Lewis G. Janes amplified this theme in a pamphlet endorsed and publicized by the New England Anti-Imperialist League. Our war in the Philippines was proof that, for the United States, "the democratic spirit" had succumbed to "the commercial and money-making power." It was the demands of commercial greed that inspired "the spirit of conquest and military domination," and our imperial policy threatened not only the destruction of the Filipinos but the vitality of popular democracy at home.[14]

Professor Felix Adler was equally convinced of the danger of American policy and angered by those who would defend it. We had destroyed the first republic in the history of Asia, and we were pursuing our destructive policy by military tactics of unexampled barbarity. Patriotic Americans had no recourse but to protest. "He loves his country best . . . who would dissuade her from doing a wrong, and who, when she has entered on a course of wrong-doing, would seek by every legitimate means in his power to persuade her to desist and to withdraw from the evil position in which she has placed herself." Our war against the Filipinos was being pursued by methods that were uncivilized and shameful. Those who argued that such means were required by the tactics of the enemy and would hasten the war's conclusion were seeking to excuse the indefensible.[15]

Although Adler and other anti-imperialist professors were undoubtedly sympathetic with the victims of American military tactics, their references to the Filipinos often had a rather patronizing tone and their emphasis was on the war's damage to American values and institutions. Perhaps the sole professorial critic who could be accused of cultural pluralism and who empathized most directly with the Filipinos was William James, professor of psychology and moral philosophy at Harvard. One of the most scathing critics of McKinley's acquisition of the Philippines—"the most incredible, unbelievable piece of sneak-thief turpitude that any nation ever practiced"—James believed that our war against the Filipinos was criminal. We had brought the Filipinos terror and destruction, in the guise of "benevolent assimilation," and were guilty of "murdering another culture." By treating the Filipinos "as if they were a painted picture, an amount of mere matter in our way," we had fallen victim to the moral insensitivity of all conquerors who confused weakness with inferiority and lost the ability to understand "the humanity of the enemy." "God damn the U.S. for its vile conduct in the Philippines."[16]

In many ways the most modern of the professorial anti-imperialists, and certainly one of the more attractive, James had little influence even within the narrow confines of the Harvard Yard. Most of his denunciations and analyses of American policy were confined to private correspondence; seldom did he engage in public declarations, and then in the form of letters to the editor of the Boston *Evening Transcript*.[17] In any case, it is unlikely that Americans were prepared to receive advice on public policy from a philosopher. Professors tended to be dismissed as impractical men, at home with the abstruse and the arcane. Only two compartments of academe could perhaps be excepted: law and history. In each of those disciplines there were scholars prepared to offer counsel, but their counsel was divided and any possible influence lost by default.

Among students of constitutional and international law there were those such as Hermann von Holst who considered McKinley's Philippine proclamation of December 1898 an example of executive usurpation and an action contrary to the precepts of international law, whereas Professor F.

Spencer Baldwin of Boston University and Professor James Bradley Thayer of the Harvard Law School believed our title to the Philippines to be unexceptionable. The views of Theodore S. Woolsey, resident authority at Yale University on "the law of nations," provide a fair summary of the confusion and division among the legal experts. Woolsey was initially something of an anti-imperialist, and in the winter of 1898–99 he opposed ratification of the Treaty of Paris and judged McKinley's decision to send army units to Luzon "an offensive measure." Subsequently, however, he became persuaded that the United States in its administration of colonial territories in the Pacific would "follow the British principle of trusteeship," rather than the commercially restrictive ways of the Dutch and Spanish empires. Once persuaded of this fact, he no longer emphasized questions of legality and began to express increasing doubts about the capacity of the Filipinos. Constitutional guarantees had to be removed from the reach of dependent peoples "like edged tools from children's hands."[18]

If there was no clear or single counsel to be received from the professors of law, no more was there from the members of the American Historical Association. For Albert Bushnell Hart and John Bach McMaster the Philippine-American War was the fault of a foolish minority of Filipinos; for Washington C. Ford and James Ford Rhodes it represented a disagreeable obstacle to the fulfillment of America's role as a world power; and for Charles Francis Adams, Jr., and Goldwyn Smith it was a source of shame and disgrace. J. Evarts Greene informed his countrymen that we had been a world power since 1776 and did not need to soil ourselves in the practice of overseas imperialism to prove our stature, but James Morton Callahan informed the readers of his history of *American Relations in the Pacific and Far East* that the only honorable course for America "was to subdue the unprovoked and wasteful insurrection." "Force must be met by force," in order that there be "the new dawn of freedom, progress and civilization" for the islanders.[19] The American Historical Association never scheduled a session on U.S. policy in the Philippines—one member observing that the Association had no proper concern for "questions of a political character"[20]—but under "Notes & Comments," its *Review* permitted discussion of historical parallels to civil-military relations in Manila and the Insular Cases. On neither past parallels nor present policies did historians agree.

Few scholars of any disciplinary persuasion were quoted in the press or the halls of Congress. Many were deeply troubled about the Philippine-American War, but their influence was restricted and a sense of futility characterized their efforts.

It is less certain that this judgment can be made of the anti-imperialist

majority within the "literary community." Surely such writers as Mark
Twain and Finley Peter Dunne were more widely quoted than Professors
Norton and Adler. Their writings failed to reverse the diplomatic and
military policies of the McKinley-Roosevelt administrations, but they
helped sustain the anti-imperialist movement and possibly had some admonitory influence on the conduct of the Philippine-American War.

If not unanimous in its response to the acquisition and subjugation of
the Philippine Islands, the literary community divided into the few and the
many. Among the supporters of American policy there were only a half-
dozen poets and authors of note: Julia Ward Howe, Bliss Carman, Richard
Hovey, Gertrude Atherton, Brooks Adams, Julian Hawthorne. These six
writers offered little poetry and prose in behalf of the nation's Philippine
policy or its military instruments, and what they offered was justifiably
soon forgotten.[21] The anti-imperialists, on the other hand, were numerous
and prolific. At least twenty were men of letters of national reputation:
George Ade, Thomas Bailey Aldrich, Ambrose Bierce, Gamaliel Bradford, George W. Cable, John Jay Chapman, Ernest Crosby, Finley Peter
Dunne, Henry Blake Fuller, Hamlin Garland, Thomas Wentworth Higginson, William Dean Howells, Edgar Lee Masters, Joaquin Miller, William
Vaughn Moody, Bliss Perry, Edwin Arlington Robinson, Lincoln Steffens,
Mark Twain, Charles Dudley Warner.

Of the prose writers, probably the most effective were the satirists,
Bierce, Dunne, and Twain. Even Theodore Roosevelt admitted to enjoying
the observations of "Mr. Dooley," Finley Peter Dunne's philosophical
Irish-American saloon keeper, who defined the policy of "benevolent assimilation" as a belief that " 'twud be a disgrace f'r to lave befure we've
pounded these frindless an' ongrateful people into insinsibility."[22] And
Samuel Clemens had created in Mark Twain a national institution almost
immune to successful attack.

Twain was slow to join the ranks of the dissenters; indeed he did not
enlist until the war in the Philippines was in its twentieth month. By the
autumn of 1900, however, influenced in some measure by his anti-
imperialist friend William Dean Howells and more decisively by the determination of the Filipino insurgents, Twain was prepared to declare
American policy a mistake and a disgrace. When interviewed by reporters
from the New York dailies upon his return from Europe, Twain informed
them that he had become convinced that the aim of American policy was
not redemption but conquest. He was opposed "to having the American
eagle put its talons on any other land."[23] After McKinley's reelection,
Twain sought to compensate for his delayed conversion with a flurry of
well-publicized labor. Between December 1900 and April 1902 there was

seldom a month that did not see an interview, essay, or public letter from Mark Twain, wherein he mocked the hypocrisy of American policy and decried the brutality and destruction that marked the war in the Philippines.[24] By the summer of 1901 he had in effect joined the Anti-Imperialist League and subsequently would sign various of its memorial protests; by February 1902 he was one of some twenty Americans petitioning Congress to arrange an armistice in the Philippines and to investigate charges of misconduct by the American army.

Twain's single most famous literary effort in denunciation of American policy in the Philippines was his article in the *North American Review* of February 1901 entitled "To the Person Sitting in Darkness." Read today, its irony seems rather labored and heavy-handed, but at points it flashes into angry eloquence. "The Person" is, of course, the benighted heathen who is being whipped into the march of progress by the "Blessings-of-Civilization Trust." While ostensibly seeking to reconcile the victim, Twain reviews the tangle of broken promises and acts of deceit that had characterized the relations of the American government with the people of the Philippines:

> There have been lies; yes, but they were told in a good cause. We have been treacherous; but that was only in order that real good might come out of apparent evil. True, we have crushed a deceived and confiding people; we have turned against the weak and the friendless who trusted us; we have stamped out a just and intelligent and well-ordered republic; we have stabbed an ally in the back and slapped the face of a guest; we have bought a Shadow from an enemy that hadn't it to sell; we have robbed a trusting friend of his land and liberty; we have invited our clean young men to shoulder a discredited musket and do a bandit's work under a flag which bandits have been accustomed to fear, not to follow; we have debauched America's honor and blackened her face before the world; but each detail was for the best.[25]

Reprinted in pamphlet form by the New York branch of the Anti-Imperialist League, Twain's essay brought him many compliments from the "antis" and charges of senility and dyspepsia from the more ardent supporters of the war and imperial expansion.[26] *The Nation* praised Twain for endangering his popularity and sales, but Twain probably realized that in America a humorist was allowed considerable leeway. It was only when he attacked the new national hero, General Frederick Funston, that he risked more than rhetorical obloquy, and this attack came only with the spring of 1902 as the war limped to a conclusion. Twain's satirical essay, "A Defense of General Funston," was not, in any case, one of his more effective antiwar efforts. He had some mordant fun with the disguises and false tricks that made possible the capture of Aguinaldo, but Twain appeared uncertain whether Funston was the perpetrator or simply the willing instrument of an evil policy.[27]

A far more effective parody of Funston's career was that published by Ernest Crosby in his novel, *Captain Jinks, Hero*. Though neither widely reviewed nor widely read, it was an ambitious effort to combine the techniques of a farcical *roman à clef* with the purposes of the propaganda novel. In Crosby's hands Funston-Jinks becomes a character both contemptible and funny. The victim of insatiable ambition and greed and the perpetrator of countless self-serving hypocrisies, he threatens to become at points almost engaging in self-serving exploits. Crosby was known in literary and anti-imperialist circles primarily as a poet, and his most famous work for the cause was his parody of Kipling's "The White Man's Burden." One of many such parodies, it was possibly the most bitter.

> Take up the White Man's burden;
>   Send forth your sturdy sons,
> And load they down with whisky
>   And Testaments and guns.
> Throw in a few diseases
>   To spread in tropic climes
> For there the healthy niggers
>   Are quite behind the times.
>
>   . . .
>
> Take up the White Man's burden,
>   And if you write in verse,
> Flatter your Nation's vices
>   And strive to make them worse.
> Then learn that if with pious words
>   You ornament each phrase,
> In a world of canting hypocrites
>   This kind of business pays.[28]

It was the duplicity of McKinley's Philippine policy that angered many of the anti-imperialist poets as much as its evil consequences. Imperialism in their eyes was made doubly wrong by being wrapped in the humbuggery of benevolent assimilation, Christian duty, and the expansion of liberty. American policy in the Philippines was identified with hypocrisy as well as sin, and the corruptions of the present day contrasted with the presumed purity of the past. The statesmen of old had not designed their policies for the satisfaction of the greedy; they had not abandoned American ideals in a covetous search for land, markets, and political boodle. The poets of protest would reveal the evil consequences of "the new departure," and bring America home again.

The call to repentance characterized the verses not only of such major poets as Joaquin Miller and William Vaughn Moody but of such lesser talents as Hezekiah Butterworth, favorite poet of *Youth's Companion*, and John White Chadwick, W. C. Gannett, William Lloyd Garrison, Jr., and James J. Dooling.[29] Many of their poems were more effective as propaganda than poetry, but several demonstrated an aptitude for imagery as well as anger, and two works of William Vaughn Moody are among the finest narrative poems in American literature.

In "An Ode in Time of Hesitation," published in the *Atlantic Monthly* in May 1900, Moody contrasted the Civil War with the Philippine-American War, the one fought to redeem the ideals of the Declaration of Independence, the other to deny them. The soldiers who had fought to free the slave had fought to enlarge liberty and had brought glory to the republic; those who fought to subjugate the Filipino were the enemies of liberty and the unwitting instruments of the nation's shame. America had fallen victim to "fluent men of place and consequence," reciting "their dull commercial liturgies." For the moment, they had persuaded their countrymen to forget their traditions, but the evil consequences of our Philippine policy would soon be made clear and its authors castigated:

> For manifest in that disastrous light
> We shall discern the right
> And do it, tardily.—O ye who lead
> Take heed!
> Blindness we may forgive, but baseness we will smite.[30]

Less than a year later Moody published what was the most elegiac of all anti-imperialist poems. Many anti-imperialists had sought to distinguish between the authors of our Philippine policy and its soldier instruments; to curse the deed while granting redemption to the doer. Not an easy task, it was never performed more effectively than in the last verse of the poem "On a Soldier Fallen in the Philippines." A soldier has been killed in Luzon while acting under orders to shoot down the Filipino guerrillas and destroy their hopes of self-government:

> Toll! let him never guess
> What work we set him to.
> Laurel, laurel, yes;
> He did what we bade him to.

> Praise, and never a whispered hint but the
> fight he fought was good;
> Never a word that the blood on his sword
> was his country's own heart's blood.[31]

Whether as a result of their medium or their temperament, the poets of anti-imperialism were usually more emotional than the essayists, more prepared to personify as well as to denounce American aggression in the Philippines. Henry Blake Fuller was more vituperative than most when he compared McKinley to Nero and pictured Mark Hanna, "coarsely fleshed and gross," following the cross of imperialism:

> Nailed upon whose either side
> Hangs a Malay crucified.[32]

But for many of the anti-imperialist poets McKinley was seized upon as the very symbol of the war and the greed and jingoism that had inspired it. Expressions of disgust with McKinley were indeed more frequent than expressions of sympathy for the Filipino. Poetic apologies were often extended to the Filipino and references made to "the slaughter of the brave," but the poets of anti-imperialism were addressing an American audience and the victim they would emphasize was the American Dream. They would set the Filipino free because America must be redeemed. When William Lloyd Garrison, Jr., wrote a poem addressed to Aguinaldo, praising his "heroic stand" and comparing him to such patriot liberators of the past as Kosciusko and Toussaint L'Ouverture, the poem ended on a note of mourning for the countrymen of Garrison, not those of Aguinaldo.[33]

The same emphasis is to be found in the poems and essays of the feminist Abbie Morton Diaz and the Boston pacifist Robert Treat Paine. It furnished mood and theme for the "chapter" in *Spoon River Anthology* in which Edgar Lee Masters struck out against the false patriotism and twisted ideals responsible for the war and its American victims.

The best poet of his generation and an anti-imperialist, Masters contributed little to the literature of dissent during the years of the Philippine-American War. It was not until the publication of *Spoon River Anthology* in 1915 that Masters made public his despair and disgust. He spoke through the voice of "Harry Wilmans" in the burial ground of Spoon River:

> I was just turned twenty-one,
> And Henry Phipps, the Sunday-school superintendent,
> Made a speech in Bindle's Opera House.
> "The honor of the flag must be upheld," he said,

"Whether it be assailed by a barbarous tribe of
    Tagalogs
Or the greatest power in Europe."
And we cheered and cheered the speech and the flag
    he waved
As he spoke.
And I went to the war in spite of my father,
And followed the flag till I saw it raised
By our camp in a rice field near Manila,
And all of us cheered and cheered it.
But there were flies and poisonous things;
And there was the deadly water,
And the cruel heat,
And the sickening, putrid food;
And the smell of the trench just back of the tents
Where the soldiers went to empty themselves;
And there were the whores who followed us, full of
    syphilis;
And beastly acts between ourselves or alone,
With bullying, hatred, degradation among us,
And days of loathing and nights of fear
To the hour of the charge through the steaming
    swamp.
Following the flag,
Till I fell with a scream, shot through the guts.
Now there's a flag over me in Spoon River!
A flag! A flag![34]

The antiwar poets occasionally served as their own publishers or saw
their verses distributed as addenda to tracts of the Anti-Imperialist League,
but a few published their poems in contemporary newspapers and magazines, and for the essayists the latter furnished an essential outlet. Any
evaluation of the literary community must take note of the position of the
periodical press and its editors. Men such as Walter Hines Page, George
Harvey, Albert Shaw, Henry B. Blackwell, Benjamin Flowers, E. L. Godkin, Edwin D. Mead, and Samuel McClure considered themselves men of
letters as well as directors of "journals of opinion." In their attitude toward
the new directions of American foreign policy and the war in the Philippines, they were more evenly divided than other components of the literary
community, but if less representative of the views of American intellectuals than the professors, satirists, and poets, they were probably of greater
influence on American public opinion.

At the turn of the century America could boast more than a score of magazines of superior literary merit, and although some refused to take a stand in support or opposition to the nation's Philippine policy, it is fairly easy to identify the predisposition of most. *The American Monthly Review of Reviews*, *Harper's Weekly*, *Lippincott's Magazine*, *The Independent*, *The Outlook*, *Century Magazine*, *Puck*, *Judge*, *World's Work*, and *McClure's Magazine* were firm supporters of the administration policy in the Philippines. *The Arena*, *The Nation*, *City and State*, *New England Magazine*, *The Dial*, *The Woman's Journal*, *The Verdict*, *Life*, and *Gunton's Magazine* were among the "antis," though in varying degrees. *The Forum*, *Munsey's Magazine*, *North American Review*, *Scribner's*, and *The Atlantic Monthly* printed articles by supporters and critics with proclaimed impartiality, but may be labeled "uneasy advocates." In brief, the nation's leading periodicals divided fairly evenly on the virtue and necessity of McKinley's Philippine policy, though with editorial advocates probably enjoying a small majority. Virtually all were critical of military censorship in Manila, and most editors offered space to serious commentators on both sides, sometimes juxtaposing contrasting articles in a "symposium."

Two of the most famous editors of the day were Albert Shaw and E. L. Godkin, men who held diametrically opposite views on insular imperialism and American-Philippine relations, and their magazines can serve as examples not only of the division of the periodical press but the arguments and emotion with which certain editors addressed the "Philippine Question."

Shaw was editor of *The American Monthly Review of Reviews*, a stalwart Republican, and a man convinced that America must play a larger and more responsible role on the world stage. He saw the anti-imperialists as obstructionists and attributed the Philippine-American War to the false encouragement given Aguinaldo by the Senate's delay in ratifying the Treaty of Paris. No informed person could believe for a minute that Aguinaldo and his Tagalog followers were capable of establishing a republic. There did not exist in the Philippine archipelago "the elements out of which a suitable autonomous government could be created," and the United States owed a duty to itself and to the other civilized nations of the world to coerce the insurgents to accept American sovereignty. Only so could the islands avoid anarchy and civil war and enjoy liberty under law:

> It is a monstrous perversion of concrete truth in the interest of mere empty words and silly argument to say that Aguinaldo represents liberty in the Philippines and that the American flag represents tyranny and oppression. . . . It is meaningless to talk about the Declaration of Independence and "government by the

consent of the governed'' as applying to the immediate situation in the Philippines.[35]

The editors of *The Nation* were among those whom Shaw would accuse of ''perversion of concrete truth'' and ''meaningless'' talk about the Declaration of Independence. His particular *bête noire* was E. L. Godkin. Though Godkin was by 1900 beginning to withdraw from active editorial management of *The Nation*, that magazine continued to represent his angry opposition to the goals and methods of American policy. Perhaps the sharpest editorial critic of ''McKinley's abuse of executive authority,'' Godkin was also one of the most forthright in defying those who would associate dissent with treason. ''The theory that any one who criticizes the war is responsible for the death of the men who die in it, and not the persons who started it'' was a doctrine fit only for fools and canting hypocrites. It was McKinley who was responsible for the war. Under his instructions, Secretary Root and General MacArthur had prepared decrees that would ''better the instruction of the cruellest Spanish general,'' decrees that would authorize the army ''to kill, burn, ravage, without rest or remorse.'' If there was anything more disgusting than McKinley's efforts to play the vandal chieftain, it was his assumption of the contradictory character of the missionary. Expressing ''a tender concern for the souls of the men he is about to kill,'' he assumed the ridiculous posture of ''a monk on the warpath.'' McKinley personified the flaws and inconsistencies of the American character and symbolized its degradation. A nation must be doomed to decay that did not stand with its ''best minds'' in denouncing ''philanthropic war . . . killing people tenderly and with tears in our eyes.'' American policy combined sin and vulgarity. A civilized man could imagine no combination more offensive to honor.[36]

The dialogue of Shaw and Godkin was repeated, though with less individuality and force, by other editors. Walter Hines Page, editor of *World's Work* and then of *The Atlantic Monthly*, would quote Shaw with approval, and George Harvey, editor of *Harper's Weekly*, paid him the tribute of unconscious imitation. Godkin considered himself less fortunate in his allies. Such anti-imperialist magazines as *The Verdict* and *Life* he judged to be rather inferior publications, and *The Arena*, though correct in its suspicions of McKinley's foreign policy, was to be censured for its support of inflationary nostrums and William Jennings Bryan. Godkin found some solace in the fact that the editors of two Boston journals, the *New England Magazine* and *The Woman's Journal*, were ''gentlemen.'' Henry B. Blackwell, editor of the latter magazine, was in fact a rather muddle-headed critic of American policy, oscillating between genteel imprecations against the barbarity of war and expressions of hope that the Filipinos might find political solace under some sort of dominion status, but the opposition of Edwin D. Mead, editor of the *New England Magazine*, was more decisive and consistent. American policy, in his eyes, was "a perversion of the Christian way." We offered the Filipino "the tyrannous alternative of unquestioning submission or ruin," and we would reap a bitter heritage.[37]

To count the pamphlets and columns of newsprint authored by members of the academic and literary communities during the years of the Philippine-American War would be an endless and a fruitless exercise, but it is not difficult to reach some rough quantitative judgments. A majority of professorial commentators denounced our Philippine policy, whereas college presidents were more circumspect; a large majority of the more distinguished poets, novelists, and belle lettrists were in opposition, but literary magazines and journals of opinion divided more evenly. The difficult questions remain unanswered, however. Did the spokesmen of these communities, on either side of the issue, influence other segments of public opinion? Did they influence public policy or the prosecution and conduct of the war? The easiest and likeliest answer to these questions is No. Policy makers and their political supporters appear to have received little inspiration from the writings of the expansionist minority in the academic and literary communities and to have viewed the anti-imperialist writers and academics as an irritation rather than an obstacle. Certainly the mood of pessimism that characterized so much of the writing of anti-imperialist intellectuals in the years 1901–2 would support the belief that they had little immediate impact on American policy in the Philippines.

To admit this, however, is not to prove that they left no imprint on public policy or the education of American public opinion. It is possible that they were of some influence in publicizing and so limiting instances of torture and military misconduct in the Philippines; it is probable that they influenced the shifting ideological rationale of the imperialists; and it is conceivable that the imprecations of the anti-imperialist Jeremiahs as well as the unexpected length of the Philippine-American War lessened the enthusiasm of policy makers and public alike for further adventures in insular imperialism.

CHAPTER IX

The Press, Military Atrocities, and Patriotic Pride

The single most dramatic development during the Philippine-American War was the commission of acts of brutality and torture by American soldiers on Filipino prisoners and civilians, and that development offers one of the more perplexing aspects of the response of the American press and public. Why was the American press so slow to publish reports of atrocities in the Philippines? What explains the eruption of criticism in the early spring of 1902, and its limits of time and intensity? Did the response of the press reflect that of its readers; did they share a conviction of the identity of military and national honor or only a moral insensitivity and emotional fatigue?

During the first years of the war there was little mention in the press of possible military misconduct by American soldiers, and those few papers that did take notice offered little concrete evidence and were admitted partisans of the anti-imperialist movement. The New York *Evening Post* in the late spring of 1899 charged that Major Wilder Metcalf and Captain Robert Bishop of the Twentieth Kansas Regiment had ordered the slaughter of prisoners after the Battle of Caloocan, and the Springfield (Mass.) *Republican* in the summer of that year quoted excerpts from a collection of "Soldiers' Letters," published by the Anti-Imperialist League in Boston, describing similar episodes at Malabon and Titatia.[1] The soldier correspondents usually requested anonymity, however; details of unit, date, and victim were vague or missing; and the accusations of the *Post* were seemingly discredited during a hurried investigation by the War Department. The editors of the *Post* proved unable to gain affidavits from their vanishing sources and finally felt obliged to issue a retraction.

The embarrassment suffered by the *Post* explains in part the reluctance of most anti-imperialist papers to give credence or space when new rumors of military misconduct began to surface in the spring of 1900. The

Albany *Press-Knickerbocker*, a Democratic paper, noted that "a story from Manila" charged Colonel Frederick Funston with summarily hanging several insurgents without benefit of trail, but only the Pittsburgh *Dispatch* and the New York *World* saw fit to express "reluctant belief."[2] Two months later there appeared the first mention and description of the "water cure torture" in the American press. It appeared in the Omaha *World* in the form of a letter from a member of the Thirty-second Volunteer Infantry. Private Miller's letter was subsequently reprinted in two anti-imperialist Philadelphia weeklies, *The Friends' Intelligencer* and *City and State*, but it caused little comment elsewhere. A few Democratic papers such as the *Atlanta Constitution* and the New York *World* were sufficiently inspired by the animosities of the presidential campaign to hint at foul deeds and "horrible measures with the natives," but such references were few in number and lacked chapter or verse.[3] H. L. Wells, correspondent for several New York papers, concurrently reported that it was a source of "great satisfaction to know that the earlier reports of the misconduct of our soldiers are disproved," though undoubtedly "our men do 'shoot niggers' somewhat in the sporting spirit."[4]

The first publication that provided specific evidence of the use of torture against the insurgents was the expansionist magazine, *The Outlook*. In its issue of 9 March, 1901, George Kennan, traveler and sometime diplomat, described the "water cure" in detail, quoting American officers as his source. Kennan sought to assure his readers that this method of extracting confession and information was performed only by the Macabebe Scouts and not their American officers, but he left little doubt that the latter were unwilling to condemn the practice.[5] Kennan's article caused a small ripple of excitement in such anti-imperialist papers as the Springfield *Republican*, but throughout the year 1901 most papers gave only infrequent attention to rumors and charges of American military misconduct in the Philippines. This was probably due less to timidity than to uncertainty. Evidence was meagre, and the proper target of attack unclear. Few papers had their own correspondents in Manila, and even for these papers the effectiveness of military censorship during the period of Otis's reign in Manila had limited the extent and accuracy of available information.[6] It must be acknowledged, moreover, that instances of military brutality were relatively infrequent in the first two years of the war and the administration of the "water cure" largely confined to the Macabebe Scouts. The chief inhibition, however, lay in an uncertainty about the proper target of attack. Even those papers most ready to attribute evil consequences to American imperialism were more ready to attribute brutality to policy makers in

Macabebe Scouts, practitioners of the "Water Cure" in the service of the United States (from William Sexton, Soldiers in the Sun, *reprinted by permission of the author)*

Washington than American soldiers in Luzon. Before they would charge the citizen-soldier with practices thought to be reserved to the hirelings of European monarchies, they would need more convincing evidence. Two markedly contrasting individuals, Herbert Welsh, the crusading editor of *City and State,* and George Frisbie Hoar, the senior Republican senator from Massachusetts, would in their separate ways make a determined effort to provide this evidence and thereby give the American press an opportunity to bemoan—however briefly—the cruelty of war.

Herbert Welsh began his campaign to expose American military brutality in the Philippines with the first week of 1902; it would provide his chief occupation for the next two years. Horrified by early reports of the "water cure," he was determined to secure evidence of this torture so conclusive that every American would share his anger. Throughout a long career as a reformer, Welsh always felt as great a need for an enemy as for a cause, and in January 1902 this opponent of war and imperialism found his enemy in the American army officer who would knock a suspected insurgent to the ground, pour water down his throat until his belly swelled like a balloon, pummel him until the water gushed forth, and then repeat the process until the man confessed and informed.

With the aid of Matthew K. Sniffen, business manager of *City and State*, and E. C. Bumpus, a privately paid assistant, Welsh sought to track down returning soldiers and obtain their testimony, in order to prove that "torture of a very horrible description" had been practiced "as a means to produce a military or political result." The "water cure" was not the inadvertent action of a few misfits; it was an expression of official policy.[7] Sending his agents to Kansas and Maryland to interview veterans who were prepared to testify against their former officers, Welsh himself made frequent trips to New England where he took depositions and sought to persuade soldier witnesses to appear before the Senate Philippine Committee. In the editorial columns of *City and State* he kept up a steady drumbeat of accusation, reminding his readers of America's collective responsibility for "crimes" committed in the Philippines under cover of the American flag and warning his countrymen not to "sacrifice exact justice to the reputation of the army" as France had done in the Dreyfus case.[8] At varying points, Welsh sought to organize the distribution of material on "Philippine atrocities" to schools and colleges; to send an agent to the Philippines who would "provide trustworthy information"; and to secure funds from Andrew Carnegie for the services of an "outside counsel" to assist the Democratic minority of the Senate Philippine Committee.[9] Henry Cabot Lodge, chairman of that committee, was denounced as an apologist for Secretary Root and General Chaffee. Lodge mouthed platitudes about "the honor of the army," while purposely obstructing the exposure of military atrocities in the hearings of the Senate Philippine Committee.[10]

However legitimate Welsh's disappointment with those hearings, they did represent a measure of official acknowledgment of the atrocity charges. Their instigation was largely the work of Senator George Frisbie Hoar. On 13 January 1902 Hoar had submitted to the Senate a resolution calling for the establishment of a special committee to "examine and report into the conduct of the war in the Philippine Islands, the administration of the government there, and the condition and character of the inhabitants."[11] Over the previous six months Hoar had been the recipient of a number of letters from soldiers and their parents reciting a variety of crimes committed by the American soldiery in the Philippines, and though these correspondents usually requested the protection of anonymity, he had reluctantly become persuaded that the evil of imperialism had corrupted the military honor as well as the diplomatic traditions of the Republic.[12] The sincerity of Hoar's disgust was not contradicted by a long-held conviction that investigation was the proper province of duly elected legislators.[13] This conviction, however, made it easier for the Republican majority in the Senate to persuade Hoar that any investigation be undertaken by that body's standing committee on the Philippine Islands. Hoar assured himself that the nature and composition of the investigating committee was comparatively insignificant. It was facts that were wanted—facts on which the Congress and public could determine its response to charges of military atrocities in the Philippines.[14]

The Lodge Committee on the Philippines would hold sporadic hearings between 31 January and 28 June 1902, and in the course of those hearings facts would emerge, but already by the spring of that year Hoar had reason to suspect that the interpretation of those facts and their impact could indeed be influenced by the nature and composition of the committee.[15] Lodge made no secret of his impatience with those who would slander the American soldier, and from the beginning Senator Beveridge assumed the role of defense counsel for the army. Only about a third of the sittings of the committee would be devoted to the subject of military misconduct, a majority of the witnesses called were sympathetic to the demands and difficulties of "pacification," and the committee chairman read into the record all of the documents and explanatory correspondence provided by the Department of War.[16] One of these documents, however, would prove a source of considerable embarrassment to the committee majority, the report of Major Cornelius Gardner, civil governor of Tayabas province in Luzon. Together with the testimony of certain soldier witnesses offering testimony on the "water cure," it provided the chief contribution of the Lodge Committee to the enlightenment of the American press and public.[17]

One of the Democratic members of the committee noted in a letter to the Secretary of War from the cantankerous Army Chief of Staff Sherman Miles a reference to a report by Major Gardner that lent support to Miles' contention that army policy in the Philippines had been characterized by "marked severity." The Democratic minority of the committee demanded a copy of the report, and it was subsequently leaked to the press. The burden of Gardner's complaints was to the effect that the conciliatory efforts of the Taft Commission were being sabotaged by the unselective animosity shown the Filipino by various junior officers and enlisted men. These officers had authorized harsh reprisals and on occasion condoned outright brutality. It was a document written in the stolid prose of a military report, and its effect was due largely to its timing. It followed the disclosure that General Franklin Bell had established concentration centers in

Batangas province; its publication was accompanied by more dramatic disclosures involving the conduct of the American army on the island of Samar.

Associated Press dispatches from Manila in the last week of January 1902 had noted without comment that General Bell had recently instituted new measures for the pacification of Batangas province. To ensure the isolation of the insurgent guerrillas, all civilians were to be driven into concentration centers where they would be under the surveillance and guard of American troops. Excerpts from Bell's order of 8 December 1901 were quoted, including the instruction that any civilian found beyond the boundaries of the camp after curfew would be summarily shot. Some two months later the AP wire from Manila carried a report of the court-martial of Major Littleton W. T. Waller, charged with ordering the death of eleven native guides on the island of Samar. The same source subsequently informed the American press that Major Waller sought exoneration on the grounds that he was only obeying the orders of General Jacob H. Smith. These disclosures would make more difficult the labors of Lodge and Beveridge to exonerate the army, and would inspire a sizable portion of the American press to address the issue of military atrocities and for a brief season express dismay and even anger.

At least two score of papers made comment on General Bell's policy of "reconcentracion," a majority of them critical of its wisdom and some prepared to judge it a "crime." The comments of the Springfield *Republican* and the New York *Evening Post* could have been predicted, but their denunciations of "the new Weyler" were matched by several papers that previously had supported American policy in the Philippines. The Baltimore *American* mourned that "we have actually come to do the thing we went to war to banish"; the Detroit *Journal* compared Bell to "Butcher" Weyler in Cuba and General Kitchener in South Africa. The Republican Philadelphia *Ledger* reminded its readers of McKinley's declaration four years earlier that "the cruel policy of concentration . . . was not civilized warfare," while the Democratic Boston *Post* insisted that Bell's inhumanity exceeded that of the hated Spaniards: "They were content with 'concentrating' the miserable women and children left after the devastation of farms and villages, but General Bell marks the husbands and fathers and brothers as criminals to be hanged when caught."[18]

For some newspaper editors, however, semantic similarities provided no proper parallel. The Pittsburgh *Times* took to task those who would compare the concentration policies of Generals Bell and Weyler; these critics ignored the fact that "General Bell does not propose to starve these people as Weyler did Cuban reconcentrados." *The Army and Navy Journal* tartly noted that what civilian critics "don't know about military affairs in the Philippines would make a wide library," and the Boston *Journal* exhibited its unwavering faith by discovering in General Bell an early exponent of urban renewal:

> The word "reconcentrado" has an ugly sound in American ears, but, after all, the question of whether it is a harsh method or not depends upon the way in which it is enforced. The hardship to the Filipinos of Batangas is not in the mere leaving of their homes, which are structures of straw and branches, only a little more elaborate than Indian wigwams. They can . . . perhaps profit by compulsory removal from abodes that long use and neglect have made unwholesome.[19]

Only the Springfield *Republican* forecast the loss of life from contagion and disease that would characterize the concentration camps in Batangas; other editorial critics of General Bell had by early March apparently lost interest in the concentration centers and their inhabitants. There was at that point a lull in press criticism of military policy in the Philippines. A few additional accounts of the "water cure" were circulated, and two papers described the army policy of burning barrios suspected of giving asylum to insurgents, but there was little news from the hearings of the Senate Philippine Committee and several papers publicly declared their belief that rumors of military "outrages" had little foundation in fact. The next month saw the release of Major Gardner's Report, the court-martial of Major Waller, and confirmation of the reprisal policy on Samar. By the end of April, General "Howling Jake" Smith and his "every-one-over-ten-order" had received national press coverage, and there was for the first and only time general public concern over military atrocities in the Philippines.

News of the court-martial of Major Waller did not inspire widespread comment until the Associated Press reported on 9 April that he had gained exoneration on the grounds that his summary execution of eleven uncooperative native guides found justification in the orders of his superior officer, General Jacob H. Smith. Then the press sought to compensate for its neglect. As earlier some commentators had compared General Bell with Weyler, now a greater number discovered a similarity between General Smith and Herod. The New York *Journal and American*, the New York *World*, the Philadelphia *North American*, the Baltimore *News*, the Boston *Advertiser*, the Chicago *News*, and the San Francisco *Chronicle* were united in labeling Smith's orders "criminal" and demanding his dismissal. The Baltimore *Herald* declared that Smith's determination to make Samar "a howling wilderness" found no precedent in "the annals of civilized warfare," and the Buffalo *Express* and the Indianapolis *News* saw in the general's orders the confessed failure of U.S. policy. We were adopting "the methods of barbarism." The New York *Evening Post* demanded that Smith be speedily tried and, when proven guilty, summarily executed.[20]

Other papers were prepared to denounce Smith's "barbarous command" but would insist that his orders neither represented American policy nor proved its failure. For the New York *Tribune*, the Chicago *Inter-Ocean*, the Philadelphia *Press*, the Pittsburgh *Gazette*, the Kansas City *Star*, and the St. Paul *Pioneer Press*, the actions of Waller and Smith, though "deplorable," had "no bearing on fundamental questions of national policy." Their crimes, announced the *Tribune*, are not "because of, but in spite of, the government's general policy in the Philippines. . . . The penalty must fall not upon the policy, but upon those men." The war and the policy of pacification were righteous and necessary; only acts of excess should be punished.[21]

If the *Tribune* was satisfied to identify and isolate the rotten apples, such papers as *The New York Times* questioned the very guilt of Major Waller and General Smith. *The Times* elaborated upon "the hardships and dangers" suffered uncomplainingly by our "brave and loyal officers," castigated the "cruel, treacherous, murderous" natives of Samar, and implied that Waller was chiefly to be criticized for his effort to seek exculpation "by fouling the military nest." The St. Louis *Globe-Democrat* believed that Smith's policy found sufficient precedent in practices of the Union Army during the Civil War, and exhibited few compunctions respecting any injuries inflicted on the native population of Samar:

> Well, suppose that the native barbarities have, in some cases, moved our soldiers to transgress the line of gentleness desirable for ordinary warfare? We are confident that, in view of the provocation received and peculiar nature of the task to be performed, the transgressions have been extremely slight. . . . It is strange, indeed, if American soldiers are to be called to the field to fight savages without hurting them.[22]

The prideful callousness of the *Globe-Democrat* was not typical, however, of the American press in the late spring of 1902. Interest and concern over possible military atrocities in the Philippines would melt with the heat of summer, but in April–May 1902 interest and concern were at their height. Although only a small minority were prepared to believe with the New York *Evening Post* that "our troops in the island of Samar have been pursuing a policy of wholesale and deliberate murder,"[23] many editors now admitted the probability that "some soldiers have disgraced their uniform" and "committed acts of excess." Secretary Root's cable to

General Chaffee of 15 April, ordering a full investigation, was widely approved,[24] and when word was received that at Smith's court-martial in Manila the defense counsel admitted "that General Smith gave instructions to kill and burn and make Samar a howling wilderness," there followed a new round of editorial condemnation.

The genteel Boston *Transcript* and the staunchly Republican Kansas City *Journal* now joined the chorus, as did an increasing number of black newspapers.[25] The *Atlanta Constitution* and a few other Democratic papers were ready to trace "these records of blood, conflagration, torture and waste" to "higher sources" and to suggest that Root and Roosevelt were "coparceners with the Jake Smith campaign of torture and murder," but even at the peak of excitement over General Smith, most papers refused to identify reprisals on the island of Samar with official American policy in the Philippines.[26]

The tendency of the press to confine its censure to individual officers and their actions made more likely that the duration of that censure would not long survive the courts-martial of Major Waller and General Smith. During the winter–spring of 1902, however, public concern was sufficient to cause some dismay among the expansionist faithful and to give a spur to the revival of anti-imperialist hopes and organization.

The correspondence file of Henry Cabot Lodge offers illustration of the distress experienced by certain politicians and businessmen in New England. George H. Lyman, Collector of the Port of Boston and the senator's loyal political agent, asked for reassurance that tales about American officers "torturing the Filipino soldiers" were "an absolute lie"; the banker Charles F. Dole requested similar assurances while expressing far less certainty of the falsehood of those tales. Henry Lee Higginson, merchant financier and a generous political supporter, demanded not only the facts but the right to inform his senator that reports of atrocities together with the war's increasing cost in lives and money had made him doubt the wisdom of "this Philippine experiment." Nor did he speak for himself alone: "A very considerable number of staunch republicans . . . who have never looked at any other ticket, would like to get out of these islands." They cared little for "the brown man," but they viewed with dread "the demoralization to our troops by atrocities committed."[27] Neither the number nor the disquiet of such correspondents was sufficient to shake the conviction of Senator Lodge and his friends in the administration respecting the necessity and righteousness of American policy in the Philippines, but such letters as those from Higginson helped inspire the counteroffensive that the Roosevelt administration launched in May. A more direct inspiration was "the mischievous labors" of the Schurz-Adams committee and the atrocity tract of Julian Codman and Moorfield Storey.

The formation of the Schurz-Adams committee was only the most obvious example of the revivifying impact of the charges of military atrocities on the determination and labors of the anti-imperialists. The anti-imperialist movement experienced a brief revival in the spring of 1902. The correspondence of Erving Winslow and Edwin Burritt Smith assumed something like its former dimensions, and certain anti-imperialists who had earlier "defected," such as Charles Francis Adams, Jr., now briefly returned to the ranks of the dissenters.

By the late winter of 1902 Adams had become convinced of the accuracy of reports that torture was now accustomed policy "for the extraction of information," and in his anger and disgust he determined to rejoin such former allies as Carl Schurz and Moorfield Storey in forcing the government to conduct a full-scale investigation. As Edmund Burke had exposed the iniquities of Warren Hastings, so would they lay bare the shameful conduct of Americans in the Philippines. Joining forces with Herbert Welsh and Edwin Burritt Smith, they held a meeting at the Plaza Hotel in New York City on 28 April. There they decided to form an "ad hoc committee" that would combine the roles of the citizen's lobby and the private investigator.[28]

Though its intention was to perform "practical tasks . . . quietly and systematically," the Schurz-Adams committee proved effective only in the area of propaganda. Plans to hire an "outside counsel" to cross-examine witnesses before the Lodge Commitee were delayed by the ill health of Wayne MacVeagh and then frustrated by the rules of the Senate; a scheme for an independent investigation of military atrocities by "a tribunal of mixed character" never materialized; and a memorial to Congress requesting the appointment of "a joint congressional committee of enquiry" to travel to the Philippines and hold hearings in Manila was quietly buried.[29] Its chief accomplishment was the publication in May 1902 of the pamphlet, *Secretary Root's Record: "Marked Severities" in Philippine Warfare: An Analysis of the Law and Facts Bearing on the Action and Utterances of President Roosevelt and Secretary Root.*[30] The most famous of all the atrocity tracts, this was the work of Moorfield Storey and his friend Julian Codman, and it bore on its frontispiece the acknowledgment: "Prepared at the request of a committee composed of Charles Francis Adams, Carl Schurz, Edwin Burritt Smith, and Herbert Welsh." Directed specifically against Secretary Root's denial of the allegations of General Miles in February and his exculpatory letter to the Senate Philippine Committee of 5 March,[31] the pamphlet was more consistent in tone than organization and focus. Beginning as a lawyer's brief against the denials and derelictions of the Secretary of War, it moved to a catalogue of thirteen "well-documented" instances of torture inflicted on noncombatants in the Philippines. This was followed by an anthology of excerpts from newspaper correspondents relating to acts of purposeful cruelty and destruction ordered by American officers, and the pamphlet concluded with an indictment against the Roosevelt administration and its harassment of those who would inform the American public of the truth. The object of attack oscillated between deceitful civilians in Washington and bloody-handed officers in Luzon, but the pamphlet found unity in a note of virulent disgust sustained for over 100 pages.

In the eyes of Theodore Roosevelt, the Storey and Codman pamphlet was a mixture of sickly sentimentalism and malevolent slander. Elihu Root was a loyal lieutenant and a man of unquestioned probity. Those who attacked him were unpatriotic mudslingers, sniping at the army and so encouraging its enemies in the Philippines. Their charges must be defused and rebutted for the sake of the honor of the army and the reputation of the administration. With the first week in May, Roosevelt set in motion a well-orchestrated counterattack. To his friend Henry Cabot Lodge was given the honor of firing the first volley.

Lodge's address to the Senate on 5 May not only set the theme of the administration's counterattack, it touched every chord. Lodge made clear the determination of the administration to attribute allegations of military misconduct to faithless fools and virulent partisans while yet assuring the American people that swift punishment would fall upon any officer who had violated the rules of civilized warfare. In defense of the army he was prepared to revive old antagonisms as well as revile the anti-imperialists. Those who sympathized with the insurgents were disappointed with the success of the army's pacification program, and consequently the army met, "as it met after Appomattox," abuse and attack. Its critics were the lineal descendants of the Copperheads. They accepted as gospel truth every rumor of misconduct by the American soldier, but they ignored the hundreds of verified incidents of assassinations and mutilations inflicted by the insurgents on Filipino natives who welcomed American guidance. Unspeakable barbarities had been committed on more than a hundred village officials alone. He was prepared to admit that on the part of the American army there had been a few cases "of water cure, of menaces of shooting, unless information was given up; of rough and cruel treatment applied to secure information." But all Americans not blinded by partisan animosity must acknowledge that the administration had made every effort to put a stop to such practices. It had moved expeditiously to punish the guilty, though with proper concern for the morale of our army and its dangerous and difficult task. Those who lived "in sheltered homes, far from the sound and trials of war" should bear in mind the temptations as well as the sufferings of our soldiers, the provocations and trials under which they labored as they sought to bring law and order to a "semi-civilized people, with all the tendencies and characteristics of Asiatics." "Let us, oh, let us be just, at least to our own."[32]

Lodge's speech was followed by public addresses from two cabinet officers, interviews by several army officers, explanatory editorials in a dozen newspapers and magazines identified with the administration, and a Memorial Day speech by Theodore Roosevelt at Arlington Cemetery. These efforts added little to the aggressive defense outlined by Lodge, but the appearance of depth is essential to any counteroffensive. Administration spokesmen, without exception, stressed the extreme provocation under which American troops had labored. Not only had Filipino sympathizers suffered unspeakable mutilation but so, too, "our soldiers, dead and alive." The *Providence Sunday Journal* was prepared to accept "the wisdom of fighting fire with fire," and to assure its readers that the water cure was in comparative terms a very mild torture, one that "does not necessarily have serious after effects." Major General O. O. Howard, the well-known Civil War and Indian fighter, Frederick Funston, home on hero's leave, and George Harvey, editor of *Harper's Weekly*, were equally certain that our soldiers had been patient and long suffering, and that the tactics of the insurgents, operating outside the laws of civilized warfare, provided a sufficient explanation for the adoption of stern "countermeasures." Like other champions of the army, however, they were quick to insist that acts of reprisals were few in number and had never been countenanced by the American military command.[33]

The treachery of the Filipino, the hardships of the American soldier, and the infrequency of American acts of reprisal formed the burden of Roosevelt's much-publicized Memorial Day speech at Arlington Cemetery, but the genius of that speech lay in Roosevelt's ability to identify the honor of the American soldier and the goals of the Roosevelt administration and imply that criticism of either was an expression of snivelling cowardice. Humanity, not severity, marked our policy in the Philippines, but we would not make the mistake of coddling our Filipino enemies and endangering our Filipino friends. Our army was engaged in a noble endeavor in support of a righteous and intelligent foreign policy. The work of pacification was nearly complete, and in our total victory rested the hope of the Filipino people, whom we would soon educate in the ways of liberty. How ungrateful were those Americans who "walking delicately" in the "soft places of the earth" would attack the brave men—their faces "marred by sweat and blood"—who were engaged in this great redemptive task.[34]

This address was Roosevelt's sole public participation in the offensive mounted against the charges of military atrocities. Further public appearances proved unnecessary. With the summer of 1902 the counterattack of the Roosevelt administration was victorious. Not only had expansionist papers recovered their voice and optimism, but the papers that had a few months before compared Bell with Weyler and Smith with Herod now made no mention of atrocities and little mention of the Philippines. Public concern did not disappear overnight, but it gradually fell victim to emotional fatigue and apathy.

Lodge adjourned the hearings of the Senate Philippine Committee on 28 June, satisfied that he had done his best to support the honor of the army and restrict the investigation of its conduct. By carefully limiting that investigation, he had prevented any full-scale review of administration policy and its relation to the tactics of military pacification. Adjournment was without limit of time, and the committee majority even avoided the need for submitting a final report. Their performance was less a whitewash than an exercise in sleight-of-hand, and the reaction of press and public was characterized not by approval so much as apathy. Benjamin Flowers would bemoan this lack of interest in the columns of *The Arena*, and Herbert Welsh would be laboring for months afterward to secure depositions from "willing witnesses," but most editors appeared content to accept the accuracy of Roosevelt's proclamation of 4 July 1902 that the "insurrection" was over and to assume that the conclusion of the war had extinguished public interest in its history. The Springfield *Republican* berated its journalistic colleagues for allowing "the victory of our arms" to cast the mantle of oblivion on the brutality of American policy.[35]

The *Republican* and a few other diehards not only bemoaned the dissipation of journalistic concern but sought an explanation. Such obvious factors as the distraction of domestic issues and the fickleness of public interest were noted, as was the ability of the administration to mollify the public with news of the surrender of the last organized insurrectionist bands. A few commentators recognized as well the inability of most white Americans to sustain sympathy for victims of another race. In answer to its rhetorical inquiry, "Where is that vast national outburst of astounded horror which an old-fashioned American would have predicted?", one newspaper had earlier suggested that its absence was the result of geographic distance and racial insularity. It was "lost somewhere in the 8,000 miles which divide us from the scenes of those abominations," and those abominations were the more easily forgotten because they were inflicted on "the darker skins of an alien race."[36]

Few of these dissenters gave sufficient credit to the skill of the Roosevelt administration's counterattack, particularly its success in reconvincing a majority of press and public that sporadic examples of cruelty by the American soldier were inspired by the more brutal and numerous outrages committed by the insurgents on the uniformed American and his Filipino sympathizers. Ours was "the lesser evil," and if it was not to be condoned, it could be forgiven. Surely it was better forgotten than exaggerated. The doctrine of "the lesser evil" offered excuse if not justification for the psychological necessity of callousness. The New York *Evening Post* observed that any war long continued "dulls the hearts and souls of men," and proclaimed its belief that "in years to come, our Philippine wrongdoing will be cited as an indisputable proof" of this unfortunate fact.[37]

What appears indisputable is that by the summer of 1902 a large majority of press and public no longer wished to debate the rights and wrongs of American military tactics. The Philippine War was best forgotten; no purpose was to be served by further discussion of military atrocities and their victims. A sense of emotional fatigue characterized the response of many Americans, and it is this mood of self-induced apathy that best explains the precipitous decline in attention paid the issue of military atrocities.

Familiarity need not breed contempt, but repetition is always an enemy to horror. A symbolic illustration of that enmity was a sick joke used by the Cleveland *Plain-Dealer* to fill out a short column:

MA.   "What's that sound of running water out there, Willie?"

WILLIE.   "It's only us boys, ma. We've been trying the Filipino water-cure on Bobbie Snow, an' now we're pouring him out."[38]

There is no reason to believe the subscribers of the *Plain-Dealer* were more callous than other Americans; rather it seems certain that by the summer of 1902 public apathy had stripped the atrocity issue of all passion and meaning.

An examination of the response of the press to the rumors and charges of American military atrocities in the Philippines does not require a judgment of moral turpitude. The opportunities given the press to alert and educate the public were at best limited. Persuasive evidence of American military misconduct was available only in the last year of the war and then it was subject to differing interpretations on the score of its frequency and military necessity. The reluctance of the press to give publicity to rumors and charges of military atrocities was probably due more to the fact that newspaper owners and editors were necessarily civilians than that they were frequently Republicans. They displayed the conditioned reflex of most civilians in wartime that military matters are best left to the military. Confusion about the facts combined with the strength of military prestige to produce uncertainty, and the safest course when one is uncertain is to write of other matters. The failure of the press was an understandable failure, made more so by the insularity of the American people and its identification of the national honor with the exploits of the citizen-soldier.

It was not to be expected that either editors or subscribers would readily accept rumors of misconduct by the citizen-soldier who was the emblem and exemplar of American bravery, courage, and patriotism. Under the drum-fire of AP dispatches from Manila a majority of the press during the winter-spring of 1902 engaged in a brief flurry of denunciation of a particular barbarity—the water cure—and of particular army officers—Bell, Waller, Smith—but the attack was limited in its targets as well as its duration. By the opening of the baseball season of 1902, the conduct of the American army in the Philippines was ignored by all but a handful of papers. Press and public were wearied of the disagreeable "insurrection" that had lasted far too long. Let it be forgotten in all its parts and pieces. The honor of the army was still an essential reflection of the honor of the nation, and the national honor demanded a sense of national pride.

The majority response of the American public to the Philippine-American War cannot be understood without an appreciation of the force of national honor and patriotic pride. Any moment in a nation's history sees many and disparate moods within the population, but there is often a dominant attitude. In America at the turn of the twentieth century, the dominant mood was one of optimism and romantic nationalism. Optimism was generated not by a belief that all was right, but rather a belief that all could be righted. At home the search for order, efficiency, and social harmony would succeed. Abroad the nation's mission to do its duty, strengthen its diplomatic power, and expand its trade would be accomplished. And as the nation's promise was redeemed at home and abroad, so the individual participant was assured a sense of purpose and self-fulfillment. For the middle-class American—and especially for those who were white, Protestant, and college-educated—there was a conviction that the nation and its "best citizens" had a common goal, and their shared purpose provided justification for a belief that progress was natural and indeed certain.

Typesetters capitalized the Flag with the same consistency and regard they showed the Deity. Americans could smile with Finley Peter Dunne as Mr. Dooley leaned over the bar to proclaim: "We're a gr-reat people. We are-re that. An' th' best iv it is, we know we are're."[39] But the humor was the more enjoyable because few doubted the essential correctness of the assumption. The greatness and so the goodness of America was accorded automatic acceptance, and the importance of "the national honor" was a natural corollary. Not all would give the term an identical definition, but as its symbol was the Flag, so its accustomed expressions were diplomatic success and military valor. Phrases such as "the highest duty," "the supreme sacrifice," "martial glory," were uttered without apology or quotation marks. Love of country was an attribute judged to be especially warranted for an American, and the year 1902 saw the publishers of Edward Everett Hale's patriotic tale, *The Man Without a Country*, make plans for a new printing, its thirteenth.

Sentiments of romantic nationalism and convictions of the certitude of progress made patriotism a necessity as well as a virtue. There was consequently a presupposition in favor of the rightness of the diplomatic and military policies of the nation. Their opponents were required to fight that presupposition and prove that in rejection lay the path of patriotism and progress. They failed. The nature and length of the Philippine War proved sufficient to inspire discouragement, but there was no time when a majority of Americans ceased to identify military success in the Philippines with the honor of the army and the Republic and so the course of duty and progress.

The Philippine-American War was our most quickly forgotten war, the war least celebrated in legend or song,[40] least marked by cenotaphs and monuments. But during the course of the war, Americans at home had little reason to believe that the army had ceased to consider itself an instrument of progress as well as patriotism, and the newly established Veterans of Foreign Wars made clear its belief that the trooper in Luzon, like his more publicized predecessor on San Juan Hill, was the exemplification of military valor and glory. Some American wars might be more inspirational than others, but the power of romantic nationalism would allow no distinction among warrior heros. By Memorial Day of 1903 most monuments to the soldiers and sailors of the Spanish-American War had chiselled on their base a reference, unashamed if brief, to those who had served their country in "the Philippine Insurrection."

The dark side of patriotism was its ethnocentric disregard of the claims and humanity of other peoples. The slaughter of Filipinos did not

inspire a general sentiment of moral outrage, because Filipinos were for-
eigners as well as enemies. A more attractive side of patriotism was reflected in the belief of many Americans that in supporting the March of the
Flag they were obeying the call of duty. This call was self-determined and
not without an element of arrogance, but for many young Americans at the
turn of the century, and particularly for college-educated men of the upper
middle class, the tasks of empire building appeared to represent a satisfying identification of national progress and personal self-fulfillment. Those
tasks had the appeal of service work for the YMCA, of labors in behalf of
good government and municipal reform, of active membership in the
Christian Endeavor League. Empire building would provide an outlet for
romantic nationalism and a release from personal boredom. By bringing
civilization, efficiency, and the institutions of America to the Philippines,
one would enhance the power and prosperity of the United States and
engage in self-improvement and self-advancement. We did not need the
historical experience or trained civil service of the British to match and
exceed them. Patriotic pride would enable the progressive-minded sons of
America to demonstrate to the world a new and superior form of colonial
achievement. America was the land of free institutions, and the extension
of its sovereignty was an extension of freedom. [41]

More than considerations of economic gain or strategic advantage, the
identification of the acquisition of the Philippines with the requirements of
national progress and national honor sustained a broad spectrum of middle-
class Americans during a long and costly war. The war's costs and character generated occasional bursts of irritation and discouragement, but only
for a minority did discouragement become dissent. Support underwent
various mutations, but for most Americans the identification of national
honor and military success remained constant. Altruism, national self-
assertion, and pride assisted the determination of a majority of the American public to see the war through to a victorious conclusion.

Although the Philippine War proved unexpectedly long and bloody,
there were no military defeats or disasters to destroy the credibility of
administration prophecies of future victory. At home the war brought
neither inflation nor recession; indeed, the years of the Philippine-American
War were years of economic prosperity and expansion of the home market.
It is more difficult to feel guilty when potentially victorious and currently
prosperous. Whatever the disagreeable features of pacification, we would
prove successful, and success would prove false the forebodings of the
Jeremiahs. To be successful in diplomacy and war was to be proven correct. At least this was so for a nation with the liberal creed and good
intentions of the United States.

CHAPTER X

The Problem of Significance

An analysis of the significance of the Philippine-American War raises a number of disagreeably difficult questions. Was the conquest of the Philippines an anomalous sport in the diplomatic history of the United States or another example of westward expansion characteristic of the nation's diplomatic behavior from the beginning? Was the "Philippine Insurrection" essentially a postscript to the Spanish-American War, or does it stand apart as the first war fought by the United States in support of its self-determined strategic and economic interests in the Far East? Did the war significantly affect our relations with England, Germany, Japan, and the other "China powers"? Did it alter or measurably influence the later course of American diplomacy?

The acquisition and subjugation of the Philippine Islands was not a sudden aberration in the history of American diplomacy, but neither was it merely another chapter in the history of the expanding American frontier. Although the history of American expansion is as old as the nation, only with 1898 did we seek to establish extrahemispheric colonies and only with 1899 did we seek to impose by force of arms American sovereignty over millions of ethnic aliens. Our Philippine policy was perhaps foreshadowed in our treatment of the American Indian and our relations with Mexico and certain of the Caribbean republics, but it is a perversion of truth in behalf of symmetry not to see in the wider ambitions, changed ideological justifications, and altered historical context of American expansion in the Pacific elements of innovation as well as continuity. The acquisition of the Philippines found only limited support in the ambitions of Franklin and Jefferson for "an empire of liberty," and to view the subjugation of the Filipinos as a variant of traditional commercial expansionism is to dismiss distinctions of means and tactics that provide the essential data of historical comparison.

Although historians have in recent years debated the question of the novelty of insular imperialism, they have tended to ignore the significance of McKinley's Philippine policy for American naval diplomacy. If McKinley did not share the geopolitical vision of Alfred T. Mahan, he was not unaware of the ambitions of naval strategists for shore facilities that would enhance American naval power in the western Pacific, nor was he unaware of the reciprocal relationship between naval strength and economic markets. Possession of the Philippines might strengthen our claim as a Far Eastern power; certainly it would enlarge the diplomatic influence of the American navy.

There can be little argument about the importance of the Philippines for the history of the American navy in the Pacific. Whether on balance the Philippines represented a strategic gain or a blunder is another matter. A good case can be made for judging the Philippines more an albatross than an advantage for the requirements of American defensive and strategic strength. But whether viewed as floating drydock or hostage to the rising sun of Japan, the acquisition of the Philippines represented a milestone in the evolution of American naval strategy. When the United States abandoned a strategy of defense limited to the continent and its appurtenances and extended its defense perimeter 7,000 miles into the Pacific, the requirements of American naval strength were permanently transformed.

With the acquisition of the Philippines, many politicians and some businessmen were prepared to see the United States demand a greater role in the politics and markets of China, but it is by no means clear that our possession of those islands had significant effect on our economic and diplomatic position in China. We had laid claim to the role of a "China power" as early as the Cushing Mission of 1844, and we had sought equal commercial rights in China long before John Hay formally enunciated the doctrine of the Open Door. Although dreams of American domination of a limitless China market partially inspired American acquisition of the Philippines, our conquest of those islands was followed neither by a sharp increase in our China trade nor by a significant augmentation of American diplomatic leverage in the tangled relations of China and the Western powers. The Open Door Notes were accorded somewhat greater attention in the chanceries of Berlin and St. Petersburg because we were masters of Manila; our participation in the suppression of the Boxer Rebellion was made more certain by the presence of the American army in the Philippines, but as our diplomatic and economic ambitions in China preceded the Treaty of Paris, so were they not much changed by the conquest of the Philippine Islands.[1]

Surely the impact of our Philippine policy on relations with China was less immediate and visible than its influence on our relations with Britain, Germany, and Japan. Our acquisition of the Philippines helped foster a sentiment of shared interests in the Far East with Britain; it stimulated an increased suspicion by the United States of the diplomatic goals of Germany; and it created a source of potential animosity and distrust in the relations of the United States and Japan.

The British government had openly advocated American retention of the Philippine Islands. Not only did it wish to prevent their annexation by Germany, but it saw a greater likelihood of British-American cooperation in China if the U.S. flag was raised in the western Pacific. The conviction of certain anti-imperialists that Britain had gulled America into sharing the white man's burden in Asia exaggerates British intentions and influence, but the ministry of Lord Salisbury made no secret of its approval of the Philippine policy of William McKinley. This approval was reenforced by the Boer War. In their mutual determination to suppress "insurrection," the governments of Great Britain and the United States felt a sense of unwonted unity, and another step was taken along the path of rapprochement that culminated in the entente of 1917. There was no Anglo-American alliance during the years of the Philippine-American War, but American possession of an archipelago believed to be an object of interest to both Germany and Japan made more desirable the goodwill and cooperation of Great Britain.

Recent research has shown that American fears of German and Japanese designs on the Philippines were highly exaggerated, although both countries would have been willing to acquire the archipelago if it could have been managed without antagonizing the United States. In any case, the significance of America's Philippine policy for relations with Germany and Japan lies in the suspicions shared by contemporary military strategists, not the researches of later scholars. After 1898 Germany had a high place on the U.S. Navy's list of possible enemies, and by 1905 so did Japan. American possession of the Philippines was only one of many factors that inspired a growing suspicion of Germany and Japan, but it was a factor.

There is no need, however, to accept the thesis that with our conquest of the Philippines the United States suffered a loss of innocence and "moral force in the eyes of the world."[2] Such a judgment assumes for the United States a diplomatic past more unspotted than a close look at the record will support and implies a larger role for morality in foreign relations than the history of international politics can offer. There is no reason to believe that the Philippine-American War, for all its grisly features, lowered American diplomatic prestige in the chanceries of Europe. The war was an object of sympathy in Whitehall, of uneasiness in Tokyo, and of limited interest to such "China powers" as Russia and Germany, but the inability of Aguinaldo to obtain diplomatic or material support from any foreign nation makes dubious the claim that among the war's costs for America was a "loss of moral force in the eyes of the world."

The most difficult questions respecting the diplomatic significance of American conquest of the Philippines concern neither its influence on naval strategy and the China trade nor its consequences for diplomatic friendships and animosities in the McKinley-Roosevelt era, but rather its impact on the subsequent course of American diplomacy.

Several theories have been offered in recent years that place great emphasis on the influence of the conquest of the Philippines for later American diplomatic history. One theory sees the Philippine-American War as a progenitive model for American aggression and intervention in the Far East and Pacific regions over the past two generations. Another sees our Philippine policy as a proving ground for the economic colonialism that has characterized American relations with the Third World in the twentieth century, and still a third theory sees the Philippines as a climactic episode in fashioning a foreign-policy consensus in behalf of open door imperialism.

It is dramatically pleasing to proclaim that American conquest of the Philippines planted the dragons' teeth that were harvested at Pearl Harbor, the Chosin reservoir, and the Mekong Delta, but rhetoric is not a proper substitute for proof, and the policy errors of McKinley furnish neither cause nor explanation for the difficulties and policies of his successors. American seizure of the Philippines made probable an increased orientation of American diplomacy toward Asia and the Pacific, but it did not predetermine the future options and decisions of that diplomacy. The judgment of Daniel B. Schirmer that "the United States suppression of the Philippine national revolution was the progenitor of the Vietnam War" confuses semblance with causation.[3] The existence of American bases in the Philippines did not require President Eisenhower to support the South Vietnam government of Ngo Dinh Diem or President Johnson to increase American combat forces in Indochina. The Philippine-American War was not without importance for American history, but its importance is more indirect and limited than theories of streamlined historical continuity will allow.

More popular and slightly more persuasive than the theory of genetic inheritance is that of conditioned behavior. Several historians have argued that American policy in the Philippines established the pattern of diplomatic behavior most characteristic of American foreign policy in the undeveloped areas of the world in the twentieth century. In their interpretation, American imperialism in the Philippines was gradually translated into a more sophisticated form of neocolonial control, and the techniques and instrumentalities of neocolonialism practiced in the Philippines subsequently typified American diplomacy in Latin America and Asia.[4] Such a thesis makes the imperialist policy of 1898 an actor in its own right with powers of procreation. Economic disadvantages currently suffered by Third World nations are primarily the result of the comparative terms of trade, and the counterrevolutionary anxieties exhibited by American policy in Asia and Latin America since World War II find their explanation more readily in the realities and neuroses of the Cold War than in the Philippine policy of William McKinley and Theodore Roosevelt.

A variant of the proving-ground thesis is the much acclaimed interpretation of William Appleman Williams. The thrust of Williams' interpretation is not that the Philippines provided the origins of American neocolonialism, but that debate over the annexation and conquest of the Philippines demonstrates the foreign-policy consensus soon reached by all interest groups within the American political and economic establishment. Although for a brief period there was some substantive distinction between McKinley and his anti-imperialist opponents, it was not long before the "expansionists" and "anti-imperialists" joined in support of open door imperialism. From the beginning, according to Williams, the debate had been but a dispute over alternative strategies to the goal of commercial expansion. Its participants had only quarreled over the most effective means for the uninterrupted development of American industrial and agricultural markets throughout the world. The Open Door Notes marked the conclusion of this carefully limited debate as they exemplified the solution of the noncolonial empire. Economic ambition joined with self-serving moralism to fashion a policy to which all politically significant economic interest groups could pledge allegiance.[5]

More subtle and sophisticated than the above paraphrase would suggest, Williams' interpretation deserves respect but not adoption. It denies the diversity of membership and complexity of motives of both the anti-imperialists and their opponents. It dismisses the influence of Social Darwinism and racism, brushes aside the factors of strategic interests and international rivalry, overlooks the role of the Philippine-American War, and, most important, ignores the essential differences of American policy aims in the Caribbean, China, and the Philippines. However one interprets the goals of the open door doctrine in China or the intent of the Platt Amendment in Cuba, the fact remains that American policy in the Philippines was fashioned for a territorial colony and for a people required to acknowledge the political sovereignty of the United States. Aguinaldo was not fighting the market ambitions of the New England Cotton Manufacturers Association but the soldiers of a colonial power, as later the Nacionalista party would direct its campaign efforts not against American railroad projects in the Philippines but against the political authority of the American governor general. To make American policy in the Philippines the exemplar of open door imperialism is to ignore essential distinctions of political control. It also requires a biased selection from a very mixed bag of evidence respecting American policy in the Philippine Islands.

An evaluation of the advantages and disadvantages of American rule for the Filipinos is the subject for another and a different book, but a few summary judgments may be offered in support of the author's conviction that American policy was characterized neither by wisdom nor consistency nor economic exploitation.

The war itself was the most costly episode in the history of the Filipino people. Approximately 18,000 Filipinos were killed in combat, at least 100,000 Filipinos died from disease, famine, and other war-related causes, hundreds of barrios were burned, half the stock of draft animals was destroyed, and thousands of acres of land were devastated. It is doubtful that a lengthy period of civil disturbance under an independent Philippine government would have been as damaging. If it was McKinley's aim to save the Filipinos from anarchy, the result of his decision was a loss of life and resources that could not help but weaken the potential of the islands for economic viability over the next generation.

Between the end of the Philippine-American War and the establishment of the Commonwealth Government in 1934, the United States followed an erratic policy of economic development, social modernization, and political cooptation. Schools were built as well as railroads, public health measures were introduced, the legal system was reformed, the Philippine Assembly received an increasing measure of domestic political influence.[6] There is another side to the record, however. If American administrators sought to promote "progress" in the islands, they frequently fell victim to the occupational disease of the pedagogue who would dominate as well as instruct and who remains reluctant to declare his pupil equipped for the freedom of graduation. Tutelage can have a crippling effect, and apprenticeship too long continued can promote a sense of psychological as well as economic dependence. It is false to say that the United States destroyed a dynamic and functional society and culture, for in 1898 the Philippines did not possess such a society and culture after three centuries of quixotic Spanish misrule. It is more accurate to say that the United States confused stability with development, directed Philippine nationalism into conservative as well as constitutional channels, and exercised a tutelage that was inconsistent in goals and methods.[7] American policy instituted a sufficient amount of social reform to make necessary a broader base of political participation, but failed to correct the maldistribution of land and wealth or alter the *cacique* tradition of the Philippine past.

The basic social structure was not changed by American rule. Efforts at land reform failed, the estates of the friars were bought by absentee landowners, and the number of peasant proprietors actually declined during the years of American rule.

There is no certainty that had the Philippines been granted independence under some international neutralization agreement in 1898 they would subsequently have evolved a viable economy, a democratic social structure, or a broad-based popular government. What can be said is that they had achieved none of these when the Commonwealth Government was established in 1934. The Philippines had not been victimized by a consistent policy of economic exploitation; nor as a territorial colony of the United States did they serve as a model of open door imperialism. Rather they offered an example of the debilitating effects of cultural coercion and economic dependence.

Coercion, dependence, and worse had been predicted by the anti-imperialist opponents of the Philippine-American War. Those critics had never recognized themselves as advocates of open door imperialism; nor did they consider themselves part of an establishment consensus at the war's end. They considered they had failed. Their judgment was correct, and their failure must be acknowledged in any analysis of the diplomatic significance of the Philippine-American War.

That significance lies more in the realm of instruction than precedent. The human and financial costs of the war served as a cautionary warning against further adventures of insular imperialism. It would be difficult to prove that the Philippine-American War altered the policy goals of American diplomats, but by dampening imperialist sentiment among the urban middle class, it had perhaps some inhibiting influence on diplomatic means and tactics. More certainly, the Philippine-American War had limited impact on our relations with Britain, Germany, and Japan, importantly affected American naval strategy, and publicized long-standing American ambitions in the Far East. But U.S. conquest of the Philippines neither predetermined the later course of American policy in the Far East nor marked a watershed in the history of American foreign policy.

If it is difficult to assess the impact of America's acquisition of the Philippines on the later course of American diplomacy, it is impossible to measure with precision the domestic political significance of the Philippine-American War. Certain consequences that appear obvious become less certain upon examination; others are subject to differing interpretations. Indeed, the more important the questions addressed to the Philippine-American War, the less susceptible they are to quantitative verification.

The consequences of the war for partisan politics were potentially important but in the long run surprisingly meagre. The Republican party was identified with the Philippine policy of the McKinley and Roosevelt administrations, and the Democratic party was at points identified with opposition to that policy. Only during the campaign of 1900, however, did the Philippines become a distinctly partisan issue, and even then the Democratic candidate was careful to distinguish between opposition and dissent and refused to endorse the position of the Anti-Imperialist League. The existence, moreover, of a few outspoken dissenters in the ranks of the Republicans and the presence of a much larger minority of jingo expansionists within the ranks of the Dixie Democrats helped to blur the line of partisan division. Some contemporary observers predicted that as a result of Bryan's brief effort to make imperialism "the paramount issue," there would be secessionist movements in both parties that would sharpen that line, but relatively few "regulars" of either party defected in consequence of their support or opposition to American policy in the Philippines. Senators Lodge and Hoar continued to recognize one another as fellow Republicans; Senators Morgan and Carmack continued to proclaim their respective allegiance to the Democratic party. Certain "Mugwump Republicans," such as Carl Schurz and Moorfield Storey, voted for Democratic candidates in the elections of 1900 and 1902, but only a few permanently joined the ranks of the Democracy. Such men were Independents when the war began and they were Independents when it ended. Neither the size nor the leadership of the major parties was measurably changed by the Philippine-American War.

Among the rank-and-file of both major parties, domestic issues aroused stronger partisan sentiments than did questions of diplomatic and military policy. The growing strength of the Republican party was due more to its identification with industrial prosperity than its identification with insular expansion. The Anti-Imperialist League brought the issue of American policy in the Philippines to the forefront of public discussion on occasion, and the human and financial costs of an unexpectedly lengthy war had the effect of generating periodic spasms of irritation, but such issues as the currency, industrial monopoly, and the price of wheat were more decisive in determining the voting behavior of the electorate. Americans then, as later, were prepared to attribute superior wisdom and information to their elected officials in the area of diplomatic and military affairs. One did not need to be a rabid imperialist to be willing to let the president have his way in foreign lands and to take a vicarious pride in battle victories in far-off places difficult to pronounce and easy to forget.

But if the war did not have significant effect for the division of the

American electorate between the major parties, did it influence the developing division within those parties? More particularly, did the war accentuate or hasten the evolution of a progressive-conservative split in either party? It has been argued that progressivism and imperialism shared a common faith in the possibility of shaping the future by the instrumentalities of human intelligence and endeavor. Both were goal-oriented, activist, and optimistic.[8] However accurate this may be, "progressivism" was still primarily a phenomenon of local and municipal politics in the years of the Philippine-American War, and though certain figures may be identified as "progressives," they exhibited no unity in their convictions about the war and American foreign policy. There were those who were opposed to territorial expansion and military expenditures as well as those who shared the romantic nationalism of Beveridge and Roosevelt. Proto-progressives who publicly opposed American conquest of the Philippines included Jane Addams, Josephus Daniels, John Dewey, Hazen Pingree, Hoke Smith, and Brand Whitlock. Similarly, there were conservatives who advocated territorial empire and others who emphasized its dangers. It would appear doubtful that any meaningful correlation can be made between the position of public figures on issues of domestic reform and their attitude toward the Philippine-American War. The war inspired controversy over its necessity and justice, but this controversy had little influence on the gradual development of progressive and old guard blocs within the major parties. That development was the product primarily of domestic issues and contrary solutions for the achievement of economic health and social harmony.

Some students believe that the expansionist turn of American foreign policy at the end of the nineteenth century had perceptible effect in erasing the sectional suspicions of North and South and unifying the nation. They suggest that internal harmony was the by-product of imperial adventure. Possibly the Spanish-American War helped to foster sectional reconciliation, or at least to publicize a development that found its basis in the nationalization of an industrial economy and its victim in the political rights of the black American, but the Philippine-American War was not an influence for national harmony. The conquest of the Filipinos served to accentuate racial antagonisms. It is more than a chronological coincidence that the years of the Philippine-American War were the years that saw the highest incidence of lynching in American history. Governmental proclamations implying the inferiority of brown men in the Philippines gave a national imprimatur to the recently formalized Jim Crow codes of the South and the segregationist practices of the cities and unions of the North. "Benevolent assimilation" was a reflection, not a cause, of racism in the

United States, but its domestic manifestations were no less significant for that fact.

On balance, the conquest of the Philippines had little permanent influence on the political life of the United States. Neither the hopes of the more zealous expansionists nor the fears of the more dedicated anti-imperialists were realized. Colonialism did not inspire the educated elite to form a corps of imperial civil servants and bring new vitality to public life, nor did it bring in its train executive tyranny, militarism, and moral bankruptcy. Anti-imperialist prophecies of a future where the Constitution was cancelled and economic oligarchs ruled in league with presidential caesars proved no more accurate than imperialist visions of limitless Oriental markets that would assure social harmony amidst perpetual prosperity. The Philippine-American War did illustrate the increasing power of the executive branch in the initiation of military and diplomatic policies, but here again its role was one of confirmation rather than genesis. The enhancement of executive power owed much more to the nationalization of political and economic institutions in the last two decades of the nineteenth century than to the Philippine policy of William McKinley.

In the final analysis, the major significance of the Philippine-American War is not to be found in its influence on either the political fabric or the foreign policy of the American Republic, but in the response of the American people to that war. Its importance lies less in its impact on future political and diplomatic developments than its demonstration of the beliefs and ambitions of American society at the turn of the century. The response of the American public to the Philippine-American War found expression in the diverse opinions of politicians, businessmen, labor leaders, churchmen, missionaries, teachers, writers, black Americans, and veterans' groups, and that response offers a mirror image of the patriotism and racism, confusion and optimism, of a people uncertain of their national future while convinced of their national superiority.

Notes

CHAPTER I

1. The anti-imperialist Springfield (Mass.) *Republican* prophesied in the spring of 1899 that "future historians will be able to show that the United States government, prior to the outbreak of the war with Spain, had abundant reason to anticipate the course of events in the Philippine islands." *The Springfield Weekly Republican*, 3 March 1899.

2. In its most extreme form this interpretation sees Roosevelt and his Washington circle as personally responsible for American acquisition of the Philippine Islands. See Howard K. Beale, *Theodore Roosevelt and the Rise of America to World Power*, pp. 70–71.

3. See Walter LaFeber, *The New Empire*, pp. 380–83, 410–11; Thomas J. McCormick, "Insular Imperialism and the Open Door," p. 158; Michael P. Onorato, "The United States and the Philippine Independence Movement," pp. 2–4; Daniel B. Schirmer, *Republic or Empire*, pp. 66–67.

4. John A. Grenville and George B. Young, *Politics, Strategy and American Diplomacy*, pp. 270–72, 294; Ronald Spector, *Admiral of the New Empire*, pp. 32–36. Kimball's memorandum of 1 June 1896 will be found in Record Group 38, General Records of the Office of Naval Intelligence, National Archives.

5. Spector, *Admiral of the New Empire*, p. 2.

6. McKinley to Secretary of War, 4 May 1898, *Correspondence Relating to the War with Spain, April 15, 1898–July 30, 1902*, 2:635. Daniel Schirmer insists that the McKinley administration had decided to send an army of occupation to the Philippines well before Dewey ever attacked the Spanish fleet, but his evidence is confined to a subsequent statement by the unreliable Secretary of War Russell Alger. Schirmer, *Republic or Empire*, p. 66.

7. *Correspondence Relating to the War with Spain*, 2:676–78 (italics added). A letter from McKinley to Secretary of the Navy John D. Long of the same date, 19 May, stressed that the army's role was to assure "order and security" in the islands. McKinley to Long, 19 May 1898, McKinley Papers, Library of Congress; William R. Braisted, *The United States Navy in the Pacific, 1897–1909*, p. 45.

8. General Wesley Merritt to Adjutant General, 1 August 1898; Adjutant General to Merritt, 17 August 1898, *Correspondence Relating to the War with Spain*, 2:743, 754; Garel A. Grunder and William E. Livezey, *The Philippines and the United States*.

9. By the terms of the armistice protocol signed in Washington on 12 August 1898, the United States would "hold the city, bay and harbor of Manila" until a final settlement determined "the control, disposition and government" of the archipelago.

10. See Uldarico S. Baclagon, *Philippine Campaigns*, p. 77.

11. A contrary view will be found in Louis J. Halle, *Dream and Reality*, pp. 189–90. It is Halle's contention that our policy was one of drift and that "there never was a decision to attach the Philippines to us until it was found that they virtually were attached already."

12. See William F. Marina, "Opponents of Empire," pp. 110–13.

13. Tyler Dennett wrote many years ago: "What else was there to do but to remain and to extend the American domain to the entire archipelago?" *Americans in Eastern Asia*, p. 631.

Robert H. Ferrell has recently suggested that McKinley's famous explanation to a delegation of Methodists how he received divine guidance when weighing alternative Philippine policies may in fact have been the invention of one of the members of the delegation, General James F. Rusling. See *American Diplomacy*, pp. 367–69.

14. John Foreman, "Spain and the Philippine Islands," pp. 20–33.

15. See, for example, Halle, *Dream and Reality*, pp. 193–94.

16. Walter LaFeber and William F. Marina cite the memoirs of John Basset Moore in support of this judgment. Moore, who accompanied the American delegation to the peace conference in Paris, wrote that "No incident in the history of the United States . . . [better] prepares us to understand the acquisition of the Philippines, than the course of our government towards the Samoan Islands." Moore's judgment followed the event by twenty-five years. "Autobiography," Moore MSS, Library of Congress, quoted by LaFeber, *The New Empire*, p. 140; Marina, "Opponents of Empire," p. 32.

17. In the summer of 1899 McKinley would take cognizance of the protectorate alternative but only to denounce its anti-imperialist advocates as political innocents. McKinley implied that they wished a permanent protectorate arrangement and this would mean "commitment without control," responsibility without authority. Margaret Leech, *In the Days of McKinley*, p. 328.

18. Several historians have in recent years emphasized McKinley's anxiety that the Philippines not become a source of international friction. See, for example, Halle, *Dream and Reality*, p. 192; James K. Eyre, Jr., "The Philippines, the Powers, and the Spanish-American War," p. 302. Halle believes that McKinley judged the Filipinos to be politically incompetent primarily because they were unable to provide for their own military defense.

19. Although Imperial Germany was not the uncouth opportunist and island-hungry villain projected by various expansionist editors in 1898, it seems clear that the Kaiser was not averse to acquiring a coaling station and naval base in the Philippines if the United States took the path of abnegation. Clara E. Schieber, *The Transformation of American Sentiment Toward Germany, 1870–1914*, pp. 116–17; Ernest R. May, *Imperial Democracy*, p. 228; Eyre, "The Philippines, the Powers, and the Spanish-American War," pp. 130–31, 139–40, 210–22.

20. Eyre, "The Philippines, the Powers, and the Spanish-American War," pp. 278–84, 301.

21. See Grenville and Young, *Politics, Strategy and American Diplomacy*, pp. 286–87.

22. For confirmation of this judgment, see particularly the stern rebuke delivered Pratt by Secretary of State William R. Day, 20 July 1898. *Senate Doc*. No. 62, 55th Cong., 3d sess., Pt. 2, pp. 340–47, 352, 357. The naive Pratt had forwarded to the State Department a clipping from the *Singapore Free Press*, describing the literary tribute that the Filipino colony in Singapore had paid Pratt in

gratitude for his "support of the cause of General Aguinaldo." The fact that Pratt was not only reprimanded but later dismissed from the consular service would indicate that the State Department believed he had given Aguinaldo promises that seriously embarrassed his government. Howard Bray to G. F. Hoar, 12 January, 13 January 1899, Hoar Papers, Massachusetts Historical Society; E. Spencer Pratt to Andrew Carnegie, 7 April 1899, Carnegie Papers, Library of Congress.

23. Aguinaldo would later claim that Dewey had earlier (March 1898) sent a Captain Wood of the gunboat *Petrel* to confer with him about the possibility of collaboration, but Dewey denied this.

24. *Senate Doc.* No. 331, 57th Cong., 1st sess., pp. 2929–59.

25. Dewey initially acknowledged the value of Aguinaldo's army, as distinct from his "revolutionary government": "I knew what he was doing—driving the Spaniards in—was saving our own troops." *Senate Doc.* No. 331, 57th Cong., 1st sess., p. 2928. See also Braisted, *The United States Navy in the Pacific*, pp. 46–47; Dewey to Aguinaldo, 16 July 1898, Dewey Papers, Library of Congress; General Thomas Anderson to Adjutant General, 21 July 1898, *Correspondence Relating to the War with Spain*, 2:809.

There is an abundance of conflicting sources respecting promises that were or were not made to Aguinaldo by American officials. For a representative sample, see correspondence of Sixto Lopez and Charles Denby in *The Independent* 52 (4 January, 8 March 1900), pp. 7–9, 579–85; G. F. Hoar to General Thomas Anderson, 22 January 1902, Hoar Papers, Massachusetts Historical Society; *Senate Doc.* No. 331, 57th Cong., 1st sess., pp. 2929–84; Louis F. Post, "Documentary Outline of the Philippine Case," *The Public* (Chicago), 19 May 1900; G. Apacible, *To the American People*.

26. *Senate Doc.* No. 62, 55th Cong., 3d sess., Pt. II, pp. 345–46, 431.

27. By August 1898 Aguinaldo had appointed an executive cabinet and a ten-member foreign affairs commission that was to seek recognition and assistance from the nations of Europe. Felipe Agoncillo was ordered to Paris to represent the interests of the Filipinos before the Spanish-American peace conference. Aguinaldo's cabinet was reflective of the strong support he then enjoyed among the wealthier and better-educated Filipinos.

28. For the conflicting and tentative advice offered by military officers in the Philippines, see *Correspondence Relating to the War with Spain*, 2:840–52; Braisted, *The United States Navy in the Pacific*, p. 66.

29. Paola Coletta observes that by his instructions, McKinley "violated the niceties of diplomatic intercourse . . . and provided the Filipinos a *causus belli*." Coletta, "McKinley, the Peace Negotiations, and the Acquisition of the Philippines," p. 348. Tyler Dennett concludes, more bluntly, that McKinley's proclamation was "equivalent to authorizing a campaign of conquest, while the Senate was discussing the question." Dennett, *Americans in Eastern Asia*, p. 631.

30. The key passage ran as follows: "It will be the duty of the commander of the forces of occupation to announce and proclaim in the most public manner that we come not as invaders or conquerors, but as friends, to protect the natives in their homes, in their employments, and in their personal and religious rights. All persons who, either by active aid or by honest submission, cooperate with the Government of the United States to give effect to these beneficent purposes will receive the reward of its support and protection. All others will be brought within the lawful rule we have assumed, with firmness if need be, but without severity so far as may be possible. . . . It should be the earnest and paramount aim of the military administration to win the confidence, respect, and affection of the inhabitants of

the Philippines by assuring them in every possible way that full measure of individual rights and liberties which is the heritage of free peoples, and by proving to them that the mission of the United States is one of benevolent assimilation, substituting the mild sway of justice and right for arbitrary rule." *Correspondence Relating to the War with Spain*, 2:719. The contents of McKinley's letter of 21 December were repeated in a cable to Otis of 28 December. See Adjutant General to Otis, 28 December 1898, telegram, Dewey Papers, Library of Congress.

31. Article III of the Treaty of Paris (10 December 1898) saw Spain cede the Philippine archipelago to the United States and receive $20 million in return. The embarrassing chronological fact that Manila was captured some twenty-four hours after the armistice was signed in Washington allowed Spain to demand payment-for-sale, and McKinley, though continuing to insist that the Philippines was ours by right of conquest, acquiesced.

32. Apolinario Mabini, *The Philippine Revolution*, p. 57; Teodoro A. Agoncillo, *Malolos: Crisis of the Republic*, pp. 357–70. A contemporary British observer, Richard Brinsley Sheridan, offered an identical view in his essay, *The Filipino Martyrs,* and Herbert Welsh, the anti-imperialist Philadelphia editor, was prepared to "surmize" that "a ruthless massacre of Filipinos was the means deliberately chosen for effecting political ends in Washington." Herbert Welsh, *The Other Man's Country*, pp. 109, 126.

33. Schirmer, *Republic or Empire*, pp. 125–32.

34. Philippine Insurgent Records, Group No. 94, File No. 1202; General Elwell Otis to General R. P. Hughes, 25 January 1899, copy, Dean Worcester Collection, University Library Special Collections, University of Michigan; Edwin Wildman, *Aguinaldo*, p. 186.

35. Other members were Colonel James F. Smith, Lieutenant Colonel E. H. Crowder, Ambrosio Flores, and Manuel Argüelles.

36. In effect, the Filipinos demanded that American recognition precede any negotiations concerning the qualifications that might be imposed upon their independence, but indicated their willingness to request American "protection," cede to the United States a site for a naval base, and grant the United States some form of trade preference. Philippine Insurgent Records, Group No. 94, File No. 1202. See also the "for-history's-later-eyes" letter from Otis to General R. P. Hughes, 25 January 1899, copy, Dean Worcester Collection, University of Michigan.

37. Laying great stress on the parallels of the American and Philippine revolutions, Agoncillo insisted that America had no more right to buy the Philippines while the Filipinos were fighting for independence from Spain than had France to purchase the Thirteen Colonies from Britain during the American Revolution. The authority of the Philippine Revolutionary Government was acknowledged throughout the archipelago when its American "ally" negotiated a treaty of cession with a nation that no longer possessed de facto control over the islands. See Maximo M. Kalaw, *The Case for the Filipinos*, pp. 63–77, for a detailed analysis of Agoncillo's memorandum; also, F. Agoncillo, "A Letter to the President and the American People," *The Independent* 50 (30 November 1899), pp. 3217–19.

CHAPTER II

1. Although captured Filipino documents would later be twisted by American intelligence officers in an attempt to prove Aguinaldo responsible for initiating hostilities, they only reveal that he judged war probable and had given instructions to his followers in anticipation of the event. See Philippine Insurgent Records,

Record Group 126, Files No. 1162, No. 1199. For the determined effort of Captain John R. Taylor to prove that Aguinaldo authored a conspiracy in January 1899 to assassinate General Otis, see PIR, File No. 1199 and Vol. 3:901–24, of Taylor's five-volume unpublished history, "The Philippine Insurrection Against the United States—A Compilation of Documents with Notes and Introduction" (microfilm of galley proof, PIR, Record Group 126). See also Annual Reports of the War Department for the Fiscal Year Ended June 30, 1900, *House Doc.* No. 2, 56th Cong., 2d sess., p. 94.

2. Karl Irving Faust, *Campaigning in the Philippines*, p. 125. For similar expressions, see William S. Christener, 19th Penna. Infantry, to Mr. Rufus Christener, 5 January, 22 January 1899, William S. Christener Papers; Claude F. Myers, 1st Tennessee Vol. Inf. to parents, 10 January 1899 (newspaper clipping), Claude F. Myers Papers, U.S. Army Military History Research Collection, Carlisle Barracks.

Various regimental histories published during the war unconsciously reflected this animus and the racism that helped inspire it. See, for example, A. Prentiss, ed., *The History of the Utah Volunteers in the Spanish-American War and in the Philippine Islands*, pp. 211–19, 226, 238–39, 281; Joseph I. Markey, *From Iowa to the Philippines*, pp. 166–67; W. D. B. Dodson, "Official History of the Second Oregon U.S.V. Infantry" in *The Official Records of the Oregon Volunteers in the Spanish War and Philippine Insurrection* edited by C. U. Gantenbein, pp. 26–27, 35, 45, 51.

3. John F. Bass, correspondent for *Harper's Weekly*, reported that the Filipinos were quick to accept stories of American cruelty being circulated by certain Spanish officers, including the charge that the American army branded the letters "U.S." on its Negro soldiers as well as its army mules. Cited in Philippine Information Society, *Facts About the Filipinos*, pamphlet No. 7, pp. 68–70.

4. The success of American arms during those forty-eight hours was described by many soldier participants. See, for example, William W. Winders, 1st Washington Vol. Inf., to parents, 10 February 1899, William W. Winders Papers; Claude F. Myers, 1st Tennessee Vol. Inf., to parents, 6 February 1899, Claude F. Myers Papers; Diary of Ernest W. Hewston for February–March 1899, E. W. Hewston Papers, U.S. Army Military History Research Collection, Carlisle Barracks. See also the broken files of two English-language papers published in Manila, *The American* and *Freedom*, for 6–16 February 1899, microfilm, Library of the Natural History Museum, Los Angeles County.

5. Teodoro A. Agoncillo, *Malolos*, p. 465; PIR File No. 1162; *Freedom* (Manila), 16–25 February 1899.

6. Meanwhile, the Americans had made their first efforts to take physical possession of the Visayan Islands, south of Luzon. Joint army and navy operations secured the capture of Iloilo on Panay and the capital city of the island of Cebu. In each case, as soon as the city was occupied, it was isolated by insurgent control of the surrounding countryside.

7. *Annual Reports of the War Department for the Fiscal Year Ended June 30, 1900*, Pt. 1 ("Report of Major-General E. S. Otis, U.S. Army, Commanding the Division of the Philippines and Military Governor of the Philippine Islands, to the Adjutant-General").

8. Teodoro M. Kalaw, *The Philippine Revolution*, p. 177; Leandro H. Fernandez, *The Philippine Republic*, p. 159.

9. In June, General Antonio Luna would be assassinated and Aguinaldo would again assume military command, while continuing as president of the Republic.

10. Aguinaldo's forces suffered a less pronounced decline of morale in the same period. The failure of foreign governments to offer recognition and the paralysis of the commercial economy of the islands steadily accentuated the problems of supply, and the defection of Buencamino and other conservatives had a discouraging effect.

11. See PIR, Roll 74, Files No. 1198–99.

12. Aguinaldo's invalid wife, sister, and son were ordered to stay behind at Bontoc. They were captured there by Major Peyton C. March on 1 January 1900.

13. Otis to Adjutant General, 24 November 1899, *Correspondence Relating to the War with Spain*, 2:1107. See also E. S. Otis, "The Situation in the Philippines," *The Independent* 52 (14 June 1900), pp. 1414–15.

14. See PIR, Roll 72, Files No. 1164, No. 1167, No. 1169; Roll 74, Files No. 1198, No. 1204.

15. Unidentified insurgent broadside quoted by William T. Sexton, *Soldiers in the Sun*, p. 239.

16. PIR, Roll 74, File No. 1198 (Order of Anbrosio Flores, 5 January 1900).

17. For a sympathetic evaluation of the "host of benevolent and humane efforts" undertaken by the American army, see John M. Gates, *Schoolbooks and Krags*, pp. viii, 54–70, 204–20, 276–79.

18. See, for example, Colonel L. W. V. Kennan's article on "The Katipunan of the Philippines" in *The North American Review* 178 (August 1901), pp. 208–20.

19. James A. LeRoy, "Race Prejudice in the Philippines," *The Atlantic Monthly* 90 (July 1902), p. 104; Lt. Samuel P. Lyon to Mrs. Samuel P. Lyon, 6 March, 29 March 1900, 13 January 1901, Lyon Papers; Letters of William E. Eggenberger, Co. K, 3d Inf., to Mrs. John A. Teel, 25 March, 11 May, 31 May, 7 July, 2 November 1899, 18 June 1900, 6 February 1901, Eggenberger Papers; Diary "Record of Events" of W. A. Damon, Co. E, 2d Inf., for 1901, Damon Papers; Diary of Claude F. Line, Co. A, 1st Washington Vol. Inf., for 1901, Line Papers; Diary of Frederick M. Presher, Troop K, 1st U.S. Cavalry, for 9 June, 22 June, 19 September, 8 October, 26 December 1901, 13 January, 11 February 1902, Presher Papers, U.S. Army Military History Research Collection, Carlisle Barracks; John Clifford Brown, *Diary of a Soldier in the Philippines*, entry for 29 October 1900.

20. Taft to Horace H. Lurton, 22 September 1900, Taft Papers, Library of Congress. For Taft's readiness to scorn the intelligence and veracity of the Filipinos, see Oscar M. Alfonso, "Taft's Early Views on the Filipinos."

21. Issued by the Adjutant General's Office during the Civil War, General Order No. 100, 1863 Series, specified that "war rebels" who rose in arms against "the occupying or conquering army" were to be "treated summarily as highway robbers or pirates."

22. PIR, Roll 74, File No. 1204; Peter W. Stanley, *A Nation in the Making*, p. 267.

23. See Emilio Aguinaldo, "The Story of My Capture."

24. It is probable that this "guard" was designed as much for Aguinaldo's protection as for his retention. The war correspondent and artist, John T. Mc-Cutcheon had reported to the readers of the Chicago *Record*, 13 August 1900: "Nearly every soldier refers to him in the bitterest way, and never without supplementing the remarks with the most revengeful and abusive profanity. I've heard many of them say that if they ever laid eyes on him there would be one more 'good nigger.'"

25. For a sample of editorial acclaim and optimism, see *Public Opinion* 30 (4, 11 April 1901), pp. 420–22, 456.

26. See John M. Gates, *Schoolbooks and Krags*, pp. 235–36.

27. PIR, Roll 74, File No. 1197.

28. See, for example, the diary of William R. Johnson, "Three Years in the Orient," edited by D. R. Carmony and K. Tannenbaum, pp. 293–94.

29. *Senate Doc.* No. 213, 57th Cong., 2d sess., pp. 1–11.

30. *Senate Doc.* No. 331, 57th Cong., 1st sess., pp. 1601–33. There is, however, little factual basis for the judgment of Daniel B. Schirmer that American methods were "in some applications . . . genocidal." Daniel B. Schirmer, *Republic or Empire*, p. 256.

31. Sexton, *Soldiers in the Sun*, pp. 19–20.

32. Henry F. Graff, ed., *American Imperialism and the Philippine Insurrection*, p. xiv.

CHAPTER III

1. Maria C. Lanzar, "The Anti-Imperialist League," pp. 7–18.

2. Two of the more active branch Leagues were those in Washington, under the leadership of W. C. Croffut and Patrick Ford, and Philadelphia, where George C. Mercer and Herbert Welsh were the prime organizers. Prior to its translation as the American League, the Chicago branch was known as the Central Anti-Imperialist League. Edwin Burritt Smith was its secretary, J. Sterling Morton its nominal leader, and Professors Hermann Von Holst and J. Laurence Laughlin its most articulate publicists.

3. The best analysis of the membership of the Anti-Imperialist League and its diversity is to be found in E. Berkeley Tompkins, *Anti-Imperialism in the United States*, pp. 126–260; 229–35.

4. When they first heard of the shooting of 4 February, even the more determined opponents of colonial expansion did not doubt that the hostilities were the result of Filipino initiative. The Springfield *Republican* suggested that the U.S. government should say to the Filipinos: "You struck, and we had to strike back; now let there be peace." *The Springfield Weekly Republican*, 10 February 1899. See also New York *Evening Post*, 15 February 1899; Philadelphia *City and State*, 9 February 1899.

5. Erving Winslow, "The Anti-Imperialist League," pp. 1347–50; Winslow, "The Anti-Imperialist Position," pp. 460–68; Winslow to Horace Boies, 2 June 1900 (copy), Anti-Imperialist League Papers, L.C.; Winslow to Herbert Welsh, 11 June 1902, Anti-Imperialist League Collection, Michigan Historical Collections, University of Michigan.

6. Perhaps the first organization to use modern methods of propaganda on a national scale, the League issued over 400 separate broadsides, public letters, and pamphlets. The total number of printed items bearing the League's imprimatur was in excess of 1 million. William J. Pomeroy, *American Neocolonialism*, p. 109.

7. See Winslow to Horace Boies, 2 June 1900 (copy), Misc. Papers, L.C.

8. See Carl Schurz to Oswald Garrison Villard, 21 July 1900, Villard Papers; Winslow to C. E. Norton, 12 August 1901, Norton Papers, Houghton Library, Harvard University.

9. The McKinley administration insisted from the beginning that the insurgents were engaged in a rebellion against the lawful authority of the United States. The very name given the war by the administration, "Philippine Insurrection," implied the rebelliousness as well as the responsibility of the Filipinos. The theme of insurgent responsibility for initiating hostilities was expressed most succinctly in a speech by President McKinley at Pittsburgh on 28 August 1899: "The first blow

was struck by the insurgents. Our kindness was reciprocated with cruelty, our mercy with a Mauser. . . . Our humanity was interpreted as weakness, our forbearance as cowardice." *Public Opinion* 27 (7 September 1899), pp. 291–92. See also the article by Charles Denby, former minister to China, "The Rights of the United States in the Philippines," pp. 3263–68.

10. George S. Boutwell, *Imperialism and Anti-Imperialism*; Boutwell, *The War of Despotism in the Philippine Islands*; Boutwell, *Republic or Empire*; Boutwell to G. F. Hoar, 31 May 1899, Hoar Papers, M.H.S.; Boutwell, *The President's Policy*; *Report of the Fourth Annual Meeting of the New England Anti-Imperialist League, November 29, 1902*.

11. See, for example, the series of letters exchanged with Charles Eliot Norton, Norton Papers, Houghton Library, Harvard University.

12. H. H. Van Meter, *The Truth About the Philippines* . . . , pp. 431–32.

13. Schurz to William Ordway, 21 May 1900, Schurz Papers, L.C.; Henry F. Graff, ed., *American Imperialism and the Philippine Insurrection*, p. xv.

14. Storey to Edwin Burritt Smith, 27 June 1899, Storey Papers, L.C. Storey was also convinced that any sort of protectorate would be manipulated by U.S. investors to their pecuniary advantage.

15. Baltimore *Sun*, 1 April 1899. See also Storey to James B. Thayer, 3 November 1899, Storey Papers, L.C.

16. See Atkinson to Hoar, 26 February, 13 August, 15 August 1900, Hoar Papers, M.H.S.; Atkinson to Erving Winslow, 17 November 1900, Atkinson Papers, M.H.S.

17. Atkinson to Howard Leslie Smith, 20 May 1900, Atkinson to Fiske Warren, 30 November 1900, Atkinson Papers, M.H.S.; Williamson, *Edward Atkinson*, pp. 227–29.

18. Atkinson to Carnegie, 19 November 1900, Atkinson Papers, M.H.S.

19. Atkinson momentarily confused Harrison Gray Otis, volunteer officer of the 1st Brigade, with Elwell S. Otis.

20. Atkinson to Hoar, 9 May 1899, Hoar Papers, M.H.S. See also Atkinson to Attorney General of the United States, 5 May 1899, Open Letter of Edward Atkinson to Boston Press, 6 June 1899, Atkinson Papers, M.H.S.; *Literary Digest* 18 (13 May 1899), pp. 541–42; *Public Opinion* 26 (11 May 1899), pp. 583–84.

21. Atkinson to Hoar, 19 January 1901, Hoar Papers, M.H.S. See also Atkinson to Erving Winslow, 31 January 1901, Atkinson Papers, M.H.S.

22. *Literary Digest* 18 (13 May 1899), pp. 541–42. The Minneapolis *Times* and the Philadelphia *Times* declared that agitators of Atkinson's stripe were "responsible for much unnecessary loss of life in the Philippines" and should be jailed; whereas *The New York Times* suggested that Atkinson would be an ideal vice presidential candidate for that other leading "aguinaldist," William Jennings Bryan. *Public Opinion* 26 (11 May 1899), pp. 583–84; *The New York Times*, 12 January 1900.

23. See, for example, the editorial in the Indianapolis *Journal*, 19 October 1899.

24. Elting E. Morison, ed., *The Letters of Theodore Roosevelt*, 3:60; E. P. Oberholtzer, *A History of the United States Since the Civil War*, 5:592; Robert L. Beisner, *Twelve Against Empire*, p. 236; New York *Tribune*, 22 October 1900.

The Chicago *Tribune* and the Providence *Journal* were equally quick to pass the white feather in an effort to publicize their loyalty and devotion to "the national honor." Philip Kinsley, *The Chicago Tribune*, 3:330–31; *Public Opinion* 26 (16 February 1899), pp. 198–99; *Literary Digest* 19 (26 August 1899), pp. 241–42.

25. See *Puck*, 22 March, 19 April 1899, 29 May 1901.
26. *Judge*, 6 October 1900. The cartoonist was Grant Hamilton.
27. Published in Boston in 1903, this essay was first offered as a Memorial Day address at Burlington, Vermont.
28. Fred C. Chamberlin, *The Blow from Behind*, pp. 92, 98, 110, 214.
29. *Springfield Daily Republican*, 27 August 1899.
30. *Literary Digest* 19 (16 September 1899), pp. 336–37. Ex-governor John P. Altgeld of Illinois also spoke in praise of Aguinaldo and was similarly denounced for his "treasonous speech."
31. Some eighteen years later Lenin, in his famous tract, *Imperialism*, would dismiss the American anti-imperialists of the Spanish-American War period as "the last of the Mohicans of bourgeois democracy." Quoted by Samuel Sillen, "Dooley, Twain, and Imperialism," p. 7.
32. Morrison I. Swift, *Imperialism and Liberty*, pp. 293, 346–53, 436–37.
33. *Senate Doc.* No. 208, 56th Cong., 1st sess., Pt. 1, 74; PIR, Roll 72, File No. 1168.
34. General Otis believed that disloyal Americans were responsible for the initiation and duration of the war, and Captain John R. Taylor and other compilers of captured insurgent records were instructed by their superiors to give particular attention to documentary evidence respecting the relations of Aguinaldo and his American friends. See *Annual Report of Maj. Gen. E. S. Otis . . . August 31, 1899*; PIR, Record Group 126, File No. 1199, Record Group 350, Roll 5 (Taylor, "History," Vol. 3). See also *Compilation of Philippine Insurgent Records, I–Telegraphic Correspondence of Emilio Aguinaldo . . .* ; *Senate Doc.* No. 208, 56th Cong., 1st sess., Pt. 2, pp. 12–13.
35. It is the contention of John M. Gates that anti-imperialist activity not only gave support to the insurgents but "had an adverse effect on the morale of the [American] army." Gates, *Schoolbooks and Krags*, pp. 172–73.
36. The Thurston Rifles' Ladies' Auxiliary of Omaha sent a cable to Company L of the 1st Nebraska Regiment with the request: "Boys, don't re-enlist; insist on immediate discharge." Omaha *World-Herald*, 16 April 1899, cited in John R. Johnson, "Nebraska in the Spanish-American War and the Philippine Insurrection," pp. 284–85. Several League members made a momentary hero of the governor of the Dakota Territory who had denounced the war as a violation of the Declaration of Independence and requested McKinley to order home the Dakota volunteers. See *Public Opinion* 26 (April 1899), pp. 520–21.
37. Military censorship was usually too effective for "treasonable telegrams" to reach their recipients. For three allegedly typical telegrams urging volunteer regiments not to reenlist, see *Correspondence Relating to the War with Spain*, 2:973.

CHAPTER IV

1. See Theodore Roosevelt's speech at Oyster Bay, 4 July 1899, quoted in *Public Opinion* 27 (13 July 1899), p. 38.
2. Speeches of 11–18 October 1899 as reported in *Public Opinion* 27 (19, 26 October 1899), pp. 484–85; 515–16.
3. Elihu Root, *The Military and Colonial Policy of the United States*, pp. 43–47; 225–46.
4. In that speech Lodge sought to prove that our annexation of the Philippines was the logical culmination of the expansion of the American people and to analyze "the Asiatic mind." "Negotiations, concessions, promises, and hesitations" are

for the Asiatic "merely proofs of weakness, and tend only to encourage useless outbreaks, crimes, and disorders." *Cong. Record*, 56th Cong., 1st sess., pp. 2616–30.

5. *Cong. Record*, 55th Cong., 3d sess., pp. 493–503; 56th Cong., 1st sess., pp. 601–02, 712–14, 4278–4306; 57th Cong., 1st sess., pp. 5788–98.

6. See, for example, *Public Opinion* 26 (19 October 1899), pp. 483–84.

7. In an interview with the *Washington Post*, 5 February 1899, Bacon had set the course for the dissident Democrats in the early days of the war: "I will cheerfully vote all the money that may be necessary to carry on the war in the Philippines [even though] . . . I still maintain that we could have avoided a conflict with these people." *Washington Post*, 6 February 1899. See also George F. Hoar to Robert Treat Paine, 9 January 1901, Hoar Papers, M.H.S.

8. Robert L. Beisner exaggerates, however, when he suggests that the Democrats were anti-imperialists "largely out of ritualistic partisanship." Champ Clark and Edward Carmack lacked the eloquence of such mugwumps as Schurz and Storey, but their criticism was neither pro forma nor "ritualistic." Robert L. Beisner, "1898 and 1968: The Anti-Imperialists and the Doves," p. 192.

9. *Cong. Record*, 56th Cong., 1st Sess. (25 May 1900), pp. 6018–19. Morgan's opinions were applauded by McKinley's champions in the Senate, and the word went out from the administration that the Republican party in Alabama should offer no obstacle to his reelection.

10. *Cong. Record*, 55th Cong., 3d sess. (7 February 1899), pp. 1528–32, 57th Cong., 1st sess. (21 February 1902), pp. 2042–43; B. R. Tillman, "Bryan or McKinley," pp. 439–46.

11. See, for example, Williams' speech of 3 April 1900 reprinted by the Washington Anti-Imperialist League in pamphlet form as *Empire or Republic*.

12. Portions of senate speeches and public addresses by Carmack will be found in folders No. 53–58 and several scrapbooks in the E. W. Carmack Papers, Southern Historical Collection, University of North Carolina. See also *Cong. Record*, 57th Cong., 1st sess. (3 February 1902), pp. 1236–42; (31 May 1902), pp. 6129, 6137–39.

13. Perry Belmont, "Congress, the President and the Philippines," pp. 894–911. Olney offers an example of a commercial expansionist confused by partisanship. With the spring of 1900, Olney would change front and suggest that American ownership of the Philippines was economically disadvantageous. During the campaign of 1900 he pledged a measure of allegiance to the Philippine plank of the Democratic party. Richard Olney, "Growth of Our Foreign Policy," pp. 289–301; Ernest R. May, *American Imperialism*, p. 208; Gerald G. Eggert, *Richard Olney*, pp. 290–92.

14. John R. Johnson, "Nebraska in the Spanish-American War," p. 325.

15. See resolution of the Omaha branch of the Irish-American Union, *Omaha World Herald*, 28 October 1900, quoted in Johnson, "Nebraska in the Spanish-American War," p. 345.

16. See Champ Clark's speech to the House of Representatives, 5 February 1900, in which he repudiated the proposition that patriotism required support of "the President's Philippine policy—right or wrong." *Cong. Record*, 56th Cong., 1st sess., pp. 1518–27.

17. See, for example, Williams A. Williams, *The Tragedy of American Diplomacy*, p. 36; Leon Wolff, *Little Brown Brother*, p. 327.

18. Kirk H. Porter and Donald B. Johnson, *National Party Platforms, 1840 1960*, pp. 113, 124.

19. In William J. Pomeroy's opinion, the Democratic platform of 1900 was "the most concise statement of . . . those who then opposed expansion through territorial colonialism, but who favored expansion through those other forms of imperialist development, the protectorate and the sphere of influence." Pomeroy, *American Neo-Colonialism*, p. 114.

20. *The New York Times*, 6 July 1900, quoted by William F. Marina, "Opponents of Empire," p. 189.

21. The alternatives proposed by the Democratic and Republican platforms were succinctly summarized by *The Outlook*, a Congregational journal generally sympathetic to the foreign policy of the McKinley administration: "Those who believe that events have made us responsible for the protection of persons and property in the Philippines, and that we cannot escape that responsibility until a system of self-government is established in those islands . . . should vote for Mr. McKinley; while those who think that our duty was fulfilled when we expelled the oppressor, and that our duty for the future is confined to protecting the people from other foreign oppressors, should, on this issue, vote for Mr. Bryan." *The Outlook*, 3 November 1900.

22. Margaret Leech, *In the Days of McKinley*, p. 543. See also Maximo M. Kalaw, *The Case for the Filipinos*, p. 112; *The Nation* 71 (20 September 1900), p. 222; *Proceedings of the Twelfth Republican National Convention*, pp. 146–51.

23. John C. Spooner, *"Imperialism, A Forced and Fictitious Issue,"* pp. 7–9. See also W. A. Peffer, *Americanism and the Philippines*, pp. 125–44.

24. Boston *Journal*, 5–31 October 1900.

25. The latter rumor reached William Howard Taft in Manila, and he was sufficiently credulous to pass it on to Elihu Root. Taft to Root, 14 July 1900, Elihu Root Papers, L.C. See also Harry R. Lynn, "The Genesis of American Philippine Policy," p. 166.

26. William Jennings Bryan, *Bryan on Imperialism*, pp. 69–92; Marina, "Opponents of Empire," p. 190.

27. James McGurrin, *Bourke Cockran*, p. 207. See also article by Charles A. Towne in *The Outlook* 60 (20 October 1900), p. 494.

28. *Literary Digest* 21 (29 September 1900), p. 364; (20 October 1900), pp. 453–54.

29. For a retrospective analysis of the failure of the anti-imperialists significantly to influence Bryan's campaign or the election, see typed memorandum, "The A.I. League and the Democratic Campaign Committee," by Erving Winslow, in "Papers of the Anti-Imperialist League," Michigan Historical Collections, University of Michigan.

30. For a sample of anti-Bryan opinion by League members, see letters to the editor of *City and State*, 9–21 August 1900. Herbert Welsh, the editor, was himself a strong advocate of united anti-imperialist support for Bryan and had little patience with those who equated the intellectual limitations of Bryan with the criminal activity of McKinley. *City and State* 9 (1900), pp. 39, 92–139.

31. Frederic Bancroft and William A. Dunning, *The Reminiscences of Carl Schurz*, 3:447; C. F. Adams to Carl Schurz, 14 July 1900, Schurz to Edward M. Shepard. 7 October 1900, Schurz Papers, L.C.; Edward Atkinson to G. F. Hoar, 15 August 1900, Hoar Papers, M.H.S.

32. The conclusions of Thomas Bailey, "Was the Election of 1900 a Mandate on Imperialism?" pp. 43–52, have been contested by neither the "consensus historians" nor those of the "New Left." Daniel B. Schirmer attempts to dramatize an "alliance" between the mugwumps of the Anti-Imperialist League and the

plebeian followers of Bryan, but he stops short of attributing McKinley's victory to the electoral appeal of big business imperialism.

An interesting evaluation of the impact of the issue of imperialism on political allegiance in the state of Indiana will be found in Göran Rystad, *Ambiguous Imperialism*.

33. *Omaha World Herald*, 9 November 1900.

34. Dale H. Peeples, ''The Senate Debate on the Philippine Legislation of 1902,'' pp. 130, 176. Senator Carmack was one of the few Democratic senators to attack the theory of political apprenticeship: ''Freedom is the only schoolmaster that can teach the lessons of freedom. No people ever learned self-government under a tutor. . . . You might as well suppose that a horse can learn to think by bearing a philosopher upon his back.'' Ibid., p. 113.

35. *Cong. Record*, 57th Cong., 1st sess., p. 77; John C. Spooner to Lodge, 18 June 1902, Lodge Papers, M.H.S. The provision for the future establishment of a bicameral legislature, with the lower house elected by Christian and propertied Filipinos, was the work of Taft and Root. Lodge initially considered it ''a dangerous experiment'' undertaken ''too fast.'' Lodge to Taft, 7 July 1902, Lodge Papers, M.H.S.

36. *Cong. Record*, 57th Cong., 1st sess., p. 7735; Schurz to Oswald Garrison Villard, 4 July 1902, Villard Papers, Houghton Library, Harvard University.

37. Woodrow Wilson, ''The Ideals of America,'' pp. 721–34.

38. See *The Daily Voice*, 3 November 1900.

39. *Worker's Call*, 13 October 1900; John C. Appel, ''The Relationship of American Labor to United States Imperialism, 1895–1905,'' pp. 176–77.

40. *Literary Digest* 21 (3 November 1900), p. 518. See also Chicago *Social Democratic Herald*, 15 June 1901, quoted in Richard A. Matré, ''The Chicago Press and Imperialism, 1899–1902,'' p. 199.

41. See, for example, Ronald Radosh, ''American Labor and the Anti-Imperialist Movement,'' pp. 91–100. Radosh's contentions are well answered by Horace B. Davies in a ''Note'' in the same issue of *Science and Society*, pp. 100–104.

CHAPTER V

1. Daniel B. Schirmer, *Republic or Empire*, p. 164; Thomas J. McCormick, ''Insular Imperialism and the Open Door,'' pp. 155–69. See also Walter LaFeber, *The New Empire*, pp. 407–17; Michael Onorato, ''The United States and the Philippine Independence Movement,'' p. 3.

2. See William J. Pomeroy, *American Neo-Colonialism*, p. 100.

3. Two recent articles by William H. Becker offer a persuasive correction of the tendency of certain students to exaggerate the number and influence of businesses interested in foreign market expansion at the turn of the century: ''American Manufacturers and Foreign Markets, 1870–1900''; and ''Foreign Markets for Iron and Steel, 1893–1913.''

4. There was in fact no appreciable trade between the Philippine Islands and China *in non-Philippine goods* prior to World War I. See, for example, C. R. Edwards to J. V. Graff, 6 February 1910, Bureau of Insular Affairs, No. 3432–15.

5. John Barrett, ''The Value of the Philippines,'' quoted in *American Monthly Review of Reviews* 20 (August 1899), p. 205. See also ''the China market argument'' of the Portland *Oregonian*, 9 January, 16 February 1900, and of R. Van Bergen in his article, ''Expansion Unavoidable,'' p. 885.

The combined import and export trade of the United States with China in 1898 amounted to only 2 percent of its total foreign trade. A. Whitney Griswold, *The Far Eastern Policy of the United States*, p. 24.

6. *Public Opinion* 29 (30 August 1900), pp. 265–66. See also Richard Olney, "Growth of Our Foreign Policy," pp. 289–301; Frank Dester, "Will the Philippines Pay?" pp. 465–70.

7. Andrew Carnegie, "Americanism *Versus* Imperialism," pp. 1–13.

8. Andrew Carnegie, "The Opportunity of the United States," pp. 606–12.

9. Carnegie to Welsh, 12 February 1903. Carnegie Papers, L.C.

10. *The Age of Steel*, 11 February, 12 August 1899; *The Literary Digest* 20 (21 April 1900), p. 487.

11. *The Railroad Gazette* 31–33 (12 May 1899; 2 November 1900; 8 February, 3 May 1901).

12. *The Wall Street Journal*, 6 February, 4 March, 7 March 1899.

13. *The Journal of Commerce* was the unofficial spokesman of the New York State Chamber of Commerce. It supported the administration and saw the "insurrection" as a disagreeable nuisance that discouraged "the orderly progress of the Filipino people in the path of modern civilization" (18 April 1902).

14. *The Commercial Bulletin*, 14 January, 4 March, 11 November 1899; 2 January, 6 January, 11 August 1900; 6 April 1901.

15. Charles A. Conant, *The United States in the Orient*, pp. 3–11; Conant, "The Economic Future of the Philippines," pp. 366–71. See also Conant, "The Economic Basis of 'Imperialism,' " pp. 326–40.

16. *The Railroad Gazette* 33 (1901), pp. 94–95; Annual Report of the Secretary of War to the President, Annual Reports of the War Department, 1901.

17. See William H. Taft, "Address Delivered Before the Union Reading College," Taft Papers, L.C.; *Statistical Bulletin No. 3 of the Philippine Islands*, p. 126.

18. Harry R. Lynn, "The Genesis of America's Philippine Policy," p. 255.

19. See Taft, "Address Delivered Before the Union Reading College," p. 75; James A. LeRoy, "Race Prejudice in the Philippines," p. 105.

20. Shirley Jenkins, *American Economic Policy Toward the Philippines*, p. 32.

21. *Cong. Record*, 57th Cong., 1st sess. (24 February 1902), p. 2108.

22. See *The Journal of Commerce and Commercial Bulletin*, 18 April 1902.

23. See, for example, John C. Appel, "The Relationship of Labor to United States Imperialism," pp. 139–59, 250–60; Delber L. McKee, "Samuel Gompers, the A. F. of L., and Imperialism, 1895–1900," pp. 187–99. For a contrary judgment, see William G. Whitaker, "Samuel Gompers, Anti-Imperialist," pp. 429–55.

24. Scrapbook, 1:132, Gompers Papers, L.C.; Boston *Globe*, 20 March 1899.

25. *The American Federationist*, September 1901; March 1902. Cf. Gompers' editorial of September 1901, "Chinese Must Be Barred," with that of Sam L. Leffingwell on the dangers of militarism for the Labor movement in the issue of April 1900.

26. When a resolution in behalf of a negotiated peace and Philippine independence had been introduced earlier at the annual state convention of the New Jersey Federation of Labor, it had precipitated fistfights as well as debate. One delegate charged that the resolution insulted his patriotism; another proclaimed Aguinaldo an upstart tyrant who deserved a good licking. *National Labor Standard*, 31 August 1899; Appel, "Relationship of Labor to United States Imperialism," p. 185.

27. *Indianapolis Journal*, 15 October 1900, as quoted by Appel, "Relationship of Labor to United States Imperialism," p. 185.

28. *Proceedings of the Knights of Labor General Assembly, Boston, Novem-*

ber 14–23, 1899, p. 80; Appel, "Relationship of Labor to United States Imperialism," pp. 178–79, 216.

29. *Cigar Makers' Journal*, April 1899, p. 11.

30. *National Labor Standard*, 27 April, 10 August 1899; 27 September 1900; 2 May, 23 May, 1901.

31. *Public Opinion* 26 (2 March 1899), pp. 261–62; Appel, "Relationship of Labor to United States Imperialism," pp. 227–34.

32. *The Journal of the Knights of Labor* did offer two editorials on "The Philippine Horrors" in April 1902, demanding that the "perpetrators of the alleged barbarities be sought out and punished." Cited in Appel, "Relationship of Labor to United States Imperialism," p. 337.

33. This conclusion follows closely the judgment of Appel, "Relationship of Labor to United States Imperialism," pp. 218, 361, and McKee, "Samuel Gompers, the A. F. of L., and Imperialism," p. 199.

34. The voice of Agricultural Labor in the debate over American policy in the Philippines was small and confused, and its presumed spokesmen comparatively inarticulate on the issue of colonialism and military pacification. Farmers who grew products that would suffer from Philippine competition were more likely to be anti-imperialist, but evidence about the response of Agricultural Labor is too limited to be coerced into any pattern. A piece of evidence cited by the Anti-Imperialist League was a poll conducted in May 1899 by *Farm and Home*, an agricultural journal published in Chicago. Its readers were asked to reply to the question, "Should the Filipinos be held in subjugation to the United States, or should they be allowed to form an independent government?" The editor reported that 20,000 readers had replied and over 12,000 had voted in favor of Philippine independence. The editor, however, was Herbert Myrick of Chicago, a strong anti-imperialist, and the circulation of *Farm and Home* makes the figure of 20,000 replies somewhat remarkable. *The Nation* 69 (17 August 1899), p. 121; William F. Marina, "Opponents of Empire," pp. 124–26. Most other agricultural papers seem to have given little space to the Philippines, although the *American Agriculturalist*, the *Nebraska Farmer*, the *Planter and Sugar Manufacturer*, and the *Northwest Miller* offered editorial opposition to American retention of the Philippines in the winter of 1898–99. John R. Johnson, "Nebraska in the Spanish-American War and the Philippine Insurrection," p. 349; A. M. Barnes, "American Intervention in Cuba and the Annexation of the Philippines," p. 390.

CHAPTER VI

1. For representative examples of editorial attack and defense, see *The Literary Digest* 20 (14 April 1900), pp. 460–62. *The Catholic News*, the *Ave Maria*, and the Baltimore *Catholic Mirror* were perhaps the most stalwart defenders of the friars.

2. Interview in *The Outlook*, 26 August 1899.

3. *The Literary Digest* 20 (10 February 1900), p. 188. Similar editorials were offered by *The Church News* of Washington and *The Catholic News* of New York.

4. *The Literary Digest* 19 (30 September 1899), pp. 409–10. It was the opinion of *The Pilot* that the 1st Colorado Company from Cripple Creek had disembarked at San Francisco with "enough church goods to fill a large store." Cited in Leon Wolff, *Little Brown Brother*, p. 254.

5. *The Literary Digest* 19 (30 September 1899), pp. 409–10; Frank T. Reuter, *Catholic Influence on American Colonial Policy, 1898–1904*, pp. 71, 73, 85, 165.

6. The strongest journalistic defender of the Republican administration and its policy of colonial expansion was the editor of *The Catholic World*.

7. Ireland was himself anxious that the election of 1900 not assume a sectarian character. He was able, with the help of Bellamy and Maria Storer, to obtain from the Vatican a statement sufficiently friendly to American ownership of the Philippines to prevent Catholic supporters of Bryan from associating expansion with anti-Catholicism. J. T. Farrell, "Background of the 1902 Taft Mission to Rome, I," pp. 1–32.

8. Ireland to D. J. O'Connell, 11 May 1898, as quoted in J. T. Farrell, "Archbishop Ireland and Manifest Destiny," p. 295; Rochester *Union and Advertiser*, 4 October 1900; New York *Herald*, 10 October 1900.

9. Springfield *Republican*, 1 May 1899.

10. Rev. Father Joseph Algué, "The Philippine Question," pp. 660–63.

11. These journals may be classified as follows: strong supporters—*Christian Work*, *The Baptist Union*, *The Missionary Herald*, *The Methodist Review*, *The Journal and Messenger*, *The Outlook*, *The Evangelist* (Presbyterian), *The Advance* (Congregationalist); moderate supporters—*The Christian Advocate* (Methodist), *The Watchman* (Baptist); neutral—*The Christian Intelligencer*, *The North and West*; dissenters—*Friends' Intelligencer and Journal*, *The Observer*.

12. Robert E. Bisbee, "Why I Oppose Our Philippine Policy," pp. 113–18.

13. The following ministers were among the more prominent and articulate clerical dissenters: Charles G. Ames, Isaac M. Atwood, A. A. Berle, Robert E. Bisbee, Charles F. Dole, E. Winchester Donald, William H. P. Faunce, Paul R. Frothingham, Frank O. Hall, Scott F. Hersey, Robert J. Johnson, A. N. Littlejohn, George C. Lorimer, Joseph May, Daniel Merriman, Charles H. Parkhurst, Leighton Parks, Francis H. Rowley, B. F. Trueblood, and Henry Van Dyke. Over a third were Unitarian pastors, and the Unitarian Church in New England was closely associated with anti-imperialist protest.

14. See, for example, the sermon of Henry Van Dyke, "The American Birthright and the Philippine Pottage," pp. 1579–85; Joseph May, *The Peril of Our Republic*; *The Moral and Religious Aspect of the So-Called Imperial Policy*, pamphlet of the New England Anti-Imperialist League; Address of A. A. Berle, in *Report of the Third Annual Meeting of the New England Anti-Imperialist League, November 30, 1901*, p. 30; Freeman Stewart, "The Preservation of the Republic," pp. 565–77.

15. *Ministers' Meeting to Protest Against the Atrocities in the Philippines*, pamphlet of the New England Anti-Imperialist League. The rabbi was Charles Fleischner.

16. Leighton Parks, *Christian Expansion*, pp. 12–16, 21–30.

17. *The Outlook*, 23 January 1899; 15, 22, 29 September, 10 November, 15 December 1900; 9 February 1901; 31 May 1902.

18. *The Advance*, 26 January, 23 February, 9 March, 13 April, 27 April 1899; 11 October, 8 November 1900; 8 May, 15 May, 10 July 1902.

19. Randolph H. McKim, "Religious Reconstruction in Our New Possessions," p. 505; Alice Byram Condict, *Old Glory and the Gospel in the Philippines*, pp. 17, 119; *The Independent*, 28 December 1899; *The Watchman*, 10 February 1901; *The Christian Advocate*, 22 May 1902.

20. *The Christian Advocate*, 9 February, 23 February 1899; 12 July, 11 October 1900; 31 January 1901; 1 May, 10 July 1902; *Central Christian Advocate*, 4 June 1902.

21. *The Literary Digest* 19 (9 September 1899), p. 317; *Public Opinion* 27, p. 292.

22. *The Watchman*, 20 July 1899.

23. *The Advance*, 31 August 1899.

24. *The Watchman*, 5 July 1900.
25. Josiah Strong, *Expansion Under New World-Conditions*, p. 298. See also ibid., pp. 288–95.
26. MacQueen to E. W. Carmack, 6 May 1902, Carmack Papers, University of North Carolina.
27. *The Advance* informed its readers that it had decided not to mention "unsavory details," for to publicize them was "a questionable measure for public health." *The Advance* 43 (3 April 1902), p. 428.
28. *The Woman's Journal*, 2 June 1900.
29. The photograph illustrated an article in *Justice* by William E. Johnson, correspondent of several Prohibitionist journals in the Middle West. Cited in *City and State* 9 (25 October 1900), p. 262.
30. *City and State*, 20 March 1902. Bishop Henry Potter, once the foremost Episcopalian anti-imperialist, had already recanted. After a trip to the Orient, Potter proclaimed that the Christian obligation of the United States was to bring to the Orientals "what we know as civilization and give them the opportunity to adopt it." *The Independent* 52 (19 March 1900), p. 787.
31. *The Watchman*, 10 July 1902.

CHAPTER VII

1. Albert J. Beveridge, "The American Soldier in the Philippines," *Saturday Evening Post*, 17 March 1900, as quoted in *Public Opinion* 28 (22 March 1900), pp. 359–60.
2. Considering the little information available respecting the career of Aguinaldo, it is remarkable how quickly he was characterized by expansionists and anti-imperialists alike. The cartoon portraiture displayed in newspaper and magazine issues of February 1899 would suffer little change over the next three years. Anti-imperialist cartoonists portrayed him as a dwarf version of Booker T. Washington reading with approval the American Declaration of Independence. In expansionist papers, he was usually portrayed as a half-naked aborigine with his bolo aimed at symbolic representations of liberty and civilization. See cartoons reprinted in *The Literary Digest* 18 (1899), pp. 141, 180, 216, 240, 260, 331.
3. Cited in Leon Wolff, *Little Brown Brother*, p. 302.
4. *The New York Times*, 6, 7 February 1899. The Washington *Post*, 10 February 1899, insisted that the Filipinos must be "forced to observe even if they could not comprehend, the practices of civilization." For both papers, Aguinaldo was a bandit-chieftain, swollen with "simian vanity."
5. John Foreman, "Spain and the Philippine Islands," pp. 20–33.
6. John Barrett, "The Problem of the Philippines," pp. 259–67; Charles Denby, "Shall We Keep the Philippines," pp. 278–81; Arthur Stanley Riggs, "A Letter from the Philippines," pp. 256–66. See also Samuel W. Belford, "Chinese Exclusion from the Philippines," p. 450; "The Native Population of the Philippines," *American Monthly Review of Reviews* 19 (1899), pp. 308–12; Ruds Virchow, "The Peopling of the Philippines," p. 518; *The Nation* 81 (6 December 1900), p. 435.
7. Schurman returned to the United States in August 1899, and in his slow progress across the country granted innumerable interviews. On each occasion he proclaimed the Filipinos' "present incapacity" for self-government. Kenneth E. Hendrickson, Jr., "Reluctant Expansionist," pp. 405–21.
8. Dean C. Worcester, one of the members of the Schurman Commission, published in the same month an article in *Harper's Weekly* expanding upon the sins

and incapacities of Aguinaldo and his "alleged government." *Harper's Weekly*, 18 November 1899. Although there was agreement that Aguinaldo was not a true representative of the Filipino "people," his critics appeared uncertain whether to denounce him as a "foolish popinjay" or as a blood-thirsty tyrant. For some he was a monkey man or rascally Sambo; others insisted he was the personification of barbarism and possessed the ability to terrorize whole provinces. See, for example, *The New York Times*, 6 February 1899; the Louisville *Courier-Journal*, 26 November 1899; Charles Denby, "Some Remarks on a 'Filipino Point of View,' " p. 9.

9. See *Report of The Philippine Commission*, particularly 1:181–82; Philip W. Kennedy, "The Concept of Racial Superiority and United States Imperialism, 1890–1910," pp. 56–58; Josiah Strong, *Expansion Under New World-Conditions*, pp. 293–94.

William Howard Taft, though suspected by many army officers of being unduly sympathetic with the Filipinos, held very similar beliefs. He informed Elihu Root that "the dishonesty of this race" was "the superlative of the quality of official corruption that prevails in the Orient anywhere." Taft to Root, 1 July 1900, Root Papers, L.C.

10. In the view of the Portland *Oregonian*, 6 August 1900, imperialism found sufficient justification in its "efficiency." It was "the rule of those who are fittest to rule, and therefore who ought to rule."

11. The Chicago *Times-Herald*, 7 February 1899, expressed the same opinion more bluntly: "The Lord made Anglo-Saxons to make poor natives hump."

12. Roosevelt to W. A. Guild, 14 April 1900, Roosevelt Papers, L.C.; Kennedy, "The Concept of Racial Superiority," p. 42; Alfred T. Mahan, "The Transvaal and the Philippines," pp. 289–91. See also "The Future of Inferior Races," *Gunter's Magazine* 17 (August 1899), p. 114; Amos K. Fiske, "Some Consecrated Fallacies," pp. 821–28. The Seattle *Times* believed that the doctrine of "the survival of the fittest" both required and justified the Philippine-American War: "True this war may mean the disappearance of a race under the slow process of assimilation, but it does mean above everything else, the survival of the fittest." Seattle *Times*, 20 January 1900, quoted by Edward H. Loy, "Editorial Opinion and American Imperialism," p. 218.

13. Considering the long history and nature of White-Indian relations, there were surprisingly few comparisons made between the Filipino and the American Indian. The Tacoma *Daily Ledger*, 22 April 1902, and a few other Republican papers, compared the battle treachery of the Filipino guerrilla with that of the Apache, but most advocates of American Philippine policy found the skin tone of the Filipinos more important than their military tactics when searching for racial comparisons.

14. Whitelaw Reid, *Problems of Expansion as Considered in Papers and Addresses*, pp. 131, 149; New York *Tribune*, 28 January 1903. The sometime expansionist editor of the Louisville *Courier-Journal*, Henry B. Watterson, believed that American expansion would inject a new vitality into the bloodstream of the caucasian American, and on one occasion identified the components of the Filipino population as "injun, nigger, beggar—man, thief—'both mongrel, puppy, whelp and hound, and cur of low degree.' " Cited in Wolff, *Little Brown Brother*, p. 304.

15. Peter H. King, "The White Man's Burden," p. 147.

16. Walter Johnson, *William Allen White's America*, p. 111.

17. See, for example, E. L. Godkin, "The Conditions of Good Colonial Government," p. 190.

18. See Ernest Crosby's parody in his collection, *Swords and Plowshares*, pp. 33–34. Crosby and Freeman Stewart were among the anti-imperialists who di-

rectly attacked the theories and arguments of Social Darwinism. See Crosby's contribution to a symposium on "The Philippine Question" in *The Arena*, pp. 10–11, and Freeman Stewart, "The Preservation of the Republic," pp. 565–77.

19. *Cong. Record*, 56th Cong., 1st sess., pp. 4278–4306 (17 April 1900). See also Hoar to Susan D. Anthony, 14 March 1900, Hoar Papers, M.H.S.

20. Springfield *Republican*, 25 April 1899. See also editorial of 5 September 1900 relating racist violence in America to the policy of "force and blood" in the Philippines.

21. George P. Marks, III, was the first scholar to investigate the editorial reaction of the black press to American colonialism. In a path-breaking essay of 1951, he concentrated on Negro papers opposed to the Philippine-American War and offered the judgment that twenty-six Negro papers opposed the war. Four of the papers listed by Marks—the Indianapolis *Recorder*, the Washington *Bee*, the Washington *Colored American*, and the New York *Age*—moved to a "pro" or neutral stance by the summer of 1900. George P. Marks, III, "Opposition of Negro Newspapers to American Philippine Policy, 1899–1900," pp. 1–25. Two decades later, Marks expanded this essay in *The Black Press Views American Imperialism*. In the latter work, Marks cites twelve Negro papers that were, on balance, favorable to McKinley's Philippine policy, twenty that were strongly opposed, and five that took a neutral or ambivalent position.

The most recent analysis of black response to insular imperialism is Willard B. Gatewood, Jr., *Black Americans and the White Man's Burden, 1898–1903*. Although some of its judgments are exaggerated, it is a valuable study based on a wide variety of source materials.

22. The Republican editor of the *Planet* did give McKinley and his party its reluctant endorsement in the campaign of 1900.

23. Quoted by Marks, "Opposition of Negro Newspapers," pp. 8, 21.

24. Exceptions to this reluctance were the *Broad Ax* and the Charlotte *Star of Zion*. Marks, "Opposition of Negro Newspapers," pp. 10–11, 15.

25. *The American Citizen*, 28 April 1899, as cited in Marks, "Opposition of Negro Newspapers," p. 7.

Mrs. Jefferson Davis briefly regained the attention of the public in January 1900 with an article in *The Arena*. According to Mrs. Davis, "the most serious objection to making the Philippines American territory" was that "three-fourths of the population is made up of negroes." Mrs. Jefferson Davis, "Why We Do Not Want the Philippines," pp. 1–14.

26. See, for example, Cleveland *Gazette*, 29 September, 13 October 1900.

27. See Marks, *The Black Press Views American Imperialism*, pp. 113, 126. *The Savannah Tribune* of 7 March 1900 quoted and apparently endorsed the enthusiasm of F. H. Crumbley, a black captain in the Forty-ninth Volunteer Infantry, respecting the value of the Philippines for the United States and the American Negro: "The young colored men and women of Christian education" would find splendid opportunities for missionary work and "every opening for the Negro in business. . . ."

28. W. S. Scarborough, "The Negro and Our New Possessions," p. 344. See also Fortune's editorial lament for the death of General Henry W. Lawton, "killed by a Filipino sharpshooter." New York *Age*, 4 January 1900.

29. Washington *Colored American*, 13 May, 16 September 1899; Marvin E. Fletcher, "The Negro Soldier and the United States Army, 1891–1917," p. 270. The Washington paper advocated independence for the Filipinos and commendation for the black soldiers engaged in their subjugation.

30. Washington *Colored American*, 16, 23 September 1899, cited in Willard

B. Gatewood, Jr., *"Smoked Yankees" and the Struggle for Empire*, p. 237. A year later its "racial sympathies" for the Filipino had diminished. Another editor quoted with approval the opinion of Captain W. H. Jackson that "all the enemies of the U.S. government look alike to us." *Colored American Magazine* 1 (August 1900), p. 149. See also the Indianapolis *Freeman*, 1 July 1899.

31. *The Guardian* began publication in November 1901 and, though strongly anti-imperialist, had only limited opportunity to reflect Negro attitudes in Boston.

32. Washington *Colored American*, 13 July 1901, cited in Gatewood, *"Smoked Yankees,"* p. 300.

33. *Voice of Missions* 6 (1 May 1899), pp. 2, 8 (1 October 1900), p. 3, cited in Willard B. Gatewood, Jr., "Black Americans and the Quest for Empire, 1898–1903," pp. 558–59; Marks, "Opposition of Negro Newspapers," pp. 15–16.

34. Marks, "Opposition of Negro Newspapers," pp. 10, 17.

35. Daniel B. Schirmer, *Republic or Empire*, pp. 15, 214–15. Scott was subsequently appointed as one of the numerous vice presidents of the New England Anti-Imperialist League, the only black man to serve as an official of any branch of the Anti-Imperialist League.

36. See editorials of the Richmond *Planet* and of Calvin Chase, Republican editor of the Washington *Bee*, for October 1900. The National Democratic League, headed by a black lawyer, George E. Taylor, received little publicity or attention during the campaign. Marks, "Opposition of Negro Newspapers," p. 22.

37. See Boston *Evening Transcript*, 19 July 1899; Schirmer, *Republic or Empire*, p. 172. The Anacostia Club of Indianapolis sent McKinley similar assurances. Marks, *The Black Press Views American Imperialism*, pp. 126–27.

38. Kelly Miller, "The Effect of Imperialism upon the Negro Race," pp. 87–91; Miller to G. F. Hoar, 3 February 1900, Hoar Papers, M.H.S.

39. Frederick L. McGhee, "Another View," pp. 92–96; Marks, "Opposition of Negro Newspapers," p. 20.

40. Boston *Post*, 16, 17 July 1899.

41. A more independent Negro effort, "The National Negro Anti-Expansion, Anti-Imperialist, and Anti-Trust and Anti-Lynching League," with headquarters in Cairo, Illinois, had similar aims and met with a similar fate. It had a paper existence in 1899–1900 and apparently dissolved after the election of 1900.

42. In the four regiments of Negro regulars, there were twenty-nine desertions, but only nine of these men defected to the Filipinos. Regimental Records, Record Group No. 94, National Archives; M. C. Robinson and F. H. Schubert, "David Fagan," pp. 68–83.

43. *Army and Navy Journal* 37 (November 1899), p. 259; 38 (13 April 1901), p. 797; letter "From a Negro Soldier in Manila," quoted in Richmond *Planet*, 14 October 1899; letter from Chaplain T. G. Steward to *The Independent* 52 (1 February 1900), pp. 312–14; letter from Patrick Mason in Cleveland *Gazette*, 29 September 1900; Record Group No. 391, National Archives.

44. See the small sample of letters from officers of the Twenty-fifth U.S. Infantry Regiment in the U.S. Army Military History Research Collection, Carlisle Barracks, especially "William A. Batson Papers" and "Samuel P. Lyon Papers"; Records of Twenty-fourth and Twenty-fifth U.S. Infantry Regiments, Old Military Division, National Archives; Fletcher, "The Negro Soldier and the United States Army," pp. 158–60; Gatewood, *"Smoked Yankees,"* pp. 246–316; Charles Steward, "Manila and Its Opportunities," p. 255; Rienzi B. Lemus, "The Enlisted Man in Action," pp. 46–54; James Cleland Hamilton, "The Negro as Soldier," *Anglo-American Magazine*, August 1899 as quoted in *Public Opinion* 27 (17 August 1899), p. 198; soldier letters in Washington *Bee*, April 1899–December 1901.

45. *The Freeman*, 18 November 1899, cited in Gatewood, *"Smoked Yankees,"* pp. 247–48.

46. Lemus, "The Enlisted Man in Action," p. 51. The black sergeant of another company expressed disappointment that his friends at home were not more enthusiastic about a struggle in which the Negro soldier "risked the sacrifice of life and health." Letter of Michael H. Robinson, Co. F, 25th U.S. Infantry, to *The Colored American*, Washington, 17 March 1900, cited in Gatewood, *"Smoked Yankees,"* p. 264.

47. AGO No. 335956; Fletcher, "The Negro Soldier and the United States Army," p. 271. It was quite literally Fagan's head that was brought to Bongabong in December 1901 after he had been ambushed by some Filipino bandits. See Diary of Frederick M. Presher, 1st U.S. Cavalry, for 13 December 1901, U.S. Army Military History Research Collection, Carlisle Barracks.

48. John W. Ganzhorn, *I've Killed Men*, pp. 172–73.

49. One of these poster appeals was reprinted in the Richmond *Planet*, 11 November 1899. It urged "Negritos Americanos" not to be the instruments of their white master's ambition to conquer another "people of color." Cited in Gatewood, *"Smoked Yankees,"* p. 15.

50. Taft to Root, 27 April 1901, Root Papers, L.C. See also "Reminiscences of James A. LeRoy" (for the year 1901), Michigan Historical Collections, University of Michigan; Stephen Bonsal, "The Negro Soldier in War and Peace," pp. 321–27.

51. "Race Discrimination in the Philippines," *The Independent* 54 (13 February 1902), pp. 416–17; Mathew F. Steel, "The 'Color Line' in the Army," p. 326.

52. *Cong. Record*, 57th Cong., 1st sess. (7 May 1902), p. 5103; Scarborough, "The Negro and Our New Possessions," pp. 340–50; A. R. Abbot, "The Employment of Negroes in the Philippines," pp. 196–201; J. O. Baylen and J. H. Moore, "Senator John Tyler Morgan and Negro Colonization in the Philippines," pp. 65–73. See also W. S. Scarborough, *The Educated Negro and His Mission*.

CHAPTER VIII

1. See for example, Charles W. Eliot, "Political Principles and Tendencies," pp. 459–60. See also the interesting letter from Eliot to Jacob Gould Schurman, 20 May 1902, copy, Letter Book No. 92, Eliot Papers, Harvard University Archives. In that letter, Eliot declared—more explicitly than in his public addresses—that America's claim of sovereignty over the Philippines "was from the beginning a plain piece of stupidity."

2. David Starr Jordan to Editor of *The Outlook*, 27 April 1899, McKinley Papers, L.C. (enclosed with letter from Lyman Abbott to William McKinley); David Starr Jordan, *Imperial Democracy*, pp. 63–81, 172, 267–74.

3. Charles Kendall Adams, president of the University of Wisconsin, was a dedicated expansionist but contributed only a single public declaration in defense of McKinley's Philippine policy. Charles Kendall Adams, "Colonies and Other Dependencies," pp. 33–46.

4. Kenneth E. Hendrickson, "Reluctant Expansionist," pp. 405–21.

5. Jacob Gould Schurman, *Philippine Affairs*, pp. 14, 107–09. See also Schurman's letter to Charles W. Eliot, 22 April 1902, Eliot Papers, Harvard University Archives, in which he sought to prove that his sympathies "have always been with the ideals and aims of the anti-imperialists."

6. Worcester Papers, Special Collections, University of Michigan. David Prescott Barrows, a California professor of anthropology, was with Worcester, one of the few academics to serve as a colonial officer in the Philippines.

7. Franklin Henry Giddings, *Democracy and Empire*, pp. 270–90.

8. See Fiske Warren Diary excerpts, Moorfield Storey Papers, Special Folder, M.H.S.; congressional petition signed by thirty-six professors from the University of Chicago, *Senate Doc*. No. 166, 57th Cong., 1st sess., pp. 1–11.

9. C. E. Norton to E. L. Godkin, 2 August 1899, 31 December 1901, Godkin Papers, Houghton Library, Harvard University.

10. Correspondence between C. E. Norton and E. L. Godkin for 1899 and 1901, Godkin Papers, Houghton Library, Harvard University; P. H. King, "The White Man's Burden," pp. 127–65.

11. Thomas E. Will, "Why I Am Opposed to Imperialism," pp. 8–9; George P. Fisher, "The Question of the Philippines," pp. 8–10; J. L. Laughlin, "Patriotism and Imperialism."

12. Frederick Merk, *Manifest Destiny and Mission in American History*, pp. 238–45; John W. Burgess, "The Decision of the Supreme Court in the Insular Cases," pp. 486–504; J. C. Guffin, "Evolution versus Imperialism," pp. 141–48; William Graham Sumner, *The Conquest of the United States by Spain*.

13. Sumner, *The Conquest of the United States by Spain*, p. 9.

14. Lewis G. Janes, *Our Nation's Peril*, pp. 6–12.

15. Felix Adler, "The Philippine War," pp. 387–99.

16. Robert L. Beisner, "1898 and 1968: The Anti-Imperialists and the Doves," pp. 198–210; William James to Carl Schurz, 16 March 1900, Schurz Papers, L.C.; William James to Charles F. Adams, Jr., 29 December 1898, Charles F. Adams Papers, M.H.S.; William James to G. Stanley Hall, 14 May 1900, William James to F. C. S. Schiller, 6 August 1902, William James Papers, Houghton Library, Harvard University.

17. See, for example, Boston *Evening Transcript*, 4 March, 15 April 1899.

18. Hermann E. von Holst, "Some Expansionist Inconsistencies and False Analogies," pp. 339–45; F. Spencer Baldwin, "Some Gains from Expansion," pp. 570–75; James Bradley Thayer, *Our New Possessions*; Henry Pratt Judson, "Our Federal Constitution and the Government of Tropical Territories," pp. 67–75; *The Literary Digest* 18 (7 January 1899), pp. 1–2, 22 (20 April 1901), pp. 467–68; Theodore S. Woolsey, "The Government of Dependencies," pp. 6–8; *The Nation* 68 (12 April 1899), p. 292; Theodore S. Woolsey, "The Legal Aspects of Aguinaldo's Capture," pp. 855–59.

19. W. C. Ford, ed., *Letters of Henry Adams*, 2:202–08; W. Cameron Forbes, *The Philippine Islands*, 2:568–69; *The Literary Digest* 20 (6 January 1900), p. 24; Henry Cabot Lodge to James Ford Rhodes, 6 August 1900, Lodge Papers, M.H.S.; George Frisbie Hoar to Goldwyn Smith, 13 July 1902, Hoar Papers, M.H.S.; James Morton Callahan, *American Relations in the Pacific and the Far East, 1784–1900*, p. 154.

20. Simeon E. Baldwin, "The Constitutional Questions Incident to the Acquisition and Government by the United States of Island Territories," pp. 315–43.

21. See, for example, "Observations" of Julia Ward Howe in Boston *Sunday Herald*, 22 January 1900; Julian Hawthorne, "A Side Issue of Expansion," pp. 441–43.

22. Finley Peter Dunne, *Mr. Dooley in the Hearts of His Countrymen*, p. 6; *The Literary Digest* 18 (11 February 1899), p. 155.

23. New York *Herald*, 16 October 1900; William M. Gibson, "Mark Twain and Howells," *The New England Quarterly* 20 (1947), pp. 443–60.

24. See, for example, "A Salutation-Speech from the Nineteenth Century to the Twentieth," 31 December 1900, which Twain sent the New York *Herald*, cited in Gibson, "Mark Twain and Howells," pp. 450–51.

25. *North American Review* 17 (February 1901), pp. 161–76.

26. The editor of *Puck* insisted that the essay was not the product of Mark Twain but that of "a certain peevish, dyspeptic Mr. Clemens with a bad case of ingrowing ethics." *Puck* 49 (13 March 1901).

27. Mark Twain, "A Defence of General Funston," pp. 613–18.

28. *The New York Times*, 15 February 1899, reprinted in Ernest Crosby, *Swords and Plowshares*, pp. 33–34. Crosby and other parodists overlooked the fact that if Kipling's poem was an example of Anglo-Saxon racism and a bid for America to join the British in performing civilization's mission in foreign lands, it was also a warning that the path of duty would prove hard and difficult. Their partial misinterpretation of Kipling's verses is analyzed with skill in E. Berkeley Tompkins, *Anti-Imperialism in the United States*, pp. 236–39.

29. See the anthology of anti-imperialist verse published by the New England Anti-Imperialist League, *Liberty Poems*; Fred Harvey Harrington, "Literary Aspects of American Anti-Imperialism, 1898–1902," pp. 651–59; William Lloyd Garrison, *The Nation's Shame*; James J. Dooling, *Rhymes Without Treason*.

30. *Atlantic Monthly* 85 (May 1900), pp. 593–98. See also Harrington, "Literary Aspects of American Anti-Imperialism," pp. 651–53.

31. *Atlantic Monthly* 87 (February 1901), p. 288.

32. Henry B. Fuller, *The New Flag*.

33. Garrison, *The Nation's Shame*.

34. Edgar Lee Masters, *Spoon River Anthology*, pp. 185–86.

35. *The American Monthly Review of Reviews* 20 (September 1899), pp. 264–65. See also ibid. 19 (March 1899), p. 264, 26 (July 1902), pp. 8–9; Albert Shaw, "From a Republican Standpoint," p. 445.

36. *The Nation* 68 (18 May 1899), pp. 368–69; 69 (24 August 1899), p. 140; 69 (7 September 1899), p. 182; 69 (21 September 1899), p. 218; 70 (22 March 1900), pp. 217–18; 70 (5 April 1900), p. 252.

Godkin, with Charles Eliot Norton and Carl Schurz, was outraged and dismayed when in 1902 *The Nation*, under the leadership of Oswald Garrison Villard, appeared to accept at face value the assurances of Elihu Root that all instances of military misconduct in the Philippines had been corrected. See Charles F. Adams, Jr., to Carl Schurz, 30 April 1902, Schurz Papers, L.C.; Schurz to Oswald Garrison Villard, 21 May, 26 July, 9 August 1902, Villard Papers, Houghton Library, Harvard University.

37. Cf. *The Woman's Journal*, 10 March 1899, and the *New England Magazine* 21 (October 1899), pp. 244–56.

CHAPTER IX

1. *Soldiers' Letters: Being Materials for the History of a War of Criminal Aggression*, pp. 5–15. See also *The Literary Digest* 18 (27 May 1899), pp. 601–03.

Albert Shaw, in the May 1899 issue of his magazine, *American Monthly Review of Reviews*, dismissed the "tales" of the Boston Anti-Imperialists as "baseless slander." *American Monthly Review of Reviews* 19 (May 1899), p. 657.

2. *Public Opinion* 28 (19 April 1900), pp. 486–87.

3. See New York *World*, 26 July 1900.

4. Quoted in *The Watchman* (Boston) 80 (27 July 1900).

5. George Kennan, "The Philippines," pp. 582–83.

6. During the Philippine-American War fourteen newspapermen served for

varying periods of time as war correspondents in Manila. They were a fluctuating group and succeeded one another in a confusing pattern of multiple assignments. Only a few of the more established journals could afford the financial cost of sustaining a correspondent in the western Pacific, and they arranged that assignments be shared. No correspondent was assigned to Manila for more than eighteen months, but at one time or another in the years 1898–1902, the following men did battle with censorship in order to inform the American public of the progress of American arms: John T. McCutcheon (Chicago *Tribune* and Chicago *Record*); Oscar King Davis (New York *Sun* and *Harper's Weekly*); Albert Gardiner Robinson (New York *Evening Post*, Boston *Transcript*, and *The Independent*); John F. Bass (New York *Herald* and *Harper's Weekly*); William Dinwiddie (New York *Herald* and San Francisco *Call*); Richard Little (Chicago *Tribune*); E. W. Harden (Chicago *Tribune*); P. G. McDonnell (New York *Sun*); Harry Armstrong (Chicago *Record*); Francis Millett (*Harper's Weekly*); Theodore W. Noyes (Washington *Evening Star*); H. L. Wells (AP and New York *Evening Post*); Frederick Palmer (New York *World* and *Collier's*); E. D. Skene (Scripps McRae Association).

7. *City and State* 12 (2 January 1902), p. 7; (9 January 1902), pp. 23–24; (6 March 1902), p .160; (17 April 1902), p. 247.

8. See *The Springfield Weekly Republican*, 28 March 1902; Herbert Welsh to Charles Eliot Norton, 3 April, 19 April, 29 April 1902, Norton Papers, Houghton Library, Harvard University; Matthew K. Sniffen to E. W. Carmack, 1 June 1902, Carmack Papers, University of North Carolina.

9. H. Parker Willis to Herbert Welch, 17 April 1902, Papers of Anti-Imperialist League, Michigan Historical Collections, University of Michigan; M. K. Sniffen to Moorfield Storey, 12 April 1902, Moorfield Storey Papers, Box 1, L.C.; M. K. Sniffen to Herbert Welsh, 14 April 1902, copy, Norton Papers, Houghton Library, Harvard University.

10. *City and State* 12 (8 May 1902), p. 292.

11. *Cong. Record*, 57th Cong., 1st sess., p. 597.

12. See two files marked "Philippine Material Preserved by Sen. George F. Hoar," Hoar Papers, M.H.S.

13. Hoar viewed Herbert Welsh as an excitable zealot, but the two men later cooperated to a limited extent in arranging the appearance of witnesses before the Senate Philippine Committee. See Hoar to Herbert Welsh, 7 March, 16 April 1902, copies, Hoar Papers, M.H.S. Hoar was also prepared to serve as the channel for the petitions of professors and literary men demanding an investigation of the conduct of the war. On 4 February 1902 Hoar presented such a petition signed by over a hundred private citizens, among them Mark Twain, William Dean Howells, and thirty-six professors from the University of Chicago. *Senate Doc.* No.166, 57th Cong., 1st sess., pp. 1–11.

14. Hoar to Lodge, 22 January, 28 January 1902, Hoar Papers, M.H.S.

15. See Hoar's eloquent but discouraged address to the Senate of 22 May 1902, *Cong. Record*, 57th Cong., 1st sess., pp. 5788–98.

16. A transcript of the committee hearings with related material and appendixes will be found in the following government documents: "Affairs in the Philippine Islands," 57th Cong., 1st sess., *Senate Doc.* No. 331 (1903); "Report of the Secretary of War for 1901," 57th Cong., 1st sess., *House Doc.* No. 2 (1901); "Charges of Cruelty, etc. to the Natives of the Philippines," 57th Cong., 1st sess., *Senate Doc.* No. 205 (1902); "Trials of Courts-Martial in the Philippine Islands in Consequence of Certain Instructions," 57th Cong., 2d sess., *Senate Doc.* No. 213 (1903).

17. The hearings of the Committee were "closed," but reporters from the three press associations and occasional observers were permitted, and such Demo-

cratic members as Senator Thomas M. Patterson of Colorado and Senator Edward W. Carmack of Tennessee kept their anti-imperialist allies informed of committee proceedings.

18. Springfield *Republican*, 10, 28 January 1902; New York *Evening Post*, 28 January 1902; *Public Opinion* 32 (30 January 1902), p. 132; *The Literary Digest* 24 (1 February 1902), p. 138. See also the series of pen-and-ink illustrations in *Collier's Weekly*, 30 November 1901–20 February 1902, depicting American pacification policy in the Philippines.

19. *The Literary Digest* 24 (1 February 1902), p. 138. A correspondent for the New York *Herald* insisted that the Filipino inhabitants of the concentration centers "merely suffered some temporary inconvenience," and that "owing to the sanitary rules which are enforced," the health of the prisoners was much improved. Ibid. (8 February 1902), pp. 1–2.

20. *The Literary Digest* 24 (19 April 1902), p. 531 (26 April 1902), p. 561; New York *World*, 12, 16, 18 April 1902; New York *Evening Post*, 9, 18 April 1902.

21. *Public Opinion* 32 (24 April 1902), p. 518. George Harvey of *Harper's Weekly* was prepared to attribute "supplementary cruelties" to the necessities of the pacification program, and expressed the conviction that America could safely trust the Secretary War to deal with "such practices as in sporadic cases [have been] . . . employed by overwrought officers and soldiers." *Harper's Weekly* 46 (26 April 1902), pp. 518, 543; (7 June 1902), p. 712.

22. *The New York Times*, 17, 27, 29 April 1902; *The Literary Digest* 24 (10 May 1902), pp. 629–30. Other papers that sought to offer a bold defense for Major Waller and General Smith were the New York *Sun*, Boston *Journal*, Cleveland *Leader*, Minneapolis *Tribune*, and Providence *Journal*.

From the beginning to end, the Providence *Journal* insisted that no consideration should be shown "Aguinaldo's mercenaries." The white man's burden demanded red blood, not "a white liver." Were we to falter in the Philippines, a chain reaction might set in and there would soon be disorder in Cuba, Puerto Rico, and Hawaii. See, for example, *The Providence Sunday Journal*, 12 , 16 February 1899.

23. New York *Evening Post*, 9 April 1902. In the opinion of the *Post*, American troops had suffered "embrutement."

24. An exception was *The Army and Navy Journal* of April 1902, which deplored political intervention in the "ordinary operations of military justice," and expressed a strong suspicion of "the influence of hostile public opinion."

25. *The Literary Digest* 24 (10 May 1902), p. 629; (17 May 1902), p. 666.

26. The *Atlanta Constitution*, 10 May 1902.

27. George H. Lyman to H. C. Lodge, 12 February 1902; Lodge to Charles F. Dole, 21 January 1902; H. L. Higginson to Lodge, 22 February, 9 May 1902, Lodge Papers, M.H.S.

28. See C. F. Adams to Charles Eliot Norton, 11, 18 April 1902, C. E. Norton Papers, Houghton Library, Harvard University.

29. C. F. Adams to Carl Schurz, 21 April 1902, Schurz Papers, L.C.; Adams to C. E. Norton, 2, 31 May 1902, Norton Papers, Houghton Library, Harvard University; Jacob Gould Schurman to Carl Schurz, 3 May 1902, Schurz Papers, L.C.

30. Boston: George H. Ellis Co., 1902.

31. Particularly against the sentences of that letter which read: "It is not the fact that the warfare in the Philippines has been conducted with marked severity. On the contrary, the warfare has been conducted with marked humanity and magnanimity on the part of the United States." *Senate Doc.* No. 205, Pt. 1, 57th Cong., 1st sess., pp. 1–3.

32. *Cong. Record*, 57th Cong., 1st sess. (4 May 1902), pp. 4030–40. Elihu Root congratulated Lodge and proclaimed his speech "worthy of the subject and the serious occasion." Root to Lodge, 6 May 1902, Lodge Papers, M.H.S.

General MacArthur's final report as military commander in the Philippines was widely publicized by the War Department as a further means of reviving popular confidence in the administration's Philippine policy. In that report MacArthur reaffirmed his belief that the long-term consequence of America's enhanced position in the Pacific was "likely to transcend in importance anything recorded in the history of the world since the discovery of America." *Annual Reports of the War Department for the Fiscal Year Ended June 30, 1901*, Pt. 3.

33. *Providence Sunday Journal*, 20 April, 11 May 1902; O. O. Howard, "Is Cruelty Inseparable from War?" pp. 1161–62; *City and State* 12 (20 March 1902), p. 184; *Harper's Weekly* 46 (7 June 1902), p. 712. See also interview of Captain Louis Lang in Buffalo *Express*, 1 July 1902.

34. Boston *Journal*, 31 May 1902; Roosevelt to Josephine Shaw Lowell, 9 May 1902, Roosevelt Papers, L.C.

35. See B. O. Flowers, "Some Dead Sea Fruit of Our War of Subjugation," pp. 647–53; *City and State* 12 (12 June 1902), p. 374, (26 June 1902), p. 406; Springfield *Republican*, 5 July 1902.

36. New York *World*, 16 April 1902.

37. New York *Evening Post*, 8 April 1902.

38. *The Literary Digest* 24 (10 May 1902), p. 635.

39. Finley Peter Dunne, *Mr. Dooley in Peace and in War*, p. 5.

40. It was not a war that inspired a significant addition to the nation's stock of martial music; only a handful of civilians could have recognized the lyrics of "Bacon on the Rind" and "On Datu Ali's Trail." For the "soldier songs of the Philippine Insurrection," see the "Introduction" to C. S. Peterson, *Known Military Dead During the Spanish-American War and the Philippine Insurrection, 1898–1901*.

41. See Peter H. King, "The White Man's Burden," pp. 135, 303–05.

CHAPTER X

1. Peter W. Stanley observes that "economic expansion, in general, and infatuation with that elusive pillar of cloud and fire, the China market, in particular, have far more affected our Asian policy than territorial possession of the Philippines. . . ." Peter W. Stanley, *A Nation in the Making*, p. 277.

2. Thomas A. Bailey, *The Man in the Street*, p. 275.

3. Daniel B. Schirmer, *Republic or Empire*, p. 3.

4. See, for example, J. W. Rollins, "The Anti-Imperialists and American Foreign Policy"; William J. Pomeroy, *An American-Made Tragedy*, pp. 6–16.

5. William A. Williams, *The Tragedy of American Diplomacy*, pp. 35–38.

6. John W. Gates is convinced that many of these achievements were begun during the period of military rule and under the aegis of U.S. Army officers who exemplified the progressive orientation soon to characterize the American political scene. John W. Gates, *Schoolbooks and Krags*, pp. 54–75.

7. Peter W. Stanley concludes that the policies of the Taft-Forbes era concerning land sales, franchises, currency reform, public education, and tariff revision were more open to the charge of political cooptation than foreign exploitation. Stanley, *A Nation in the Making*, pp. 269–73.

8. William E. Leuchtenburg, "Progressivism and Imperialism," pp. 483–504.

Bibliography

MANUSCRIPT COLLECTIONS

Duke University Libraries:
  Papers of James A. Le Roy
Harvard Archives, Harvard University:
  Papers of Charles W. Eliot
Houghton Library, Harvard University:
  Papers of Gamaliel Bradford
  Papers of E. L. Godkin
  Papers of William James
  Papers of Charles Eliot Norton
  Papers of Oswald Garrison Villard
Library of Congress (L.C.):
  Papers of William Jennings Bryan
  Papers of Andrew Carnegie
  Papers of William A. Croffut
  Papers of George Dewey
  Papers of William McKinley
  Papers of Theodore Roosevelt
  Papers of Elihu Root
  Papers of Carl Schurz
  Papers of Moorfield Storey
  Papers of William Howard Taft
Massachusetts Historical Society
    (M.H.S.):
  Papers of Charles Francis Adams, Jr.
  Papers of Edward Atkinson
  Papers of George S. Boutwell
  Papers of George F. Hoar
  Papers of Henry Cabot Lodge
  Papers of Moorfield Storey
  Papers of Winslow Warren

Michigan Historical Collections,
    University of Michigan:
  Papers of Anti-Imperialist League
  Papers of Dean C. Worcester
National Archives:
  Philippine Insurgent Records, 1896–
    1901, Microcopy No. 254: Roll 72
    (folders No. 1161–75) and Roll 74
    (folders No. 1191–1205)
  Bureau of Insular Affairs Records,
    file No. 13949
  Philippine Insurgent Records com-
    piled by Captain J. R. Taylor,
    Record Group No. 126, general
    files, Bureau of Insular Affairs
New York Public Library:
  Papers of Edward W. Ordway
Southern Historical Collection,
    University of North Carolina:
  Papers of Edward W. Carmack
United States Army Military History
    Research Collection, Carlisle
    Barracks:
  Papers of William A. Batson
  Papers of W. A. Damon
  Papers of William E. Eggenberger
  Papers of Claude F. Line
  Papers of Samuel P. Lyon
  Papers of Frederick M. Presher

NEWSPAPERS

The Advance
The Age of Steel
The American (Manila)
American Exporter
American Federationist
Baltimore *Sun*
Boston *Herald*
Boston *Journal*
Chicago *Broad Ax*
Chicago *Record*
Chicago *Times-Herald*
Chicago *Tribune*
The Christian Advocate
City and State
The Commercial Bulletin
Commercial and Financial Chronicle
The Evangelist
Freedom (Manila)
The Guardian (Boston)
The Journal of the Knights of Labor
National Labor Standard
New York *Age*
New York *Evening Post*
New York *Herald*
The New York Times
New York *Tribune*
New York *World*
The Pilot
Providence *Journal*
The Public (Chicago)
Railway Age
Springfield (Mass.) *Republican*

The Wall Street Journal
Washington *Colored American*
Washington *Post*
The Watchman.

PERIODICALS

The American Monthly Review of Reviews
The Arena
Army and Navy Journal
Atlantic Monthly
Century Illustrated Magazine
Collier's Weekly
The Colored American Magazine
Contemporary Review
Cosmopolitan
The Forum
Harper's Weekly
The Independent
Judge
Literary Digest
Living Age
McClure's Magazine
Munsey's Magazine
The Nation
The New England Magazine
North American Review
The Outlook
Overland Monthly
Public Opinion
Puck
Scribner's Magazine
The Verdict
The Woman's Journal

PUBLIC DOCUMENTS

Correspondence Relating to the War with Spain, April 15, 1898– July 30, 1902. 2
    vols. Washington, D.C., 1902.
Papers Relating to the Foreign Relations of the United States (for the years 1898–
    1902).
Congressional Record (for the years 1898–1902).
The United States and the Philippine Islands, 1900–1904. Washington, D.C.,
    1905.
Report of the United States Philippine Commission. Washington, D.C., 1901.
Reports of the War Department: Reports of the Secretary of War (1899–1902).

United States Congress. 56th Congress. Senate Documents No. 138, No. 148, No. 208, No. 218, No. 426, No. 432, No. 435.
United States Congress. 57th Congress. Senate Documents No. 166, No. 205, No. 213, No. 259, No. 273, No. 286, No. 331, No. 347.

BOOKS AND ARTICLES

Abbot, A. R. "The Employment of Negroes in the Philippines." *The Anglo-American Magazine* 6 (September 1901);196–201.
Abelarde, Pedro E. *American Tariff Policy Towards the Philippines, 1898–1946.* New York: King's Crown Press, 1947.
Adams, Charles Francis, Jr. "Imperialism and 'The Tracks of Our Forefathers.' " Pamphlet. Boston: Dana Estes & Co., 1899.
Adams, Charles Kendall. "Colonies and Other Dependencies." *The Forum* 27 (March 1899):33–46.
Adler, Felix. "The Philippine War: Two Ethical Questions." *The Forum* 33 (June 1902): 387–99.
Agoncillo, Teodoro A. *Malolos: Crisis of the Republic.* Quezon City: University of the Philippines Press, 1960.
———. *Revolt of the Masses: The Story of Bonifacio and the Katipunan.* Quezon City: University of the Philippines Press, 1956.
Aguinaldo, Emilio; and Pacis, Vincente. *A Second Look at America.* New York: Speller, 1957.
———. "The Story of My Capture." *Current Literature* 31 (September 1901): 269–70.
Alfonso, Oscar M. "Taft's Early Views on the Filipinos." *Solidarity* (Manila) 4 (1969):52–58.
———. *Theodore Roosevelt and the Philippines, 1897–1909.* Quezon City: University of the Philippines Press. 1970.
Algué, Fr. Joseph. "The Philippine Question." *The Independent* 52 (15 March 1900):660–63.
Apacible, G. *To the American People.* Pamphlet. Boston: New England Anti-Imperialist League, 1900.
Appel, John C. "The Relationship of American Labor to United States Imperialism, 1895–1905." Ph.D. dissertation, University of Wisconsin, 1950.
Armstrong, William M. *E. L. Godkin and American Foreign Policy, 1865–1900.* New York: Bookman Associates, 1957.
Atkinson, Edward. "Criminal Aggression: By Whom Committed"; "The Cost of a National Crime"; "The Hell of War and Its Penalties." Boston: privately printed, 1899.
Austin, O. P. "Does Colonization Pay?" *The Forum* 28 (November 1899):621–31.
Baclagon, Uldarico S. *Philippine Campaigns.* Manila: Graphic House, 1952.
Bailey, Thomas A. "America's Emergence as a World Power: The Myth and the Verity." *Pacific Historical Review* 30 (1961):1–16.
———. *The Man in the Street.* New York: Macmillan Company, 1948.
———. "Was the Election of 1900 a Mandate on Imperialism?" *Mississippi Valley Historical Review* 24 (June 1937):43–52.

Baldwin, F. Spencer. "Some Gains from Expansion." *The Arena* 22 (November 1899):570–75.

Baldwin, Simeon E. "The Constitutional Questions Incident to the Acquisition and Government by the United States of Island Territories." *Annual Report of the American Historical Association for the Year 1898*. Washington, D.C., 1899.

Bancroft, Frederic; and Dunning, William A. *The Reminiscences of Carl Schurz*. 3 vols. New York: McClure, 1907–8.

————,ed. *Speeches, Correspondence and Political Papers of Carl Schurz*. 6 vols. New York: G. P. Putnam's Sons, 1913.

Barnes, Arthur M. "American Intervention in Cuba and the Annexation of the Philippines: An Analysis of Public Discussion." Ph.D. dissertation, Cornell University, 1948.

Barrett, John. "The Problem of the Philippines." *North American Review* 167 (September 1898):259–67.

————. "The Value of the Philippines." *Munsey's Magazine* 21 (August 1899):689–703.

Barrows, David P. "The Governor-General of the Philippines Under Spain and the United States." In *The Pacific Ocean in History*, edited by H. M. Stephens and H. E. Bolton, pp. 238–65. New York: Macmillan Company, 1917.

Baylen, Joseph O.; and Moore, John Hammond. "Senator John Tyler Morgan and Negro Colonization in the Philippines, 1900 to 1902." *Phylon* 29 (Spring 1968):65–73.

Beale, Howard K. *Theodore Roosevelt and the Rise of America to World Power*. Baltimore: Johns Hopkins Press, 1956.

Becker, William H. "American Manufacturers and Foreign Markets, 1870–1900: Business Historians and the 'New Economic Determinists.' " *Business Historical Review*, 47 (1973), pp. 466–81.

————. "Foreign Markets for Iron and Steel, 1893–1913: A New Perspective on the Williams School of Diplomatic History." *Pacific Historical Review*, 4 (May, 1975), pp. 233–48.

Beisner, Robert L. "1898 and 1968: The Anti-Imperialists and the Doves." *Political Science Quarterly* 85 (June 1970):187–216.

Belford, Samuel W. "Chinese Exclusion from the Philippines." *The Arena* 23 (May 1900):450.

Belmont, Perry. "Congress, the President and the Philippines." *North American Review* 169 (1899):894–911.

Bernstein, Barton J.; and Leib, Franklin A. "Progressive Republican Senators and American Imperialism, 1898–1916: A Reappraisal." *Mid-America* 50 (1968):163–205.

Bisbee, Robert E. "Why I Oppose Our Philippine Policy." *The Arena* 28 (August 1902):113–18.

Blount, James. *The American Occupation of the Philippines, 1898–1912*. New York: G. P. Putnam's Sons, 1912.

Blumentritte, Ferdinand. "Race Questions in the Philippine Islands." *Appleton's Popular Science Monthly* 55 (August 1899):472–80.

Bonis, H. "Imperial Republicanism." *The Arena* 33 (April 1900):321–31.

Bonsal, Stephen. "The Negro Soldier in War and Peace." *North American Review* 186 (June 1907):321–37.

Boutwell, George S. *Imperialism and Anti-Imperialism: Address at a Conference of Anti-Imperialists, Boston, May 16, 1899*. Pamphlet. New York: Anti-Imperialist League, 1900.

_____. *The President's Policy: War and Conquest Abroad, Degradation of Labor at Home*. Pamphlet. Chicago: American Anti-Imperialist League, 1900.

_____. *Reminiscences of Sixty Years in Public Affairs*. 2 vols. New York: McClure, Phillips, 1902.

_____. *Republic or Empire*. Boston: Anti-Imperialist League, 1900.

_____. *The War of Despotism in the Philippine Islands: Address at Springfield, Mass., September 5, 1899*. Pamphlet. Boston: New England Anti-Imperialist League, 1899.

Bowers, Claude. *Beveridge and the Progressive Era*. Boston: Houghton Mifflin Company, 1932.

Braisted, William R. *The United States Navy in the Pacific, 1897–1909*. Austin: University of Texas Press, 1958.

Brooks, Francis A. *The Unauthorized and Unlawful Subjugation of Filipinos in the Island of Luzon by President McKinley*. Pamphlet. Cambridge, Mass.: Caustic and Claflin, 1900.

Brown, John Clifford. *Diary of a Soldier in the Philippines*. Portland, Me.: privately printed, 1901.

Bryan, William Jennings. *Bryan on Imperialism*. New York: Arno Press, 1970 (reprint).

_____. *Republic or Empire? The Philippine Question*. Chicago: The Independence Company, 1899.

Burgess, John W. "The Decision of the Supreme Court in the Insular Cases." *Political Science Quarterly* 16 (September 1901):486–504.

Callahan, James Morton. *American Relations in the Pacific and the Far East, 1784–1900*. Baltimore: Johns Hopkins Press, 1901.

Campbell, Charles S., Jr. *Anglo-American Understanding, 1893–1903*. Baltimore: Johns Hopkins Press, 1957.

_____. *Special Business Interests and the Open Door Policy*. New Haven, Conn.: Yale University Press, 1961.

Carleton, William G. "Isolationism and the Middle West." *Mississippi Valley Historical Review* 33 (December 1946):371–90.

Carmony, Donald F.; and Tannenbaum, Karen, eds. "Three Years in the Orient: The Diary of William R. Johnson, 1898–1902." *Indiana Magazine of History* 63 (1967):263–98.

Carnegie, Andrew. "Americanism *Versus* Imperialism." *North American Review* 168 (1899):1–13.

_____. "The Opportunity of the United States." *North American Review* 184 (1902):606–12.

Chamberlain, Mary Endicott. "An Obligation of the Empire." *North American Review* 170 (April 1900):493–503.

Chamberlin, Fred C. *The Blow from Behind*. Boston: Lee & Shepard, 1903.

Chetwood, John. *Manila or Monroe Doctrine*. New York: Robert Lewis Weed Company, 1898.

Coletta, Paola E. "Bryan, McKinley, and the Treaty of Paris." *Pacific Historical Review* 24 (May 1957):131–46.

——. "McKinley, the Peace Negotiations, and the Acquisition of the Philippines." *Pacific Historical Review* 30 (1961):341–50.

Colquhoun, Archibald Ross. *The Mastery of the Pacific*. New York: Macmillan Company, 1902.

Conant, Charles A. "The Economic Basis of 'Imperialism.'" *North American Review* 168 (September 1898):326–40.

——. "The Economic Future of the Philippines." *Atlantic Monthly* 89 (March 1902):366–71.

——. *The United States in the Orient: The Nature of the Economic Problem*. Boston: Houghton Mifflin Company, 1900.

Condict, Alice Byram. *Old Glory and the Gospel in the Philippines*. Chicago: Fleming H. Revell Company, 1902.

Corpus, Onofre D. *The Philippines*. Englewood Cliffs, N.J.: Prentice-Hall, 1965.

Crosby, Ernest. *Captain Jinks Hero*. New York: Funk & Wagnalls, 1902.

——. "The Philippine Question." *The Arena* 25 (July 1902):10–11.

——. *Swords and Plowshares*. New York: Funk & Wagnalls, 1902.

Curti, Merle. *Bryan and World Peace*. Northampton, Mass.: Smith College, 1931.

——. *Peace or War: The American Struggle, 1636–1936*. New York: W. W. Norton & Company, 1936.

Davis, Mrs. Jefferson. "Why We Do Not Want the Philippines." *The Arena* 23 (January 1900):1–14.

Denby, Charles. "The Rights of the United States in the Philippines: A Reply to Senor Agoncillo." *The Independent* 51 (7 December 1899):3263–68.

——. "Shall We Keep the Philippines." *The Forum* 26 (November 1898): 278–81.

——. "Some Remarks on a 'Filipino Point of View.'" *The Independent* 52 (4 January 1900):9.

Dennett, Tyler. *Americans in Eastern Asia: A Critical Study of the Policy of the United States*. . . . New York: Macmillan Company, 1922.

Dester, Frank. "Will the Philippines Pay?" *The Arena* 25 (May 1901):465–70.

Dooling, James J. *Rhymes Without Treason*. Lexington Mass.: privately printed, 1899.

Dulles, Foster Rhea. *America's Rise to World Power, 1898–1954*. New York: Harper Brothers, 1955.

——. *The Imperial Years*. New York: Crowell, 1956.

Dunne, Finley Peter. *Mr. Dooley in Peace and War*. Boston: Small, Maynard, 1898.

——. *Mr. Dooley in the Hearts of His Countrymen*. Boston: Small, Maynard, 1899.

Eggert, Gerald G. *Richard Olney: Evolution of a Statesman*. University Park, Pa.: Pennsylvania State University Press, 1974.

Eliot, Charles W. "Political Principles and Tendencies." *The Outlook* 66 (20 October 1900):459–60.

Elliott, Charles B. *The Philippines to the End of the Military Regime*. Indianapolis: Bobbs-Merrill, 1916.

Esty, Thomas Bruce, ed. *Views of the American Press on the Philippines*. New York: Esty & Esty, 1899.

Eyot, Canning, ed. *The Story of the Lopez Family*. Boston: James H. West Company, 1904.

Eyre, James K., Jr. "The Philippines, the Powers and the Spanish-American War: A Study of Foreign Policies." Ph.D. dissertation, University of Michigan, 1940.

Farrell, John T. "Archbishop Ireland and Manifest Destiny." *Catholic Historical Review* 33 (1947):269–301.

———. "Background of the 1902 Taft Mission to Rome, I." *Catholic Historical Review* 36 (1950):1–32.

Faust, Karl Irving. *Campaigning in the Philippines*. San Francisco: Hicks-Judd Company, 1899.

Ferguson, John H. *American Diplomacy and the Boer War*. Philadelphia: University of Pennsylvania Press, 1939.

Fernandez, Leandro H. *The Philippine Republic*. New York: Columbia University Press, 1926.

Ferrell, Robert H. *American Diplomacy: A History*. 3d ed. New York: W. W. Norton & Company, 1975.

Fisher, George P. "The Question of the Philippines." *The Moral and Religious Aspects of the So-Called Imperial Policy*. New Haven, Conn.: Tuttle, Morehouse & Taylor, 1899.

Fiske, Amos K. "Some Consecrated Fallacies." *North American Review* 169 (December 1899):821–28.

Fiske, Bradley A. *War Time in Manila*. Boston: Richard G. Badger, 1913.

Fletcher, Marvin E. *The Black Soldier and Officer in the United States Army, 1891–1917*. Columbia: University of Missouri Press, 1974.

———. "The Negro Soldier and the United States Army, 1891–1917." Ph.D. dissertation, University of Wisconsin, 1968.

Flowers, Benjamin O. "Some Dead Sea Fruit of Our War of Subjugation." *The Arena* 27 (June 1902):647–53.

Forbes, W. Cameron. *The Philippine Islands*. 2 vols. Boston: Houghton Mifflin Company, 1928.

Ford, Worthington C., ed. *Letters of Henry Adams*. 2 vols. Boston: Houghton Mifflin Company, 1930–1938.

Foreman, John. "Spain and the Philippine Islands." *Contemporary Review* 74 (July 1898):20–33.

Francisco, Luzviminda. "The First Vietnam: The U.S.-Philippine War of 1899." *Bulletin of Concerned Asian Scholars* 5 (1973):2–16.

Fuller, Henry B. *The New Flag*. Chicago: privately printed, 1899.

Funston, Frederick. *Memoirs of Two Wars: Cuban and Philippine Experiences*. New York: Scribner's, 1911.

Ganzhorn, John W. *I've Killed Men: An Epic of Early Arizona*. New York: Devin, 1959.

Gantenbein, C. U. *The Official Records of the Oregon Volunteers in the Spanish War and Philippine Insurrection*. Salem, Ore.: J. R. Whitney, 1908.

Garrison, William Lloyd. *The Nation's Shame: Sonnets*. Boston: privately printed, 1899.

Gates, John M. *Schoolbooks and Krags: The United States Army in the Philippines*. Westport: Greenwood Press, 1973.

Gatewood, Willard B., Jr. "Black Americans and the Quest for Empire, 1898–1903." *Journal of Southern History* 38 (1972):545–66.

_____. *Black Americans and the White Man's Burden, 1898–1903*. Urbana: University of Illinois Press, 1975.

_____. *"Smoked Yankees" and the Struggle for Empire: Letters from Negro Soldiers, 1898–1902*. Urbana: University of Illinois Press, 1971.

Gibson, William M. "Mark Twain and Howells: Anti-Imperialists." *The New England Quarterly* 20 (December 1947):435–70.

Giddings, Franklin H. *Democracy and Empire: With Studies of Their Psychological, Economic, and Moral Foundations*. New York: Macmillan Company, 1900.

Godkin, E. L. "The Conditions of Good Colonial Government." *The Forum*, 27 (1 April 1899):190–203.

_____. "Imperium et Libertas." *The Nation* 68 (18 May 1899):368–69.

_____. "Rich Men and Democracy." *The Nation* 71 (8 November 1900):362.

Gookin, Frederick W. *A Liberty Catechism*. Pamphlet. Chicago: American Anti-Imperialist League, 1899.

Graebner, Norman A. "The Year of Transition—1898." In *An Uncertain Tradition: American Secretaries of State in the Twentieth Century*, edited by Norman A. Graebner. New York: McGraw-Hill Book Company, 1961.

Graff, Henry F., ed. *American Imperialism and the Philippine Insurrection: Testimony Taken from Hearings on Affairs in the Philippine Islands before the Senate Committee on the Philippines–1902*. Boston: Little, Brown, and Company, 1969.

Greenberg, A. A. "Public Opinion and the Acquisition of the Philippine Islands." Master's thesis, Yale University, 1937.

Grenville, John A.; and Young, George B. *Politics, Strategy and American Diplomacy*. New Haven, Conn.: Yale University Press, 1966.

Griswold, A. Whitney. *The Far Eastern Policy of the United States*. New York: Harcourt, Brace & Co., 1938.

Grunder, Garel A.; and Livezey, William E. *The Philippines and the United States*. Norman: University of Oklahoma Press, 1951.

Guffin, J. C. "Evolution versus Imperialism." *The Arena* 23 (February 1900):141–48

Halle, Louis J. *Dream and Reality: Aspects of American Foreign Policy*. New York: Harper Brothers, 1959.

Harrington, Fred H. "The Anti-Imperialist Movement in the United States, 1898–1900." *Mississippi Valley Historical Review* 22 (1935):211–30.

——. "Literary Aspects of American Anti-Imperialism, 1898–1902." *The New England Quarterly* 10 (December 1937):650–67.

Hawthorne, Julian. "A Side Issue of Expansion." *The Forum* 27 (June 1899):441–43.

Hayden, Joseph Ralston. *The Philippines: A Study in National Development*. New York: Macmillan Company, 1942.

Hendrickson, Kenneth E., Jr. "Reluctant Expansionist—Jacob Gould Schurman and the Philippine Question." *Pacific Historical Review* 36 (1967):405–21.

Hoar, George F. *Autobiography of Seventy Years*. 2 vols. New York: Scribner's, 1903.

——. "Our Duty to the Philippines." *The Nation* 51 (9 November 1899): 2995–3000.

Holbrook, Franklin F. *Minnesota in the Spanish-American War and the Philippine Insurrection*. St. Paul, Minn.: privately printed, 1923.

Holli, Melvin G., ed. "A View of the American Campaign Against 'Filipino Insurgents': 1900." *Philippine Studies* 17 (January 1969):97–111.

Hollingsworth, J. Rogers, ed. *American Expansion in the Late Nineteenth Century: Colonialist or Anticolonialist?* New York: Holt, Rinehart and Winston, 1968.

Holt, W. Stull. *Treaties Defeated by the Senate*. Baltimore: Johns Hopkins Press, 1933.

Howard, Oliver O. "Is Cruelty Inseparable from War?" *The Independent* 54 (15 May 1902):1161–62.

Howe, M. A. DeWolfe. *Portrait of an Independent: Moorfield Storey, 1845–1929*. Boston: Houghton Mifflin Company, 1932.

Janes, Lewis G. *Our Nation's Peril: Social Ideals and Social Progress*. Pamphlet. Boston: James H. West Company, 1899.

Jenkins, Shirley. *American Economic Policy Toward the Philippines*. Stanford, Calif.: Stanford University Press, 1954.

Johnson, Guion Griffis. "The Ideology of White Supremacy, 1876–1910." In *Essays in Southern History*, edited by Fletcher M. Green. Chapel Hill: University of North Carolina Press, 1949.

Johnson, John R. "Nebraska in the Spanish-American War and the Philippine Insurrection: A Study in Imperialism." Ph.D. dissertation, University of Nebraska, 1937.

Johnson, Walter. *William Allen White's America*. New York: Henry Holt & Co., 1947.

Jordan, David Starr. *Imperial Democracy*. New York: Appleton, 1899.

Judson, Henry Pratt. "Our Federal Constitution and the Government of Tropical Territories." *The American Monthly Review of Reviews* 19 (January 1899):67–75.

Kalaw, Maximo M. *The Case for the Filipinos*. New York: Century Company, 1916.

———. *The Development of Philippine Politics, 1872–1920*. Manila: Oriental Commercial Company, 1926.

Kalaw, Teodoro M. *The Philippine Revolution*. Quezon City: University of the Philippines Press, 1969.

Kennan, George. "The Philippines: Present Conditions and Possible Courses." *The Outlook* 67 (9 March 1901):576–84.

Kennan, George F. *American Diplomacy, 1900–1950*. Chicago: University of Chicago Press, 1951.

Kennedy, Philip W. "The Concept of Racial Superiority and United States Imperialism, 1890–1910." Ph.D. dissertation, St. Louis University, 1962.

Kennon, L. W. V. "The Katipunan of the Philippines." *North American Review* 173 (August 1901):208–20.

Kidd, Benjamin. *The Control of the Tropics*. New York: Macmillan Company, 1898.

King, Peter H. "The White Man's Burden." Ph.D. dissertation, University of California at Los Angeles, 1958.

Kinsley, Philip. *The Chicago Tribune: Its First Hundred Years*. 2 vols. New York: A. A. Knopf, 1946.

Kirk, Grayson. *Philippine Independence: Motives, Problems, and Prospects*. New York: Farrar & Rinehart, 1936.

Knapp, Arthur May. "Japan and the Philippines." *Atlantic Monthly* 83 (June 1899):737–42.

Kohlsaat, Herman H. *From McKinley to Harding*. New York: Scribner's, 1923.

LaFeber, Walter. *The New Empire: An Interpretation of American Expansion, 1860–1898*. Ithaca, N.Y.: Cornell University Press, 1963.

Lanier, Osmos. "Anti-Annexationists of the 1890's." Ph.D. dissertation, University of Georgia, 1965.

Lanzar-Carpio, Maria C. "Anti-Imperialist Activities between 1900 and Election of 1904." *Philippine Social Science Review* 4 (July 1932; October 1932):182–98; 239–54.

Lasch, Christopher. "The Anti-Imperialists, the Philippines, and the Inequality of Man." *Journal of Southern History* 16 (August 1958):319–31.

Laughlin, J. L. *Patriotism and Imperialism*. Pamphlet. Chicago: American Anti-Imperialist League, 1899.

Lee, Henry. "The War Correspondent and the Insurrection, A Study of American Newspaper Correspondents in the Philippines, 1898–1900." Senior honors thesis, Harvard University, 1968.

Leech, Margaret. *In the Days of McKinley*. New York: Harper Brothers, 1959.

Lemus, Rienzi B. "The Enlisted Man in Action, or the Colored American Soldier in the Philippines." *Colored American Magazine* 5 (May 1902):46–54.

Lens, Sidney. *The Forging of the American Empire*. New York: Thomas Y. Crowell, 1971.

Leopold, Richard W. "The Emergence of America as a World Power: Some Second Thoughts." In *Change and Continuity in Twentieth-Century America*, edited by John Braeman, Robert H. Bremmer, Everett Walters. Columbus: Ohio State University Press, 1964.

Le Roy, James A. *The Americans in the Philippines*. 2 vols. Boston: Houghton Mifflin Company, 1914.

———. "Race Prejudice in the Philippines." *Atlantic Monthly* 90 (July 1902): 100–112.

Leslie's Official History of the Spanish-American War. New York: 1889.

Leuchtenburg, William E. "Progressivism and Imperialism: The Progressive Movement and American Foreign Policy, 1898–1916." *Mississippi Valley Historical Review* 39 (1952):483–504.

Liberty Poems. Boston: New England Anti-Imperialist League, 1900.

Linderman, Gerald F. *The Mirror of War: American Society and the Spanish-American War*. Ann Arbor: University of Michigan Press, 1974.

Lininger, Clarence. *The Best War at the Time*. New York: Robert Speller & Sons, 1964.

Lodge, Henry Cabot, ed. *Selections from the Correspondence of Theodore Roosevelt and Henry Cabot Lodge, 1884–1918*. 2 vols. New York: Scribner's, 1925.

———. *The War with Spain*. New York: Harper Brothers, 1900.

Loy, Edward H. "Editorial Opinion and American Imperialism: Two Northwest Newspapers." *The Oregon Historical Quarterly* 72 (September 1971):209–24.

Lynn, Harry R. "The Genesis of America's Philippine Policy." Ph.D. dissertation, University of Kentucky, 1935.

Mabey, Charles R. *The Utah Batteries: A History*. Salt Lake City, 1900.

Mabini, Apolinario. *The Philippine Revolution*, translated by Leon M. Guerrero. Manila: National Historical Commission, 1969.

McCormick, Thomas J. "A Commentary on the Anti-Imperialists and Twentieth-Century Foreign Policy." *Studies on the Left* 3 (1962):28–33.

———. "Insular Imperialism and the Open Door: The China Market and the Spanish-American War." *Pacific Historical Review*, 23 (1963):155–69.

McGhee, Frederick L. "Another View." *Howard's American Magazine* 5 (October 1900):92–96.

McGurrin, James. *Bourke Cockran: A Free Lance in American Politics*. New York: Scribner's, 1948.

McKee, Delber E. "Samuel Gompers, The A.F. of L. and Imperialism, 1895–1900." *The Historian* 21 (February 1959):187–99.

McKim, Randolph H. "Religious Reconstruction in Our New Possessions." *The Outlook* 63 (28 October 1899):504–6.

Mahan, Alfred Thayer. "The Transvaal and the Philippine Islands." *The Independent* 52 (1 February 1900):289–91.

Majul, Cesar Adib. *The Political and Constitutional Ideas of the Philippine Revolution*. Quezon City: University of the Philippines Press, 1957.

March, Alden. *The History and Conquest of the Philippines and Our Other Island Possessions*. New York: 1899.

Marina, William F. "Opponents of Empire: An Interpretation of American Anti-Imperialism, 1898–1921." Ph. D. dissertation, University of Denver, 1968.

Markey, Joseph Ignacius. *From Iowa to the Philippines: A History of Company M, Fifty-first Iowa Infantry Volunteers*. Red Oak, Iowa: Thomas D. Murphy Company, 1900.

Marks, George P. *The Black Press Views American Imperialism*. New York: Arno Press, 1971.

————. "Opposition of Negro Newspapers to American Philippine Policy, 1899–1900." *Midwest Journal* 4 (Winter 1951–2):1–25.

Martin, Harold. "The Manila Censorship." *The Forum* 31 (June 1901):462–71.

Masters, Edgar Lee. *Spoon River Anthology*. New York: Macmillan Company, 1915.

Matré, Richard A. "The Chicago Press and Imperialism, 1899–1902." Ph.D. dissertation, Northwestern University, 1971.

May, Ernest R. *American Imperialism: A Speculative Essay*. New York: Atheneum Press, 1968.

————. "An American Tradition in Foreign Policy: The Role of Public Opinion." In *Theory and Practice in American Politics*, edited by William H. Nelson and Francis L. Loewenheim. Chicago: University of Chicago Press, 1964.

————. *Imperial Democracy: The Emergence of America as a Great Power*. New York: Harcourt, Brace & World, 1961.

May, Joseph. *The Peril of Our Republic*. Pamphlet. Philadelphia: privately printed, 1900.

Mead, Edwin D. "British and American Imperialism." *New England Magazine* 21 (October 1899):244–56.

Means, D. G. "Imperialism and Protection." *The Nation* 67 (22 September 1898):217–18.

Merk, Frederick. *Manifest Destiny and Mission in American History: A Reinterpretation*. New York: Alfred A. Knopf, 1963.

Miller, Kelly. "The Effect of Imperialism upon the Negro Race." *Howard's American Magazine* 5 (October 1900):87–91.

Millis, Walter. *The Martial Spirit: A Study of Our War with Spain*. Boston: Houghton Mifflin Company, 1931.

Minger, Ralph E. "Taft, MacArthur, and the Establishment of Civil Government in the Philippines." *The Ohio Historical Quarterly* 70 (October 1961):308–31.

Moody, William Vaughn. "An Ode in Time of Hesitation." *Atlantic Monthly* 85 (May 1900):593–98.

————. "On a Soldier Fallen in the Philippines." *Atlantic Monthly* 87 (February 1901):288.

Morgan, H. Wayne. *William McKinley and His America*. Syracuse, N.Y.: Syracuse University Press, 1963.

Morison, Elting, ed. *The Letters of Theodore Roosevelt*. 8 vols. Cambridge, Mass.: Harvard University Press, 1951–54.

Mott, Frank Luther. *A History of American Magazines*. 5 vols. Cambridge, Mass.: Harvard University Press, 1938–68.

Neale, R. G. *Great Britain and United States Expansion, 1898–1900*. East Lansing: Michigan State University Press, 1966.

Neely, F. Tennyson, ed. *Fighting in the Philippines*. London: F. Tennyson Neely Publishers, 1899.

Nevins, Allan. *The Evening Post, a Century of Journalism*. New York: Boni & Liveright, 1922.

Newman, Philip Charles. "Democracy and Imperialism in American Political Thought." *Philippine Social Sciences and Humanities Review* 15 (December 1950):351–67.

Noyes, Theodore W. *Oriental America and Its Problems*. Washington: Judd & Detweiler, 1903.

Olney, Richard. "Growth of Our Foreign Policy." *Atlantic Monthly* 85 (March 1900):289–301.

Onorato, Michael P., ed. *Philippine Bibliography, 1894–1946*. Santa Barbara: American Bibliographical Center, 1969.

————. "The United States and the Philippine Independence Movement." *Solidarity* 5 (1970):2–15.

Palmer, Frederick. "White Man and Brown Man in the Philippines." *Scribner's Magazine* 27 (January 1900):76–86.

Parker, John H. "What Shall We Do with the Philippines." *The Forum* 32 (February 1902):662–70.

Parks, Leighton. *Christian Expansion: Ancient and Modern*. Pamphlet. Boston: New England Anti-Imperialist League, 1902.

Parks, Samuel C. "Causes of the Philippine War." *The Arena* 27 (June 1902):561–72.

Parsons, Frank. "The Giant Issue of 1900." *The Arena* 23 (June 1900):561–65.

Peabody, George Foster. *Some Moral Results of the Imperial Policy*. Pamphlet. Brooklyn, N.Y.: privately printed, 1901.

Peeples, Dale Hardy. "The Senate Debate on the Philippines Legislation of 1902." Ph.D. dissertation, University of Georgia, 1964.

Peffer, William A. *Americanism and the Philippines*. Topeka, Kan.: Crane & Company, 1899.

————. "Imperialism, America's Historic Policy." *North American Review* 171 (August 1900):246–58.

Peterson, C. S. *Known Military Dead During the Spanish-American War and the Philippine Insurrection, 1898–1901*. Baltimore: privately printed, 1958.

Pettigrew, Richard F. *Imperial Washington*. Chicago: C. H. Kerr & Company, 1922.

Philippine Information Society. *Facts About the Filipinos*. Pamphlets. Boston: privately printed, 1900–1901.

————. *The Philippine Review*. Pamphlets. New York: privately printed, 1901–2.

Pierce, Edwin C. *Expansion Means Industrial Disaster*. Pamphlet. Boston: privately printed, 1900.

Pomeroy, William J. *An American-Made Tragedy: Neo-Colonialism and Dictatorship in the Philippines*. New York: International Publishers, 1974.
———. *American Neo-Colonialism: Its Emergence in the Philippines and Asia*. New York: International Publishers, 1970.
———. "Pacification in the Philippines." *France-Asie* 21 (1967):427–46.
Porter, Kirk H.; and Johnson, Donald B. *National Party Platforms, 1840–1960*. Urbana: University of Illinois Press, 1961.
Potter, Henry Codman. *The East of To-Day and To-Morrow*. New York: The Century Company, 1902.
———. "National Bigness or Greatness—Which?" *North American Review* 168 (April 1899):433–44.
Pratt, Julius W. *America's Colonial Experiment: How the United States Gained, Governed, and in Part Gave Away a Colonial Empire*. New York: Prentice-Hall, 1951.
———. *Expansionists of 1898*. Baltimore: Johns Hopkins Press. 1936.
Prentiss, A., ed. *The History of the Utah Volunteers in the Spanish-American War and in the Philippine Islands*. Salt Lake City: William F. Ford, 1900.
Radosh, Ronald; and Davies, Horace B. "American Labor and the Anti-Imperialist Movement: A Discussion." *Science and Society* 28 (1964):91–104.
Randolph, Carman F. *The Law and Policy of Annexation*. London: Longmans, Green, 1901.
Reid, Whitelaw. *Problems of Expansion, as Considered in Papers and Addresses*. New York: The Century Company, 1900.
Reuter, Bertha A. *Anglo-American Relations During the Spanish-American War*. New York: Macmillan Company, 1924.
Reuter, Frank T. *Catholic Influence on American Colonial Policies, 1898–1904*. Austin: University of Texas Press, 1967.
Reyes, Jose S. *Legislative History of America's Economic Policy Toward the Philippines*. New York: Columbia University Press, 1923.
Richardson, George A. "The Subjugation of Inferior Races." *Overland Monthly* 35 (January 1900):49–60.
Riggs, Arthur Stanley. "A Letter from the Philippines." *Atlantic Monthly* 92 (August 1903):256–66.
Robinson, Albert Gardner. *The Philippines: The War and the People; A Record of Personal Observations and Experiences*. New York: McClure, Phillips, 1901.
Robinson, Michael C.; and Schubert, Frank N. "David Fagan: An Afro-American Rebel in the Philippines, 1899–1901." *Pacific Historical Review* 44 (February 1975):68–83.
Rollins, J. W. "The Anti-Imperialists and American Foreign Policy: A Reappraisal." Master's thesis, University of Wisconsin, 1961.
Root, Elihu. *The Military and Colonial Policy of the United States; Addresses and Reports*. Cambridge, Mass.: Harvard University Press, 1916.
Rystad, Göran. *Ambiguous Imperialism: American Foreign Policy and Domestic Politics at the Turn of the Century*. (Lund Studies in International History 6). Stockholm: Esselte Stadium, 1975.

Salamanca, Bonifacio. *The Filipino Reaction to American Rule, 1901–1913*. Norwich, Conn.: Shoe String Press, 1968.

Scanland, J. M. "Our Asiatic Missionary Enterprise." *The Arena* 24 (September 1900):258–67.

Scarborough, W. S. *The Educated Negro and His Mission*. Washington, D.C.: The Academy, 1903.

———. "The Negro and Our New Possessions." *The Forum*, 31 (May 1901): 341–49.

Schieber, Clara E. *The Transformation of American Sentiment Toward Germany, 1870–1914*. Boston: Cornhill, 1923.

Schirmer, Daniel B. *Republic or Empire: American Resistance to the Philippine War*. Cambridge, Mass.: Schenkman, 1972.

Schott, Joseph L. *The Ordeal of Samar*. Indianapolis: Bobbs-Merrill, 1964.

Schurman, Jacob Gould. *Philippine Affairs: A Retrospect and Outlook*. New York: Scribner's, 1902.

Seed, Geoffrey. "British Views of American Policy in the Philippines Reflected in Journals of Opinion, 1898–1907." *Journal of American Studies* 2 (April 1968):49–64.

Sexton, William T. *Soldiers in the Sun*. Harrisburg, Pa.: The Military Service Publishing Company, 1939.

Shaw, Albert. "From a Republican Standpoint." *The Outlook* 66 (20 October 1900):441–49.

Shenton, James P. "Imperialism and Racism." In *Essays in American Historiography: Papers Presented in Honor of Allan Nevins*, edited by Donald Sheehan and Harold C. Syrett. New York: Columbia University Press, 1960.

Sheridan, Richard Brinsley. *The Filipino Martyrs: A Story of the Crime of February 4, 1899*. London: John Lane, 1900.

Sillen, Samuel. "Dooley, Twain and Imperialism." *Masses and Mainstream* 1 (1948):6–14.

Small, Melvin, ed. *Public Opinion and Historians: Interdisciplinary Perspectives*. Detroit: Wayne State University Press, 1970.

Smith, Goldwin. "Imperialism in the United States." *The Contemporary Review* 75 (May 1899):620–28.

Soldiers' Letters: Being Materials for the History of a War of Criminal Aggression. Boston: Anti-Imperialist League, 1899.

Spector, Ronald. *Admiral of the New Empire: The Life and Career of George Dewey*. Baton Rouge: Louisiana State University Press, 1974.

Spooner, John C. *Imperialism, A Forced and Fictitious Issue*. Pamphlet. Washington, D.C.: 1900.

Stanley, Peter W. *A Nation in the Making: The Philippines and the United States, 1899–1921*. Cambridge, Mass.: Harvard University Press, 1974.

Steele, Mathew F. "The 'Color Line' in the Army." *North American Review* 186 (June 1907).

Steward, Charles. "Manila and Its Opportunities." *The Colored American Magazine* 3 (August 1901):255.

Stewart, Freeman. ''The Preservation of the Republic: Christianity and Imperialism.'' *The Arena* 23 (June 1900):565–77.

Stillman, James W. *A Protest Against the President's War of Criminal Aggression*. Pamphlet. Boston: George H. Ellis, 1899.

Storey, Moorfield; and Lichauco, M. P. *The Conquest of the Philippines by the United States, 1898–1925*. New York: G. P. Putnam, 1926.

————.; and Codman, Julian. *Secretary Root's Record: ''Marked Severities'' in Philippine Warfare: An Analysis of the Law and Facts Bearing on the Action and Utterances of President Roosevelt and Secretary Root*. Boston: George H. Ellis, 1902.

Strong, Josiah. *Expansion Under New World-Conditions*. New York: Baker & Taylor, 1900.

Sullivan, Mark. *Our Times: The United States, 1900–1925*. 6 vols. New York: Scribner's, 1926–1935.

Sumner, William Graham. *The Conquest of the United States by Spain*. Boston: D. Estes, 1899.

Swift, Morrison I. *Imperialism and Liberty*. Los Angeles: Ronbroke Press, 1899.

Taft, William Howard. ''Shall We Promise Independence?'' *The Outlook* 71 (31 May 1902):305–21.

Taylor, James O., ed. *The Massacre at Balangiga: Being an Authentic Account by Several of the Few Survivors*. Joplin, Mo.: McCorn Publishing Co., 1931.

Taylor, John R. M. ''History of the Philippine Insurrection Against the United States, 1899–1903.'' Galley proofs in 5 vols., National Archives.

Thayer, James Bradley. *Our New Possessions*. Pamphlet reprint from *Harvard Law Review*, March, 1899. Cambridge, Mass.: 1899.

Tillman, Benjamin R. ''Bryan or McKinley: Causes of Southern Opposition to Imperialism.'' *North American Review* 171 (October 1900):439–46.

Tompkins, E. Berkeley. *Anti-Imperialism in the United States: The Great Debate, 1890–1920*. Philadelphia: University of Pennsylvania Press, 1970.

————. ''The Old Guard: A Study of the Anti-Imperialist Leadership.'' *The Historian* 30 (May 1968):366–88.

Twain, Mark. ''A Defence of General Funston.'' *North American Review* 174 (1902):613–24.

————. ''To the Person Sitting in Darkness.'' *North American Review* 172 (February 1901):161–76.

Van Bergen, R. ''Expansion Unavoidable.'' *Harper's Weekly* 44 (1900):885–86.

Vanderbilt, Kermit. *Charles Eliot Norton: Apostle of Culture in a Democracy*. Cambridge, Mass.: Harvard University Press, 1959.

Van Dyke, Henry. ''The American Birthright and the Philippine Pottage.'' *The Independent* 50 (1 December 1898):1579–85.

Van Meter, Henry Hooker. *The Truth about the Philippines from Official Records and Authentic Sources*. Chicago: The Liberty League, 1900.

Veeder, Russell. ''The Philippine Question in the Red River Valley Press, 1898–1901.'' *North Dakota Quarterly* 42 (October 1974):96–112.

Vevier, Charles. ''American Continentalism: An Idea of Expansion, 1845–1910.'' *American Historical Review* 65 (January 1960):323–35.

———. "Brooks Adams and the Ambivalence of American Foreign Policy." *World Affairs Quarterly* 30 (1959):3–18.

Virchow, Ruds. "The People of the Philippines." *Annual Report of the Board of Regents of the Smithsonian Institution for the Year Ending June 20, 1899*. Washington, D.C.: 1901.

Von Holst, Hermann E. "Some Expansionist Inconsistencies and False Analogies." *University of Chicago Record* 3 (1899):339–45.

Wall, Joseph Frazier. *Andrew Carnegie*. New York: Oxford University Press, 1970.

Warren, Winslow. *Governor Taft in the Philippines: A Review of Evidence Given Before the Senate Philippine Commission of the 57th Congress*. Boston: privately printed, 1902.

Weinberg, Albert. *Manifest Destiny: A Study of Nationalist Expansion in American History*. Baltimore: Johns Hopkins Press, 1935.

Welsh, Herbert. *The Other Man's Country: An Appeal to Conscience*. Philadelphia: J. B. Lippincott, 1900.

Whitaker, William G. "Samuel Gompers, Anti-Imperialist." *Pacific Historical Review* 38 (1969):429–55.

Wilcox, Marrion, ed. *Harper's History of the War in the Philippines*. New York: Harper Brothers, 1900.

Wildman, Edwin. *Aguinaldo: A Narrative of Filipino Ambitions*. Boston: Lothrop, 1901.

Wilkerson, Marcus. *Public Opinion and the Spanish-American War*. Baton Rouge: Louisiana State University Press, 1932.

Will, Thomas E. "Why I Am Opposed to Imperialism." *The Arena* 28 (July 1902):8–9.

Williams, Daniel R. *The Odyssey of the Philippine Commission*. Chicago: A. C. McClurg, 1913.

———. *The United States and the Philippines*. New York: Doubleday, Page, 1926.

Williams, John Sharp. *Empire or Republic: Retention of the Philippines; An Imperial Army Has A Destiny–Its Destiny Is To Destroy Free Institution*. Pamphlet. Washington: 1900.

Williams, William A. *The Tragedy of American Diplomacy*. Cleveland: World Publishing Company, 1959.

Williamson, Harold F. *Edward Atkinson: The Biography of an American Liberal, 1827–1905*. Boston: Old Corner Book Store, 1934.

Wilson, Woodrow. "The Ideals of America." *Atlantic Monthly* 90 (December 1902):721–34.

Winslow, Erving. "The Anti-Imperialist League." *The Independent* 51 (18 May 1899):1347–51.

———. "The Anti-Imperialist Position." *North American Review* 171 (October 1900):460–68.

Wolff, Leon. *Little Brown Brother: How the United States Purchased and Pacified the Philippine Islands at the Century's Turn*. Garden City: Doubleday, 1961.

Woolsey, Theodore S. "The Government of Dependencies." *Supplement to the Annals of the American Academy of Political and Social Sciences* 13 (1899):6–8.

———. ''The Legal Aspects of Aguinaldo's Capture.'' *The Outlook* 67 (13 April 1901):855–59.

Worcester, Dean C. *The Philippines Past and Present*. 2 vols. New York: Macmillan Company, 1914.

Zaide, Gregorio F. *Philippine Political and Cultural History*. 2 vols. Manila: Philippine Education Company, 1949.

———. *The Philippine Revolution*. Manila: The Modern Book Company, 1954.

Index

The Author

Richard E. Welch, Jr., professor of history at Lafayette College, is author of *Theodore Sedgwick: Federalist, George Frisbie Hoar and the Half-Breed Republicans*, and *Imperialists vs. Anti-Imperialists*.

The Book

Typeface: Mergenthaler V-I-P Times Roman
Design and composition: The University of North Carolina Press
Paper: Sixty pound Olde Style by S. D. Warren Company
Binding cloth: Roxite B 53565 Linen by The Holliston Mills, Incorporated
Printer and binder: Edwards Brothers, Incorporated

Published by The University of North Carolina Press